Bloom's Modern Critical Interpretations

Erich Maria Remarque's
All Quiet on the Western Front
New Edition

Edited and with an introduction by
Harold Bloom
Sterling Professor of the Humanities
Yale University

**BLOOM'S
LITERARY CRITICISM**
An imprint of Infobase Publishing

Bloom's Modern Critical Interpretations:
All Quiet on the Western Front—New Edition

Bloom's Literary Criticism
An imprint of Infobase Publishing
132 West 31st Street
New York NY 10001

Library of Congress Cataloging-in-Publication Data
Erich Maria Remarque's All quiet on the western front / edited and with an introduction by Harold Bloom. — New ed.
    p. cm. — (Bloom's modern critical interpretations)
  Includes bibliographical references and index.
   ISBN 978-1-60413-402-5 (hardcover : acid-free paper) 1. Remarque, Erich Maria, 1898–1970. Im Westen nichts Neues. I. Bloom, Harold. II. Title. III. Series.

  PT2635.E68I665 2009
  833'.912—dc22
                                         2008045705

Bloom's Literary Criticism books are available at special discounts when purchased in bulk quantities for businesses, associations, institutions, or sales promotions. Please call our Special Sales Department in New York at (212) 967-8800 or (800) 322-8755.

You can find Bloom's Literary Criticism on the World Wide Web at
http://www.chelseahouse.com.

Contributing editor: Portia Williams Weiskel
Cover design by Ben Peterson

Printed in the United States of America
IBT EJB 10 9 8 7 6 5 4 3

This book is printed on acid-free paper.

All links and Web addresses were checked and verified to be correct at the time of publication. Because of the dynamic nature of the Web, some addresses and links may have changed since publication and may no longer be valid.

Contents

Contents

Editor's Note

My introduction fuses the confirmed, rather antithetical authority of two great critics, Samuel Johnson and Oscar Wilde, to justify my dismissal of *All Quiet* as just another honorable period piece.

Christine R. Barker and R.W. Last exhaustively and rather disconcertingly praise Remarque's novel, even to the point of comparing it to Shakespeare, while George J. Mitchell gives an account of the motion picture, a great improvement on the tale.

For Modris Eksteins, *All Quiet* was Remarque's personal struggle with sorrow, redeemed when the Nazis publicly burned the book.

Hans Wagener emphasizes the novel's reception, after which Ariela Halkin considers the novel's place in the flood of war fiction in the 1920s, while David Midgley yet once more contemplates remembrance as a theme.

For Hilton Tims and also for Helmuth Kiesel, *All Quiet* is a permanently compelling document, after which Brian Murdoch ends this volume by seeing Remarque as a celebrant of "the life force."

HAROLD BLOOM

Introduction

All Quiet on the Western Front was first published in book form in 1929 and was translated soon after into English. It was Erich Maria Remarque's third novel and has always remained his most popular, though several of his later works were very successful with the public in the 1940s and 1950s. But his other books have faded away and are now scarcely readable. *All Quiet on the Western Front* remains very popular and is widely read, but whether it is more than another period piece seems quite questionable to me.

As a literary critic, I have always tried to follow Dr. Samuel Johnson, who warned that contemporary literary fame has a way of vanishing:

> Of many writers who filled their age with wonder, and whose names we find celebrated in the books of their contemporaries, the works are now no longer to be seen, or are seen only amidst the lumber of libraries which are seldom visited, where they lie only to show the deceitfulness of hope, and the uncertainty of honour.
>
> Of the decline of reputation many causes may be assigned. It is commonly lost because it never was deserved, and was conferred at first, not by the suffrage of criticism, but by the fondness of friendship, or servility of flattery. The great and popular are very freely applauded, but all soon grow weary of echoing to each other a name which has no other claim to notice, but that many mouths are pronouncing it at once.

1

Let me add, to the great Samuel Johnson, the sublime Oscar Wilde with his two critical adages: everything matters in art, except the subject, and all bad literature is sincere. What matters most in *All Quiet on the Western Front* indeed is the subject, World War I, and the book is very sincere. It is therefore not a work of art, but a period piece and a historical document.

To be even more autobiographical, I discovered recently how much fury can be generated by naming a currently popular work as just another period piece. After I discussed the Harry Potter fad in the *Wall Street Journal*, the *Journal* received 80 negative letters and none positive. J.K. Rowling, like Stephen King and Danielle Steele, will join the thousands of other writers in "the lumber of libraries" and the dustbin of the ages. Popularity is an index to popularity and to nothing more.

Remarque's *All Quiet on the Western Front*, still popular, remains an effective enough antiwar tract, but it hardly competes with Hemingway's *A Farewell to Arms* or even with Norman Mailer's *The Naked and the Dead*. Though Remarque's style is terse and tense, his protagonist lacks significant personality or mind to be of lasting interest to the reader. Paul Bäumer doubtless was meant to be a kind of everyman, but he is drab as he is desperate, and his yearnings are too commonplace to be interesting. Lew Ayres, playing Paul Bäumer in the American film version (1931), invested the character with more integrity and stubborn honor than Remarque had been able to suggest.

Remarque's novel is narrated by Bäumer in the first person. It is ironic that the book's most effective paragraphs are the final ones, in which Bäumer's voice ceases, and we are glad to receive a third-person narration though it be of the young man's death:

> He fell in October 1918, on a day that was so quiet and still on the whole front, that the army report confined itself to the single sentence: All quiet on the Western Front.

> He had fallen forward and lay on the earth as though sleeping. Turning him over one saw that he could not have suffered long; his face had an expression of calm, as though almost glad the end had come.

CHRISTINE R. BARKER AND R.W. LAST

All Quiet on the Western Front

In 1936, the National Socialist newspaper *Völkischer Beobachter* made this proud announcement to its readers:

> After all the lies told by people like Remarque, we now bring to you the experience of a soldier who took part in the war, of which you will say at once: that is what it was really like.[1]

There then follows an extract from an account of life at the front which, on closer examination, turns out to be nothing other than part of Remarque's *Im Westen nichts Neues* (presumably sent in anonymously by a third party), and this really was heaping insult on injury, since Joseph Goebbels's *Angriff* had already been similarly duped into printing a "genuine tale from the front line" at the height of his anti-Remarque campaign, which had also turned out to have been culled from the pages of *Im Westen nichts Neues*.[2] These were among the more bizarre consequences of the publication of what rapidly became one of the most successful books ever written—that is, if success is to be measured in terms of the number of copies sold, a proposition which many might be inclined to challenge.

When *Im Westen nichts Neues* was serialized in the *Vossische Zeitung* in November and December 1928, the paper's circulation tripled as eager readers

From *Erich Maria Remarque*, by Christine R. Barker and R.W. Last, pp. 32–68, 159–162. © 1979 Oswald Wolff Ltd.

snatched the latest issue from the news vendors with an avidity matched only by those in quest of the latest news of Pickwick or the fate of Little Nell in nineteenth-century England. The book edition, preceded by a concentrated advertising campaign in the press and on street hoardings, sold a million copies in a single year; its author was nominated for the Nobel literature prize; and the work set in train the most amazing storm of controversy, in the course of which it was hailed by one faction as the greatest anti-war novel of all time, denounced by the National Socialists as denigratory to the German *Volk*, and ultimately burned in the Opernplatz in Berlin during the infamous Nazi book-burning ceremony on 10 May 1933 (in such distinguished company as the works of Thomas and Heinrich Mann, Kästner, Brecht, Joyce, Hemingway and Gorki), to the accompaniment of these solemn words:

> As a protest against the literary betrayal of the soldiers of the Great War, and on behalf of the education of our people in the spirit of truth, I consign to the flames the writings of Erich Maria Remarque.[3]

Remarque found himself pilloried by his opponents, and accused of all manner of misrepresentation and misconduct; books and articles galore were written about him and his bestseller, many of them factually inaccurate, not to say libellous; a parody appeared, transposing the setting from the Western front to the Greek camp outside the walls of Troy; and the writer and critic Dr Salomo Friedlaender, under his pseudonym of Mynona, published a full-length attack on Remarque and his masterpiece in mediocrity, as he was pleased to call it.

Not surprisingly, the circumstances surrounding the composition of *Im Westen nichts Neues* and its submission to publishing houses are surrounded with confusion and contradictions. One thing, however, is clear, and that is that Remarque did not compose the novel as a deliberate money-making exercise, as Rowley for one seems to indicate: "The particular blend of suffering, sensuality and sentiment suggests that Remarque had gauged public taste".[4] In an interview with Axel Eggebrecht in 1929, Remarque presents his own reasons for writing the novel. He had, he states, been suffering from serious bouts of depression, the underlying cause of which remained a mystery to him until he made a sustained effort to ascertain why his mood was so consistently bleak:

> It was through these deliberate acts of self-analysis that I found my way back to my war experiences. I could observe a similar phenomenon in many of my friends and acquaintances. The shadow of war hung over us, especially when we tried to shut our

minds to it. The very day this thought struck me, I put pen to paper, without much in the way of prior thought.[5]

Working quickly during the evenings after doing a day's work at the offices of *Sport im Bild*, Remarque completed the novel in a mere six weeks—keeping himself awake with strong cigars and large quantities of coffee, if we are to believe a rather inflated account by Riess, who also cuts the time of composition in half.[6]

The finished work was submitted to S Fischer Verlag, the celebrated publishers of that other great German success of this century, Thomas Mann's *Buddenbrooks*, who were an obvious choice for any novelist eager to establish a solid reputation for himself. The manuscript was read by Bermann Fischer, who is recorded as having said that, to the best of his recollection,

> he read the novel at a single sitting, the night before a month's holiday touring, placed it before Samuel Fischer on the following morning and urged him to read it at once and draw up a contract with the author without delay, before any other publishers got sight of it.[7]

Bermann Fischer was convinced that he had brought off a really outstanding coup, but Samuel Fischer would go no further than to tell Remarque that he would take the book if no other publisher was prepared to accept it. When he heard about this, Bermann Fischer anxiously sought to retrieve the manuscript from Remarque, but by this time it was too late.

Remarque records that Samuel Fischer had informed him that, in his opinion, the book would not sell, since no one wanted to hear about the war any more.[8] But the real reason was that Samuel Fischer had very fixed ideas about what his firm should or should not put into print, and he was convinced that *Im Westen nichts Neues* did not accord with his notion of a work suitable for publication under the Fischer imprint, and he held to this view, apparently without a trace of regret, even when the novel turned out to be a huge and instantaneous success.

In the Eggebrecht interview, Remarque does not refer to the Fischer episode, but this seems more attributable to the fact that he was a reluctant interviewee than to any more sinister motive on his part; instead, he simply states that the manuscript lay untouched in his writing desk for close on six months until, at the insistence of friends, he put it in the hands of Ullstein's Propyläen Verlag.

As to the exact circumstances of its acceptance by Ullstein, there was a brief, if acrimonious, exchange of views in the correspondence columns of the *Frankfurter Allgemeine Zeitung* in 1962.[9] Professor Paul Frischauer claimed that it was he who came to know Remarque when the latter was working for *Sport im Bild*, and as a result of their meeting mentioned *Im Westen nichts Neues* to Dr Franz Ullstein at a social gathering. Ullstein then ensured that the work was seen by his reader Max Krell, who instantly recognized its qualities. So much for Professor Frischauer's account; Ullstein himself went on record as stating that it was a certain Herr Ross who first read it and strongly recommended its acceptance. In his memoirs, Krell does at least confirm that the novel came on to his desk shortly after Whitsun 1928.

Whatever the details, the Propyläen Verlag decided to give the work the full treatment: it was to come out first in installments in the *Vossische Zeitung* and then—in a slightly revised form—in a blaze of publicity in a first edition of 50,000 copies. The rest is history.

The reaction to the novel in Germany was violent in the extreme, and opinions soon polarized; but it is instructive to turn first to the response on the other side of the Channel, where a more stable political climate and the fact that Britain was not smarting under a humiliating defeat and the crippling terms of the Versailles treaty enabled the novel to be considered more dispassionately, first and foremost as a piece of literature rather than as a political manifesto.

The traditionally anonymous reviewer in the *Times Literary Supplement* accorded *Im Westen nichts Neues* a muted reception when it appeared in English translation by AW Wheen under the title *All Quiet on the Western Front*, published by Putnam for the princely sum of seven shillings and sixpence. The reviewer expresses surprise at the outstanding popularity of the work, which sold, as he records, 275,000 copies in just over six weeks:

> Very good as it undoubtedly is, this figure is astonishing; and one finds oneself wondering whether an extra nought has not slipped in.[10]

The *Times Literary Supplement* article sets the pattern for other English reviews, both in the slight note of incredulity at such success attending a novel of this nature and also in the careful reading which the reviewer undertakes of the work on its own merits which, even at this early stage, resulted in the emergence of interesting if somewhat inaccurate observations, such as the suggestion that the tale is "obviously autobiographical", or that "the real hero of the story is the narrator's particular friend, Katczinsky".

Im Westen nichts Neues in its English guise must have come as a welcome change from the tidal wave of what might be dubbed the "soft porn" of war literature flooding the British market. On the column adjacent to the *Times Literary Supplement* review, an advertiser announces—with unwitting irony and uncomfortable propinquity—the publication of *War Birds*:

Still the best-selling war book. Life, death, praying, cursing, women and the snarl of shrapnel! All the wild ecstasy and stark tragedy in this unexpurgated diary of a flying man!

The advertisement closes with a glowing extract from the review of *War Birds* by Gerald Gould of the *Daily Express*, who must have been busily preparing to eat his words: "It is the finest book on the war that has ever appeared, and a finer will never be written!"

The *Times Literary Supplement* reviewer also takes up one issue raised in the lurid apotheosis of *War Birds*, namely, that the novel contains references to certain areas of life not normally discussed in polite company and, significantly, he adds that such references are "of a type that (the reader) will not find in English novels". This prudish British insularity was particularly strong in the 1920's; indeed, it had continued unabated from the early years of the century, and is epitomized by the chauvinistic assertion in Erskine Childers's anti-German spy novel, *The Riddle of the Sands*: "It was something in his looks and manner, you know how different we are from foreigners".[11]

The review in *The New Statesman* reflects a similar cast of mind, and points out in mitigation that, of course, the Germans had the worst of it in the Great War,

> for on that side everything was a little more so—militarism was a little more militaristic; parade ground imbecilities were a little more imbecile; the squalor of the trenches (in the last year or two) was more squalid.[12]

And it concludes on a not untypical note of faint praise, commending the strengths of the work on the one hand, yet on the other stating that this level of achievement was not beyond the reach of any competent writer who happened to have served in the trenches:

> For the rest, anyone who was sufficiently in the thick of it for a long period, on one side or the other, might have written this grim, monotonous record, if he had the gift, which the author has, of remembering clearly, and setting down his memories truly, in naked and violent words.

Grudging though the recognition may have been in many quarters, the reception of *Im Westen nichts Neues* in Britain did at least focus attention on the novel as literature, but, when we turn to the reaction within Remarque's home country, it is clear that we find ourselves faced with an entirely different situation.

In Germany, the emphasis was not so much on the book as on the impact which it had on individuals and political factions alike. All the varied reactions have one thing in common, as can be illustrated by the case of the angry Doctor of Medicine Karl Kroner, writing in the *Neue Preussische Kreuz-Zeitung*, who protests mendaciously that nowhere in *Im Westen nichts Neues* is the medical profession depicted with humanity or sympathy. Even the ancillary staff, he complains, come off badly. No one would believe from Remarque's novel that there were actually doctors up in the front line itself, facing the salve dangers as the troops in action. Remarque, claims Dr Kroner, gives the totally erroneous impression that the wounded soldier was obliged to pick his own way back to the field stations. And, worse still,

> all the old tales of horror about the Germans, now happily long forgotten, and which sprang up in the war psychosis, will now be resurrected. People abroad will draw the following conclusions: if German doctors deal with their own fellow countrymen in this manner, what acts of inhumanity will they not perpetrate against helpless prisoners delivered up into their hands or against the populations of occupied territory?[13]

Dr Kroner reads *Im Westen nichts Neues* as documentary fiction, as if it staked some kind of claim to being representative both of German attitudes and German actions at the front and behind the lines during the Great War.

The novel is also regarded as aspiring to present the "truth" on a literal, autobiographical level. The *Times Literary Supplement* and *New Statesmen* reviewers were far from being alone in their insistence that the reader is being presented with an account of events that actually took place, and more than one critic has gone so far as to chastise Remarque for not giving precise details of time or place, so that they might be checked for accuracy.[14] A certain Peter Kropp, who had been a patient in the same military hospital at Duisberg as Remarque, and who knew him, as Erich Remark, of course, was outraged at his former comrade's descriptions of the hospital in *Im Westen nichts Neues*.[15] Remarque, he protests, presents a very partial view which is not without its serious inaccuracies. Of course there was a great deal of suffering in the hospital, but there was much silent heroism too. The hospital, asserts Kropp, was run in an exemplary fashion, the patients were tended by a nursing order of Catholic nuns, and Remarque is entirely erroneous in his assertion that the patients were disturbed by the noisy praying of the sisters in the corridors. (*Im Westen*, p. 226) Kropp goes on to describe the exact location of the chapel in the hospital, thus "proving" that their prayers could not have been heard by the wounded soldiers, as Remarque claims in his novel. From this point, Kropp proceeds to try and identify individual patients with characters in the novel, and lights in particular on the forty-year-old Lewandowski, who has been in the hospital for ten months, and who in the novel is excitedly anticipating a first visit from his wife. Lewandowski tells the others—"for in the army we have no secrets of that kind" (*Im Westen*, p. 238)—that he is desperate to make love to his wife when she comes to see him, and the others stand guard as the blushing couple embrace in the hospital bed. This is too much for Kropp, who protests that this kind of thing simply could not have happened: "I should certainly have known about it," he complains.

In more general terms, Kropp castigates Remarque for accentuating the negative:

> I find no front-line spirit in Remark's book. There were other front-line soldiers who were different from the way Remark depicts them. There were such soldiers to whom the protection of homeland, protection of house and homestead, protection of the family was their highest objective, and to whom this will to protect their homeland gave the strength to endure any extremities.[15]

This assumption that, in *Im Westen nichts Neues*, Remarque was seeking to encapsulate a piece of personal and national history in literary form was immediately taken up by both sides in the critical debate.

In his celebrated review for *Die literarische Welt*, the dramatist Ernst Toller claims that Remarque "has spoken on behalf of all of us".[16] Not only does the book describe in unforgettably graphic terms the horrific experiences and privations to which the front-line soldier was exposed, but so exemplary is it, Toller argues, that it should be read by everyone as an anti-war document, and especially in the schools. *Im Westen nichts Neues* says more about the nation and its involvement in the Great War than any statistics or weighty historical tomes ever could.

A publicity pamphlet produced by the Ullstein Propyläen Verlag entitled *Der Kampf um Remarque* (The Battle over Remarque),[17] which consists of a compilation of criticism, both positive and negative, of *Im Westen nichts Neues*, cites a letter from a war-blinded schoolteacher who welcomes the novel with open arms as the one book with which to instruct the minds of the young on the subject of the Great War. This work, he writes, fortuitously employing a turn of phrase which, as we shall see later, is crucial to a proper understanding of the novel, represents "my own release (= Erlösung) from the front".

Almost alone among the reviews of *Im Westen nichts Neues*, the Berlin *Die Welt am Montag*, quoted in the Propyläen Verlag pamphlet, at least begins to spell out the nature of the real problem posed by the novel:

> What makes it so unique? … the fact that Remarque does not
> spoon-feed his reader page by page with ready-made attitudes, but
> leaves him to draw his own conclusions from the book.

But, by and large, *Im Westen nichts Neues* came to be regarded by the vast
majority of people as the anti-war book *par excellence* (or the worst kind of
pacifist propaganda, depending on which camp one belonged to), a succes-
sor to Bertha von Suttner's *Die Waffen nieder!* (Lay down your Arms, 1892),
which had been instrumental in giving an early impetus to the International
Arbitration and Peace Association because of its stark portrayal of the horrors
of war, not least in its famous depiction of the heroine, Martha von Tilling,
picking her way among the dead and dying on the battlefield of Königgrätz
in search of her missing husband. Suttner it was who persuaded her life-long
admirer, the industrialist Alfred Nobel, to institute his peace prize, one of
whose recipients she became in 1905.[18] But, although this peace movement
outlived the First World War in various forms, it had already passed its
second peak in Germany before the appearance of *Im Westen nichts Neues*,
and the right-wing backlash was already in full swing; and, as Shuster has
pointed out, "the excesses of the earlier pacifism only served to swell the
forces which were now ushering in a rebirth of militarism".[19]

This militarism assumed two forms in the context of the onslaught
launched against *Im Westen nichts Neues* and its author. In its milder manifestation, it outraged all those who were instinctively appalled at the desecration,
as they saw it, both of the sacrifices made by the front-line soldiers and of the
idea of the German nation. The most closely-argued contemporary critical
attack on the novel by Heisler states that, for all its undoubted merits, the
work represents a threat, since it tends to sap the energies of the German
nation at a time when it has to assert itself in the face of a hostile world if it
is to survive.[20]

Not unexpectedly, the main opposition to *Im Westen nichts Neues* came
from the National Socialists, who regarded the book—which, as they were
not slow to point out, was produced by a Jewish publisher—as part of a well-
financed international conspiracy on the part of Bolshevists and Jews against
the German *Volk*. At that time, the theorists of National Socialism were
claiming insistently that the Great War represented nothing less than the fire
in which the spirit of the emergent German Reich had been forged, and that,
as a consequence, *Im Westen nichts Neues* constituted a betrayal of all that is
great and noble in Germany and the German nation.

Remarque is accused of partiality in his depiction of the front-line soldier, since he presents only "how a few emotionally unbalanced people conducted themselves before they ever went into battle".[21] What the National
Socialists found most offensive in Remarque's portrayal of the men in the

trenches was his demythologizing of front-line warfare, of the concept of the "hero" which is so crucial to the National Socialist foundation myth. Life, it is argued, is a relentless Darwinian struggle, in which the individual, if he is to survive, has to assert himself in the face of others; and similarly, the strongest nation is the one that has the will to survive more successfully than any of its rivals. The individual cannot exist as a separate selfish entity—to coin a phrase, no man is an island—since he is part of a greater whole, the race or nation, and the selfless surrender of his own life on the part of the hero in order that the whole might survive, is the greatest and noblest act that a human being can perform.

Remarque's negative attitude to war in general was equally anathema to the National Socialists in that it embodied two of their *bêtes noires*: namely, pacifism and internationalism. The proponents of internationalism may proclaim from the rooftops that the life of the individual is the highest good, but the ineluctable laws of nature, which antedate the appearance of man on this planet and to which he is subordinate, dictate that this simply is not so. In a grotesque prefiguration of the biogeneticists' concept of "non-selfish" behaviour, the National Socialists argue that it is the survival of the race, the nation, that matters, not that of the individual. Hence internationalism, which is more or less equated with Marxism, is, like pacifism, a dangerous aberration: "Pacifism is the same heresy on the ethical plane as is Marxism in the social sphere".[22] If the life of the individual is sacred, as the pacifists claim, then how much more sacred must be the life of the nation:

> The projected utopia of the pacifists has one thing in common with that of the Marxists—and that is, that it will never be realized. As long as men are men, as long as death remains a fact of life, its twin servants, sickness and war, will remain with us too.[23]

Disease is equated with war, and the argument goes that getting rid of doctors will not result in the disappearance of disease, but will inevitably bring about its spread and ultimate domination. Therefore the soldier is not fomenting war and militarism; on the contrary, he is actually fighting *against* war, just like the doctor combatting disease.

This insidiously plausible line of argumentation was brought to bear with particular force on the figures in *Im Westen nichts Neues* who violated the notion of the Great War as a positive rather than a destructive force—regrettable though it was, of course, and rendered necessary only by the aggression of others:

> The war was a test; in the thunder of the cannon all masks fell away, and men stood there naked, in their true qualities. He who had eyes

to see and ears to hear learned at the front to distinguish the wheat from the chaff.[24]

And, in contrast to Remarque's negative concept of comradeship, the community of soldiers of the front in reality paved the way for the new national community of the coming Reich, under the leadership of the Führer, of course.

Despite their vocal protests, the National Socialists were unable to prevent the publication and sale of *Im Westen nichts Neues*, but Joseph Goebbels, at the time Gauleiter of the Berlin section of the National Socialist party, found himself presented with a golden opportunity to bring off a major propaganda coup when the celebrated American film based on the book, *All Quiet on the Western Front*, was screened in the German capital. The film, directed by Lewis Milestone and produced by Universal Pictures, was one of the early talkies and has since come to be recognized as one of the great classics of the cinema. The National Socialists seemed to be losing the initiative in the parliamentary battle in the *Reichstag*, but Goebbels leaped at this unique chance of bringing the fight out on to the streets. He organized a gang of Hitler Youth to storm the auditorium where the film was to be premiered, and they rampaged through the building, hurling stink bombs, scattering white mice and shouting "Germany awake!" Goebbels's tactic of stirring up controversy over an issue at the centre of public attention certainly paid off; not only did he attract considerable publicity, he even succeeded in getting the film banned in Germany. And, as we saw earlier, the book itself was also burned—and banned—when the dream of a Third Reich became a political reality in 1933.

Remarque was also the object of attack from a quite different quarter, this time on largely unpolitical grounds. The slight but acid parody *Vor Troja nichts Neues* (All Quiet before the Walls of Troy), supposedly by one Emil Marius Requark, has an overweening first-person narrator whose sole ambition it is to amass great wealth after the war is over: "I will become a rich man, all Greece will read my book".[25] And, in fact, the whole Trojan war seems to be taking place simply so that he can write a book about it. Nor is the narrator inclined to underestimate his own abilities: "One has such incredibly clever thoughts and one gets to feel the importance of one's person".[26] He inflates his ego to its fullest extent and proclaims: "Thus it is that I am writing a war diary. It will contain a great deal about me and just a very little about the war".[27] The rest of the world is in a state of utter confusion; the soldiers alone have retained their clear-sightedness and integrity.

The great poet Homer is also present, compiling the official version of the war and evidently enjoying himself. The narrator, hearing him mutter hexameters out loud, assumes that he is inebriated, and bids him forget about noble heroes and all that kind of thing and write instead about the sordid re-alities of war, the mud and the lice (to which latter the narrator has, it seems, become quite attached). The soldiers, as a sentence picked out in large type stresses, "belong to a generation which will never recover from the impact of war. Our lives are ruined beyond recall".[28] The parody in *Vor Troja nichts Neues* is directed partly against Remarque's pacifist tendencies, but even more against his personal vanity in arrogating to himself the rôle of the omniscient recording angel of the Great War, the sole repository of the whole truth about the armed conflict on the Western front.

This latter view is also espoused by Mynona's *Hat Erich Maria Remarque wirklich gelebt?*[29] an exceedingly witty and entirely libellous assault on Re-marque, which follows the pattern of Mynona's equally venomous onslaught on Freud, in the publisher's announcement for which he is elevated to the dubious status of the "Chaplin of German philosophy". Employing the time-honoured principle that the least strenuous means of demolishing the work is to discredit the man, Mynona summons up every pun, turn of wit, and allusion to his victim's life, employment and previous writing—especially his advertising career (there is much play on Conti-dummies for babies and the like) and, of course, *Die Traumbude*—in his character assassination attempt, and tops the whole thing off with a "Documentary Appendix for Sceptics" quoting Remarque's birth certificate and other information "proving" that he falsely assumed the French tail on his name. The book closes with a list of "Erich Maria Remark's Collected Werques" (sic). He finds Remarque guilty of outstanding mediocrity, and expresses his utter astonishment that such a thoroughly ordinary piece of pen-pushing should have attracted such a huge-ly disproportionate amount of public attention and stand at the epicentre of such an earth-shattering storm of controversy.

Osnabrück—"the mouse that gave birth to this mountain"[30]—has a great deal to answer for, claims Mynona, since in *Im Westen nichts Neues* that town's celebrated son does little more than hold up a dull mirror to a drab age. Mynona reminds his readers of the orator in Classical times who started with fright when he received universal applause, fearful that he might have said something ridiculous, for "only the uttermost folly gains instant thun-derous approbation, the truth in contrast is greeted by an audience of deaf mutes".[31]

Mynona describes his attack as a satirical apotheosis; but, in reality, it is no more than an enormous ego-trip, a romp of *Schadenfreude* on the part of a writer who really ought to have known better. His attack becomes more understandable—but even less forgivable—when it is realized that, under his real appellation of Dr Salomo Friedlaender, Mynona was a less than suc-cessful poet and writer, a minor member of the circle of contributors to the Expressionist periodical *Der Sturm* with pretensions as a philosopher in the

wake of Nietzsche. He had, he was convinced, "solved" the post-Kantian dilemma of subjectivity and the destruction of absolute values by means of a
strong creative individual operating a positive, but still subjective ethic, Unfortunately, no one was inclined to listen to him.[32] And nothing could have
been more repugnant to the aspirations of Dr Friedlaender than the attitudes
of the characters in *Im Westen nichts Neues*. The instinctive revulsion on the
part of Mynona, of our anonymous parodist, and indeed of others, to the
popularity of this work prefigures most of what little critical attention the
novel has been accorded in the West in recent years.

* * *

Im Westen nichts Neues hardly receives more than a passing—and not
always accurate—mention in histories of contemporary literature published
in the West: Soergel and Hohoff only accord it a handful of lines in a nine-
page section on the First World War in literature, stating that "in the case of
Remarque, too, comradeship and sacrifice were values which outlived the war"
(the first part of the assertion may be true, the second certainly is not);[33] a
five-hundred page compendium on German literature in the Weimar Republic is even more parsimonious, squeezing out just three mentions of *Im Westen
nichts Neues* by title in a whole section devoted exclusively to the novel of the
Great War;[34] Lange, skating across the surface of modern literature between
1870 and 1940, simply refers to the novel as "one of the first, but not one of
the most substantial of the war books",[35] an *ex cathedra* pronouncement not
untypical of this brand of general survey; a more considered reaction from
Rühle none the less insists that the work is political and pacifist, which "explains the hypnotic mass impact of the novel and its effectiveness as a pacifist
manifesto";[36] and Kerker goes to the other extreme in a somewhat idiosyncratic interpretation of the work, in which he claims that, far from being an
anti-war novel, it actually helped to bring about the Second World War, but
he is clearly confusing analysis of the novel as such with the impact which it
happened to have in certain quarters.[37]

Of the handful of scholars who have undertaken detailed consideration
of *Im Westen nichts Neues* in the West, Liedloff has some kind words to say
about it, but his attention is diverted by the fact that he is writing a descriptive comparatist essay, relating it to Hemingway's *A Farewell to Arms*;[38] Swados defends the artistic value of the novel, praising its directness in depicting
the horrors of war;[39] in another comparatist study, this time with reference to
F. Manning's *Her Privates We*, Klein underlines the literary merit of *Im Westen
nichts Neues* and stresses its highly organized structure, although he does not
go into a great deal of detail on this vital issue;[40] and Rowley, in a sensitive
essay, echoes Klein's views about the novel's structure, and stresses that the

style—which he dubs "journalistic"[41]—is deliberately chosen by Remarque, and not a sign of weakness on his part.

One suspects that the scant attention now paid to Remarque in the West is attributable, in part at least, to the huge success of the work—for how, the argument goes in the groves of academe, can something so overwhelmingly popular be great literature in an age when the true artist seems inevitably to be alienated from the public at large? Such considerations seem to loom particularly large for the German academic critic: witness, for example, the very mixed reception accorded to a dramatist like Fritz Hochwälder, who insists on writing "well-made plays" when everyone knows they are *passé* in an era of theatrical experimentation, or another dramatist, Rolf Hochhuth, who actually has the nerve to write about individual responsibility when the fashionable critic has long since pronounced it dead and buried—both, needless to say, very successful writers who have attracted a large public following. And, apart from the issue as to whether the novel can be regarded as "serious literature" or not, *Im Westen nichts Neues* has become almost totally submerged under the weight of the political and ideological battles that have been waged around it.

* * *

In the East, on the other hand, there have been no aesthetic reservations, for the social—not to say socialist—content of a work far outweighs any such decadent Western consideration, and *Im Westen nichts Neues* has attracted a fair amount of interest in academic circles there, largely as an illustration of a liberal Western piece which, on the social plane, puts a finger on the evils of the world but regrettably goes no further.

With not untypical circular argumentation, Marxist critics assert that the novel *is* political despite itself—its inability to advocate positive action being itself regarded as the assumption of a political stand. The principal complaint of the Marxist critic is that *Im Westen nichts Neues* fails in its social obligations: having recognized the disease, it avoids taking the next logical step, that of pronouncing a means (Marxist-Leninist, perhaps?) towards a cure. Remarque, and others like him, "indeed recognized the growing Fascist threat but did not have the will to make the revolutionary response to it".[42]

So the wheel turns full circle, and once more *Im Westen nichts Neues* is regarded as a representative work, but this time it is criticized for failing to draw any positive conclusions from the evils it detects and depicts in the militarism of Germany in World War One, which at least makes a change from being attacked for not being militaristic enough.

The novel is also found wanting on the grounds that, in its portrayal of the war scene, it is too limited in perspective: in presenting, for example, the martinet figure of the corporal Himmelstoss, Remarque is accused of concentrating shortsightedly on the symptoms, not the root cause, and for this reason if for no other the novel is incapable of advancing any kind of positive solution. Left-wing totalitarianism comes close to its arch-enemy, Fascism, when one Marxist critic, Wegner, complains that Remarque is only depicting the "little man" of the time who needs, but lacks entirely, some sense of spiritual direction, a purposeful rôle for himself in society.[43] One can almost hear a demand for the *Führerprinzip* behind these words.

* * *

Hardly any of the host of reviewers, critics and political theorists who have put pen to paper on the subject of *Im Westen nichts Neues*—or, more frequently, on issues raised by the novel—have made any real contribution to a proper understanding of the actual work itself; in fact, most of them have succeeded in going beyond the point at which the novel ceases to be relevant to their discussion. The first English critics tended to misconstrue it because of its "foreign-ness"; the Germans because it was used as ammunition in the battle between the liberals and pacifists on the one hand and the militarists and National Socialists on the other; and, after the Second World War, Western critics were either preoccupied with whether or not it was fit to be considered as "art" at all, or were again busily looking at the circumstances surrounding the work, either as comparatists or practitioners of the currently fashionable art of the aesthetics of the reception of literature; and, behind the Iron Curtain, the Marxist critics have been holding it up against the yardstick of social and political commitment and finding it wanting.

But, for all that, *Im Westen nichts Neues*—like many another work—has managed to survive its critics; yet the main issue still remains largely unanswered: What makes it such a compelling and successful work? And the only way to answer that question is actually to take a look at the novel itself.

* * *

Im Westen nichts Neues concerns the war experiences of a school class of young men who volunteer for active service under patriotic pressure from Kantorek, their schoolmaster, and another group of men whom they have closely befriended in the army. Of the class, originally twenty in all, only a handful remain, and the attention is focussed on four of them—Kropp, Müller, Leer and Bäumer—and this quartet is balanced by four others: Tjaden, a mechanic, Westhus, a turf-cutter, Detering, a farmer, and Katczinsky (referred to by the nickname of "Kat"), at forty the oldest of the group.

This numerical equilibrium which Remarque establishes between the more intelligent but inexperienced young soldiers on the one hand and the academically less able ex-workers on the other, who compensate for their lack of intellectual attainment by a wider experience of life, points to a strong sense of organization on the part of the author which, as we shall see in due course, is fundamental to the entire work and has been studiously ignored by most critics.

It is told, principally in the historic present (which will be retained in quotations although it rings awkwardly in English), by a first-person narrator, Paul Bäumer, whose surname has been assiduously dismembered by Liedloff into "Baum" (= tree) and "Träumer" (dreamer), which by a tangential leap of the imagination is caused to represent two supposedly key constituents of Bäumer's nature: his "yearning for beauty" encapsulated in the "organic growth" of the tree; and his reflective and inward-turned personality.[44] However, there is not a shred of evidence, internal or external, which might indicate that this is anything other than a perfectly ordinary German name, chosen precisely because of its ordinariness. The "Paul," on the other hand, is a direct reference to Remarque's original second Christian name and suggests that the novel is obliquely autobiographical. (Until Mynona dredged up the "truth" about Remarque's "real" name, of course, that autobiographical element remained hidden from the reader.) The problem is, to what extent and in what manner does it reflect the life and convictions of the author? This question could equally be posed in relation to the vast majority of Remarque's output. Critics—especially those hostile towards *Im Westen nichts Neues*—have all too eagerly tended to fall into the trap of arguing themselves into a logically absurd position: on the one hand, Remarque is castigated for not adhering faithfully to the "facts" of his own personal life, and yet on the other he is reprimanded by the same people for presenting a personal, partial and biased picture of the war on the Western front.

To some extent, at least, Remarque is to blame for this state of affairs; he describes the experiences and emotions of his central figure with such vividness and with such an aura of authenticity that one is all too readily tempted to assume that the events described actually took place precisely as he depicts them, or, if they did not, that some kind of fraud is being perpetrated; it is, to borrow an observation from an entirely different context, "a reproof to that large body of readers, who, when a novelist has really carried conviction to them, assert off-hand: 'O, that must be autobiography!'"[45] The sentiments are Remarque's, the words those of Arnold Bennett.

The most superficial examination of, say, place-names, in *Im Westen nichts Neues*, makes it abundantly clear that Remarque has selectively plundered his own past experiences and environment in the composition of his novel. When Bäumer (why do critics patronizingly tend to refer to him as "Paul" all the time?) is entering his home town by train on leave from the front, for example, he passes over the Bremer Strasse before entering the main station. And there is no denying that the railway line to Remarque's home town of Osnabrück does precisely that (but the more pernickety critic might have observed that this is the route from the *east*, and therefore less likely to have been travelled upon by a soldier returning from the Western front). When Bäumer leaves the station, he sees the river rushing out from the sluices under the mill bridge; he looks up at the old watch tower, now used as a wash house; he crosses the bridge, finds his way home, climbs the stairs to his parents' flat, and later sits at his bedroom window looking out at the chestnut tree in the garden of the inn across the way—and every detail is "almost photographically accurate".[46]

Although Remarque keeps close to reality in his depiction of the setting of his home town, leaving the front line deliberately imprecise because of its uniformity of appearance and the irrelevance of geographical designations, there is much less to be found in the way of parallels between the characters and their actions and any real life equivalents, save on the most superficial level: Bäumer's class "volunteers" under the chiding tongue of Kantorek, whereas all but three of Remarque's class waited until they were conscripted in 1916 (including our author himself). Other parallels are more or less on the level of, for example, the name of the corporal Himmelstoss being based on that of a family living in the Jahnstrasse in Osnabrück.[47]

So it is quite evident that we are considering here a writer who, by preference, draws fairly directly but none the less selectively on his own experiences and background, although he is by no means seeking to present us with fictionalized autobiography. The reader unfamiliar with the topography of Osnabrück is not one whit the poorer. Were it not for all the nonsense penned about Remarque and his supposed "distortions" of reality, it would hardly be necessary to state the obvious; namely, that Remarque uses his home town or city and experiences close to his own as a convenient basis for his imaginative work.

Instead of fussing about the supposed authenticity or otherwise of Remarque's work, it might be less quixotic to consider the internal parallels between novel and reality. In order to do so, we must return to the words of the blind schoolteacher in the Propyläen publicity pamphlet, for whom the novel represented a release or "Erlösung" from the experiences of the war, a cathartic purging of the emotional residue of the front line. It enabled him to sort out within himself the tangled memories and emotions of the Great War, and to come to terms with them. And it is precisely in this light that Remarque himself regarded *Im Westen nichts Neues*. In the interview with Eggebrecht, Remarque too talks of a sense of release that came with the writing of his novel, and he uses exactly the same word, "Erlösung".[48] He had experienced an inexplicable sense of depression, and the act of writing had enabled him to recognize the symptoms and their cause and to work towards some kind of accommodation with the past.

But more than that: Remarque succeeded in transcending his own personal situation; he touched on a nerve of his time, reflecting the experiences of a whole generation of young men on whom the war had left an indelible mark. Remarque uses his own personal experiences in a similar fashion as the starting point for nearly all his subsequent novels. This exorcism of his own doubts and conflicts enabled him to make a huge step forward away from the preciosities of *Die Traumbude* and of the little prose and verse pieces penned for *Die Schönheit*.

* * *

Although the novel is divided into twelve chapters of varying length, they do not necessarily point to more than one facet of the basic structure of *Im Westen nichts Neues*. In this novel he is introducing a structural technique—which he was to refine in his subsequent works—which involves a series of small episodes as building bricks, not necessarily related to one another causally (that is to say, the "plot" is not particularly important), but cumulative in effect. Bäumer's account is very much like a diary, consisting in the main of either description of a sequence of events or internal monologue, without linking passages of any kind. It is, one might say, without seeking to over-stretch the comparison, a kind of "Stationenroman" on the lines of the Brechtian epic theatre with its "Stationendramen", that is, a novel held together, not by the traditional glue of a developing action culminating in a climax and denouement, but rather by broader thematic links, such as character or ideas. And, as far as Remarque's novels in general are concerned, there is a strange inverse relationship between their literary quality and the tightness of their plot.

Im Westen nichts Neues falls into three parts plus a contemplative interlude. The first part (Chapters I–VI) explores the experiences of the private soldier at the front and behind the lines, together with reflections back on home, the last days in school and life in the training barracks. It opens with a depleted company newly returned from the front, only eighty men out of a hundred and fifty, and concludes in similar vein with the return of another company, this time reduced to a mere thirty-two men. The central section (Chapter VII, the longest in the book) deals partly with women (of whom a little more later), aspirations towards a world of love beyond the war, and partly with Bäumer's disastrous experience of leave, when he fails to regain contact with his past. There then follows a contemplative interlude (Chapter

VIII), principally devoted to Bäumer's thoughts as he stands guard over a group of Russian prisoners of war; in this section, he actually ponders on the wider political and moral issues raised by the armed conflict (not a few critics must have had faulty copies of *Im Westen nichts Neues* with these particular pages expunged!). In the final section (Chapters IX–XII), the action becomes more concentrated: vignettes of fellow soldiers, each ending in their death, are sandwiched between periods of reflection and contemplation, and the narrative technique—unusually for Remarque—switches over from blocks of description and action with a high content of dialogue to a summarized, compressed account of the concluding phase of the war, as time seems to become suspended and the comrades' emotions utterly numbed. And, at the end, Bäumer dies, just as peace is approaching.

Reading critics of *Im Westen nichts Neues*, one might all too readily gain the impression that the novel is a succession of nightmarish situations and unrelieved gloom, but this is far from being the case. Remarque skilfully paces the development of the action, interposing scenes of real happiness and contentment, some of which contain episodes that are extremely funny. On one such occasion, Bäumer clumsily attempts to "liberate" a brace of geese from a farmyard; he is cornered by the farm bulldog and pinned to the ground by that animal; and, finally, he manages to extricate his revolver:

> When I get my revolver in my hand, it starts to shake. I press my hand on to the ground and tell myself: raise the revolver, fire before the dog can get at me and make myself scarce. Slowly I take my breath and calm down. Then, holding my breath, I jerk the revolver into the air, it goes off, the dog leaps yowling to one side, I reach the stable door and go head over heels over one of the geese which had fled from me. (*Im Westen*, p. 89)

So he makes a grab for it, hurls it over the wall to Kat, who puts the bird out of its misery; and Bäumer joins them, having just escaped the fangs of the frustrated bulldog. (Almost as funny, but unintentionally so, is the National Socialist critic Nickl's accusation against Remarque that this is another instance of double standards: on the one hand, men protest violently against the sufferings of horses in warfare, but on the other they are quite prepared to kill and eat geese. Nickl must have been a vegetarian as well as a National Socialist.)[49]

Another amusing episode which is equally concerned with food, but this time, so to speak, from a different point of view, relates to the inevitable outcome of gastronomic excess. Kat manages to acquire two sucking pigs, and these are roasted with all the trimmings:

We fall asleep chewing. But things get bad in the night. We have eaten too much fat. Fresh roast sucking pig has a devastating effect on the bowels. There is an incessant to-ing and fro-ing in the dugout. Men are squatting about outside in twos and threes with their trousers down, cursing. Getting on for four in the morning we achieve a record: all eleven men ... on their haunches outside together. (*Im Westen*, p. 213–14)

Even the tyrannical corporal Himmelstoss gives occasion for some amusement, as when the soldiers obey his orders with excessive slowness, thus whipping him into a hoarse frenzy (*Im Westen*, p. 28); but there is a grimmer side to the humour, too, both in the scene where Himmelstoss is swathed in a sheet and beaten by the vengeful group of comrades, (*Im Westen*, p. 48f) and when their ex-teacher Kantorek is also humiliated by a former pupil of his in the barracks when the rôles are reversed and Kantorek is actually a subordinate to his erstwhile student. (*Im Westen*, p. 160)

Such episodes, however, are not scattered randomly about the novel; in this, as in all else, Remarque pays considerable attention to the detailed organization of his material. Opening on a positive note, the novel alternates light and dark episodes, the intensity of both increasing as the narrative progresses. In Chapter I, the comrades sit *al fresco* on latrine buckets in a circle playing cards in a scene of tranquil contentment; and this sequence is closely followed by a visit to the dying Kemmerich. Chapter V brings the *contretemps* with the goose, which is then consumed with considerable relish in an atmosphere of peace and fulfilment; and this comes just before the comrades move up to the front line past coffins piled high in readiness for the victims of the coming offensive. And, finally, in Chapter X there is a sequence in an evacuated village—"an idyll of guzzling and sleeping" (*Im Westen*, p. 210)—which they are supposed to be guarding, and where they have been left more or less to their own devices; and this is immediately followed by Bäumer and Kropp sustaining wounds in action. Each of the positive scenes, it will have been noted, is concerned with basic functions of the human body; and we shall be returning to this preoccupation with the essentials of life later.

Similarly, Remarque establishes a series of contrasts between scenes at the front and behind the lines, in an alternating sequence in which more and more stress comes to be placed on the front as the struggle becomes grimmer and the small group of comrades finds its numbers gradually whittled down. This aspect of the novel's structure is reflected in the chapter endings, each of which—with the exception of the Russian prisoners interlude in Chapter VIII—is concerned with a departure or a return of some kind, and the novel ends with the final departure from this life by Bäumer.

The process being depicted is one of a decreasing freedom of action and a growing sense of claustrophobia; there is, it becomes increasingly evident, no way out save through death. This relentless crushing of life and the closing in of death is underlined by the motif of Kemmerich's English flying boots. At the beginning of the novel, he lies dying, one leg amputated, and Müller is obsessed with the desire to inherit them. When Kemmerich realizes that he is close to death, he hands them over to Müller. When the latter dies in Chapter XI and Bäumer comes into their possession, we know that he too is marked for death. Of the original group of eight comrades, only one remains, Tjaden, and he in turn inherits the boots; but "Tjaden has luck as always" (*Im Westen*, p. 120) and he alone also will survive, despite the ill-fated boots, and indeed he reappears in the sequel *Der Weg zurück*.

The whole of *Im Westen nichts Neues* is in fact based on a series of antitheses which reflect various levels of alienation in the minds of the small and dwindling band of comrades. The first of these to come to light is that between "them" and "us".

> Whilst they were still writing and speechifying, we saw field hospitals and dying men;—whilst they were proclaiming service of the state as the highest good, we knew already that fear of death is the stronger. This did not turn us into rebels, deserters, or cowards—all these words came so readily to their lips—we loved our homeland just as much as they did, and we advanced bravely with every attack;—but . . . we had suddenly had our eyes opened. And we saw that of their world nothing remained. (*Im Westen*, p. 17)

There are two immediate consequences that flow from this gulf: the first is that the private soldiers form a closed and self-contained group, that is, they acquire and foster a sense of "comradeship" which dominates every aspect of their existence, but not in the meaning of the word coined by the National Socialists: this is not a case of the "Frontgemeinschaft" (brotherhood of the front)[50] which is such a key concept in their interpretation of the rôle of the First World War, far from it. It is, rather, a negative state, a protective shrinking within a cocoon of intense intimacy with fellow soldiers as an essential means towards self-preservation and the maintenance of sanity in a world gone mad. After being lost for endless hours in No Man's Land, Bäumer hears the voices of his comrades who are out searching for him:

> An uncommon warmth flows through me all of a sudden. Those voices, those few, softly-spoken words, those footsteps in the trench to my rear suddenly wrench me out of the terrible isolation of the mortal fear to which I had all but succumbed. Those voices

mean more to me than my life ... they are the most powerful and protective thing that there can ever be: they are the voices of my comrades. (*Im Westen*, pp. 191–92)

The second consequence of the gulf between "them" and "us" is, that the comrades have lost all sense of belonging to that hierarchy of rôles that sustained them as they grew up: father, mother, schoolmaster and the rest have forfeited their validity; and anew hierarchy has come to be established within the confines of the closed group of comrades. In *Im Westen nichts Neues*, it is Kat, twice the age of the others, who acts out the rôle of the father: he is the source of authority, the leader, the indestructible one whose death by a stray piece of shrapnel as Bäumer is carrying him to a field station to have his wounds dressed so poignantly parallels the wasting away of Bäumer's disease-stricken mother at home. Parent substitute and "real" parent are now both irretrievably lost. (Of Bäumer's father we hear virtually nothing, save that he is a book-binder; and the French soldier Gérard Duval, whom Bäumer stabs in a crater in No Man's Land, and who dies slowly and in great pain before his eyes, also followed that trade.)

Significantly, Kat's qualities are vastly different from those of the group's parents and other figures of authority: he is admired for his ability both to survive in a cruel environment and to care for the needs of his comrades. This finds its sharpest expression in relation to his skill at conjuring food and other necessities of life apparently out of empty air. And so it is hardly surprising to find Bäumer writing about Kat in these terms when he wakens in the night during a rest-break after a wire-laying party, frightened by a sudden sound:

> It is so strange, am I a child? ... and then I recognize Katczinsky's silhouette. He is sitting there quietly, the old soldier ... I sit upright: I feel strangely alone. It is good that Kat is there. (*Im Westen*, pp. 58–59)

And again, as the captured goose is being roasted in the gathering gloom, Bäumer falls into a reverie and is roused by Kat:

> Is my face wet, and where am I? Kat stands before me, his giant shadow bent over me like home. (*Im Westen*, p. 91)

But, for Kat, as for the rest of them, "home" is the barracks (*Im Westen*, p. 63); and the nostalgic reminiscences of the group are directed, not back at their schooldays and childhood, but towards their experiences in the training barracks, when, for example, the order was given for piano-players to take two paces forward, and the unfortunates who did so were briskly marched off to the cookhouse for spud-bashing; or when Himmelstoss made them practise time and again what he evidently regarded as the difficult art of "changing trains in Löhne", which meant that they were obliged to crawl beneath their beds—which served to simulate the underpass at the station—and emerge smartly on the other side. (*Im Westen*, p. 43)

Thus a second area of alienation is on the temporal plane. The little group of comrades is effectively cut off from the past: "Since we have been here, our earlier life has been excluded from us, without our having done any-thing to bring that about." (*Im Westen*, p. 23) The years prior to the outbreak of war, and the values and knowledge which the comrades had acquired then have no meaning for them now. "Between today and the past there is a gulf . . . it is a different world." (*Im Westen*, p. 155) The past is an alien realm to which they could return only as strangers. It is as if the past has died; and, in order to underline this, Remarque twice employs the image of the photograph: when Kemmerich is expiring of his wounds in the hospital bed, he is described as looking blurred and indeterminate in outline, "like a photographic plate which has been double exposed", (*Im Westen*, p. 19) just a hazy shadow of the man he once was. And this image recurs when Bäumer is on guard duty in the darkness reflecting back on the scenes and experiences of his younger days and recognizes that, for him, they are irretrievably lost:

> It would be just like pondering over a photograph of a dead comrade; it is his features, it is his face, and the days we spent together would acquire a deceptive life in our memory, but it is not the thing itself. (*Im Westen*, p. 115)

In the front line, what they learned in school is utterly useless to them. At one point, the comrades joke about the knowledge they acquired in school, throwing the old questions at one another: "How many inhabitants has Melbourne?" "What were the goals of the Göttinger Hain?" (A circle of sentimental eighteenth-century poets.) "How many children has Charles the Bold?"

> We can't remember very much about all that rubbish. Nor has it been of any use to us. No one taught us in school how to light a cigarette under attack in the rain, how to make a fire with wet wood or that the best place to thrust a bayonette is in the stomach, because it doesn't get stuck fast there like it does in the ribs. (*Im Westen*, p. 82)

On entering the army, they were thoroughly brainwashed into forgetting their previous scale of values, although these simply lay dormant at first; it was not until their exposure to front-line fighting over an extended period of time that they became obliterated altogether. In another example of Remarque's skilful use of theme and variation, the recruits were taught "that a polished button is more important than four volumes of Schopenhauer". (*Im Westen*, p. 25) This is then neatly stood on its head in the sequence where Bäumer is observing to his amusement his former schoolmaster Kantorek being drilled in the barracks square by his former pupil, Mittelstaedt, who cries out: "Landsturmmann Kantorek, is that what you call cleaning buttons? You never seem to learn. Unsatisfactory, Kantorek, unsatisfactory". (*Im Westen*, p. 161) He turns the schoolmaster's words against him, destroying all the man's values in a sour act of revenge for the fact that Kantorek, in encouraging his pupils to enlist, had caused precisely the same fate to befall them. This rupture with the past is one of the dominant themes of Remarque's work, the discontinuity of life, this jolting from one plane of existence to another for which man is completely unprepared.

Not only are they cut off from the past; a gulf also extends between them and the future. The inability of those who survive the war to readjust to peacetime conditions is suggested by the way in which Bäumer, walking along the streets of his home town while on leave, starts with fright at the screeching sound of the tramcars, mistaking the noise for that of a grenade whistling through the air. (*Im Westen*, p. 153. The identical motif is repeated in *Der Weg zurück*, p. 82.) The knowledge they have acquired in the trenches is as useless to them in time of peace as their school lessons in time of war.

Only those of the older generation, like Kat, will be able to slip back more or less unscarred into civilian life, since they came to war as mature adults, with a firm foundation in life, and they have something to build on when they return; Kat, for example, has his wife and, significantly, a young son to provide hope for the future. But, as Bäumer writes of his own generation: "The war has ruined us for everything". (*Im Westen*, p. 84) They have been caught up in the war when the hold of school and parents was slackening, but before they had had the opportunity to enter upon adult life: none are married, none have a job, none know which direction they want their future to take.

The young comrades feel equally alienated from the political and social issues of the day; it is not "their" war, and they can see no sense in the notion, say, of a nation actually wanting to attack another nation, a personification of abstractions which, to them, is nonsensical. And when the Kaiser himself appears to review the troops, their reaction is one of bemused disappointment; surely he cannot be the much-vaunted embodiment of the highest ideals of the German nation, they ask themselves; and this leads them on to challenge the whole question of the war, its origins and objectives. In the end, Albert Kropp speaks for them all when he bursts out: "It's better not to talk about all this nonsense at all". (*Im Westen*, p. 187)

Worse still, they feel cut off from reality itself and from their own humanity by the horrific routine of death and suffering in the trenches. They come to lose all sense of time,

> and all that keeps us going is the fact that there are even weaker ...
> yet more helpless men who look up at us with wide-open eyes as
> gods who are able for awhile to evade death. (*Im Westen*, p. 125)

All they possess is life and freedom from injury. They have even lost all sense of their youthful vitality:

> Iron youth. Youth! None of us is more than twenty years old. But
> young? Youth? That's way back in the past. We are old men. (*Im
> Westen*, p. 22)

And in the trenches they are coming to discover that even life itself does not belong to them. At the very beginning of the novel, when Kemmerich is dying it is stressed that the life has already drained out of him, that "the face already bears the alien lines" of death, that "there is no life pulsing under the skin any more", that he has the mark of death upon him. (*Im Westen*, pp. 18–19) When Kemmerich has expired, Bäumer's reaction is one of terrible exultation, for he is alive, he has life within him, and he is filled with the most powerful desire to cling on to that elusive force whatever the cost:

> Streams of energy flow through the earth, surging up into me
> through the soles of my feet.... My limbs move freely, I feel
> my joints strong.... The night lives, I live. I feel a hunger, more
> powerful than for mere food. (*Im Westen*, p. 35)

The ground is frequently referred to in *Im Westen nichts Neues* as the source of a life-giving power, and the strength and significance of the "life force"—which has been conveniently overlooked by the critics—lies at the heart of all Remarque's mature work, and, as we shall see, it is a concept which he develops in the novels which follow upon *Im Westen nichts Neues*. One of them, *Der Funke Leben* (meaning: the spark of life) has the life force as its central theme, and the title of this novel, which explores the power of life in the midst of death and torture in the concentration camps, is prefigured in the scene where the goose is being roasted, and Bäumer describes Kat and himself as "two tiny sparks of life" in the darkness. (*Im Westen*, p. 90)

So when Bäumer and his comrades state that "we want to live at any price", (*Im Westen*, p. 130) the sentiments expressed have nothing to do with cowardice or selfishness. Running away from the fighting is never once contemplated as a possibility (the only exception being the farmer Detering, whose mind snaps when he catches sight of some cherry blossom which swamps him with recollections of his home). Life seems all the more precious when death is so close, but this does not cause them to falter when the call comes to attack the enemy. They fight like dangerous animals, but their adversary is not the French or the British—it is death itself, the negation of the life force:

> We are not hurling grenades against people, we are oblivious of all that at this moment, for there is Death in full cry against us. (*Im Westen*, p. 108)

This existence on the border of death causes them to concern themselves only with the basic essentials; and this is why the episodes of happiness we discussed earlier all concerned the basic physical needs of the comrades: food, defecation, sleep.

The one thing that keeps Remarque's characters determined to maintain their hold on life, even in the face of the most terrible injuries, or frightful tortures in *Der Funke Leben*, is hope; and when Bäumer confesses in the closing pages of *Im Westen nichts Neues* that "we are without hope", (*Im Westen*, p. 251) we know that his end is near. If, Bäumer acknowledges, the war had been over in 1916, it would have been possible for them to return to normality, but now they have been exposed to the front line for too long, they know nothing else any more, and in the words of one study of war fiction, "the front line has become the soldier's home, and it is best to die at home".[51]

Despite all the critical assertions to the contrary, however, the comrades do not actively embrace their lives as savages, for perhaps the most tragic level of alienation which the novel explores is their separation from their true nature as human beings. When Bäumer comes out of the hospital ward where Kemmerich has just died of his wounds, he is filled, not with grief, but with an overwhelming longing, a hunger greater than that for mere sustenance could ever be, a burning desire to reach out and capture life itself.

Their adjustment to life at the front is more apparent than real; they adopt a deliberately superficial mode of existence, cutting themselves off from all emotion and passion in order to be able to survive at all. This causes them to yearn all the more intensely to be able once more to live as complete human beings. The goal of their aspirations is, however, far beyond their grasp: "It is unattainable, and we know it. It is as vain as the expectation of becoming a general". (*Im Westen*, p. 115)

When Bäumer returns home on leave, he recognizes that even those once attainable and modest aspirations which used to fill him—pursuing his studies, reading his books—have been driven out of by the experience of war.

The last words that Bäumer writes before he is killed reflect this loss of hope of ever returning to normality, although the life force within him will continue to "seek its way" (*Im Westen*, p. 263) for as long as he or others of his contemporaries are spared; and the use of the word "way" ("Weg" in German) forges the link with the title of the sequel *Der Weg zurück*, in which Bäumer's generation tries to find a way back to normality, even though the impossibility of the task is clear from the outset. The life force within them will struggle on, just as it now does in Bäumer, whether they will or no.

But the hardest lesson of all that the group of comrades is forced to learn in the war is that the ordered and meaningful pattern of life which they had once found in parents, home and school is a lost illusion; the causality which they had been taught was one cornerstone of their lives does not exist in the front line. There all life hangs on a sequence of blind chances, and chance is the only faith left to the soldier:

> The front is a cage in which you have to wait nervously for whatever is going to happen ... When a shot comes towards me I may duck down, but that is all; where it strikes I can neither know exactly nor influence.... Every soldier only remains alive by a thousand chances. And every soldier believes and trusts in chance. (*Im Westen*, p. 96)

The good do not necessarily prosper, nor do the bad meet their just deserts; in fact, the exact opposite seems to obtain. Joseph Behm, for example, a fat contented lad, does not want to go to war, but lets himself be persuaded, for fear that he would have been branded a coward. Behm is one of the first to fall; wounded in the eyes, he rushes aimlessly about blind and crazed with pain, and is shot down before any of his comrades can reach him and bring him back to safety. Even the apparently indestructible Kat, who has a wife and son to return to, is killed by a tiny stray splinter of shrapnel.

The only apparent exception to this total disruption of causality is the fate of Himmelstoss, the corporal whose reign of terror over the comrades when they are undergoing their basic training culminates in his vicious treatment of Tjaden and another soldier. The two are bed-wetters, and he assigns them to a two-tier bunk, where each is to take turns at sleeping in the lower bunk. Vengeance for this and his other actions is meted out to him on the night before the trainees depart for the front line: Himmelstoss is caught as he returns from his favourite bar, covered in a sheet, tied up, and soundly beaten. When he subsequently appears behind the lines, Tjaden and Kropp insult him, but only receive token punishment when Tjaden explains in the orderly room about the bed-wetting episode. So in this case, it seems, justice is done and seen to be done twice over; the wicked Himmelstoss does not profit from his evil ways, and later in the novel he is shown to be a reformed character; when one of the kitchen orderlies goes on leave, he puts Tjaden in charge of supplies and ensures that the rest of the group are assigned to three days on kitchen fatigue so that they get "the two things which the soldier needs to be happy: food and rest". (*Im Westen*, p. 130)

The semblance of causality in this sequence of events relating to Him-melstoss only serves to heighten the overall absence of causality from the prin-cipal strand of the action. And, if the Himmelstoss subplot is considered in the light of Remarque's later novels, it soon becomes evident that it really has little to do with causality as such; it is rather related to the motif of revenge which becomes so prominent in the novels of emigration, where the act of revenge is a protest against the absence of causality in a blindly cruel world.

Since the soldier lives by chance, all the skill and moral probity in the world are powerless to protect him against a falling shell or a stray bullet; and this situation is reflected in the structure of *Im Westen nichts Neues*, which has no real plot in the proper sense of the term at all, but operates instead on the basis of theme and variation, a sequence of antithetical patterns, and also of a highly developed substructure of recurrent images. We have already encoun-tered the motif of the English flying boots and the photographic plate, but the most poignant of such motifs relates back to the days before the war; the two most important of these are butterflies and poplar trees. Like Remarque himself, Bäumer used to collect butterflies as a child, and when he returns home on leave he looks again at his collection, and reflects on the past which is now irretrievably lost:

> My mother is there, my sister is there, my case of butterflies there
> and the mahogany piano there—but I am not yet quite there ...
> There's a veil, a gap between us. (*Im Westen*, p. 149)

Needless to say, the optimism expressed in the words "not yet quite there" is far from justified.

Earlier in the novel, this same gulf between the world beyond the trenches and the front line is underlined by a grotesque juxtaposition of two incidents, again in the context of the butterfly: two brimstone butterflies (in German, "Zitronenfalter", i.e. "lemon butterflies") flutter all morning over the trench in which the comrades are on duty, and rest for a while on the teeth of a skull, A few lines further on comes a description of a huddle of corpses after a grenade attack; two of them have literally been blown to pieces, and one

> rests his head in death on his chest in the trench, his face is lemon
> yellow, in his bearded mouth a cigarette is still glowing. It glows
> until it hisses out on his lips. (*Im Westen*, p. 121)

The colour of the butterflies is transferred to the face of the dead soldier, and their alighting on the skull's teeth is paralleled by the glowing cigarette on the lifeless lips.

The butterfly motif is taken up to very great effect in the film *All Quiet on the Western Front*; in its celebrated closing sequence, Bäumer's hand is seen reaching out to touch a butterfly, only to fall back limply in death as he is fatally wounded. In a parallel sequence in the novel, in which Detering is overwhelmed with a longing to return to the past, it is the delicate colour of cherry blossom which causes him to lose his reason. His comrades find him holding a twig of cherry blossom, and ask him why he has picked it. He replies that this is the time of year when his cherry orchard back home is transformed into a sea of white blossom; and so powerful is the pull of this recollection of past happiness that Detering simply disappears, presumably seeking to find his way back home. The comrades hear no more of him, but his fate is almost certainly that of the deserter: "For what do court martial judges a hundred kilometres behind the lines understand about that kind of thing?" (*Im Westen*, p. 248)

For Bäumer, the trenches represent the antithesis of the fragile, gentle and ever-present beauty of Nature the "lost world of beauty", as Liedloff puts it.[52] As far as Nature is concerned, Remarque never quite shakes off the sentimentality of his *Jugendstil* days. The butterfly and the cherry blossom symbolize the irrevocable disappearance of the comrades' past lives. Towards the end of the novel—it is the summer of 1918, and it is clear that the Germans have lost the war—Bäumer writes: "The days stand like angels in gold and blue, beyond our grasp, over the circle of destruction". (*Im Westen*, p. 254) Nature is totally detached from the conflict being acted out beneath.

Only once in the novel is there a reference to any military object as being pictorially attractive, and the circumstances are quite special: the comrades are waiting behind the lines for transport; it is a misty night, and there is a strange atmosphere of suspension from reality. A column of men goes past, but they are not like men, only a pattern of shapes against the gloom. And then more men pass, this time on horseback, but equally unreal: "The riders with their steel helmets look like knights of a past age; in some strange way it is beautiful and stirring". (*Im Westen*, p. 56) But, overwhelmingly, the war is bereft of all beauty; and it is significant that even the aspirant poet and dramatist Bäumer cannot share with an artist like Paul Nash a sense of awe at "these wonderful trenches at night, at dawn, at sundown".[53] Nothing can compensate for the destructiveness and horror of this war, because it has cut them off from beauty and all that it represents. Nash may observe and paint with all the "inspired egotism of the artist who is sure of his vocation",[54] but for Bäumer and his comrades such sublimation of the experiences of war is an impossibility.

Alongside the butterfly, poplar trees also represent the unattainability of the lost world; these are the trees of Bäumer's home town along the Pappelallee (Poplar Avenue; the equivalent in Osnabrück is Am Pappelgraben, and poplars find frequent mention throughout Remarque's novels). There Bäumer and his schoolfriends used to catch sticklebacks in the brook running the length of the avenue, but it is all now no more than a golden memory of a hopelessly lost time. And, significantly, the sight and sound of the poplars occur again on the last page of the novel as symbolic of Bäumer's vain aspiration to find his way back to his past and to make use of the foundation laid in those early years to build himself a positive future.

Remarque also employs the repetition of certain key words, of which "Erde" (earth) and "Stille" (tranquillity) are the most significant, in order to express certain central concepts. We have already encountered "earth" as representing the source of the life force, of the energy that flows through Bäumer when he is overwhelmed by the recognition that he is alive, and Kemmerich dead; and, ultimately, it is to the earth that man finally returns. The notion of "tranquillity" is associated with the lost past, and in the last lines of the novel both these key terms are stressed once again: the day of Bäumer's death is "quiet and tranquil", and his body lies "as if in sleep on the earth". (*Im Westen*, p. 263)

Bäumer dies on one of those days in the final stages of the war when military activity is on such a relatively subdued level that the report from the front line states merely that all is quiet on the Western front. Death and suffering have become so routine that it requires a major offensive or a particularly gory occurrence to force the war back into the headlines.

As a result, language too is alienated, words are stripped of their true import, and the most horrific experiences are depicted in flat, matter-of-fact terms, just as in Kafka's chilling fantasies. Again and again, Bäumer admits the inadequacy of mere words such as attack, counter-attack, mines, gas, machine-guns and the rest to encompass the terrors they purport to describe. This does not only hold true for his experiences in the front line: when he is at home on leave, words also come to him only with great difficulty, and he finds that the words of his books fail to reach him any more. He is unable to explain what things are like in action; and, when he pays a visit to Kemmerich's mother, he admits his total inability to put down on paper words adequate to depict the sufferings of the bereaved mother.

Bäumer's only recourse is to state quite baldly what happens when, for example, raw recruits—whom the comrades describe as children even though they are scarcely a few months younger than the majority of them—dying under a gas attack, failing to take cover at the right moment, or going berserk with fear.

So everything is reduced to a numbing routine: in the descriptions of battle, of waiting behind the lines, thinking of home, enjoying the basic pleasures of food and sleep, the same formulae appear time and again to stress the sameness of every aspect of their lives, the treadmill of war from which there is no escape. Feeling and emotion dare not be allowed any room for expression, or insanity would inevitably result; and equally the words used describe the surface of the life to which they have been reduced, a string of bare utterances, an Expressionist sequence of substantives, as here:

> Grenades, gas clouds and flotillas of tanks—crushing, corrosion, death. Dysentery, influenza, typhus—throttling, incineration, death. Graves, field hospital, mass grave—no more possibilities exist. (*Im Westen*, pp. 252–53)

This routine of suffering and the necessity for the suppression of feeling and emotion are to become a key motif in Remarque's later novels under the guise of the cliché, of which more later.

The recurrent motifs that express the lives of the comrades also stress the basic essentials of the life to which their animal existence has reduced them. They concentrate, as we have seen, on food and defecation. Only fleeting reference is made to tobacco, although it is stressed as vital to the soldier, and there is also relatively little emphasis on alcohol, a state of affairs that is more than remedied in Remarque's subsequent novels. Surprisingly, perhaps, there is not very much in the way of references to sexual matters (especially for those who have read the reviewers and the critics rather than the novel itself). Early critics claimed that *Im Westen nichts Neues* was read by some for its questionable aspects, but it is far from being a rich stamping-ground for those in pursuit of titillation, even by the standards of the 1920's. There is little to cause linguistic offense, apart from references to a certain portion of the anatomy and its defecatory rôle, and there is no specific reference to details of the sexual act. There are a couple of allusions to adolescent curiosity about sex, and to Leer's fascination with girls from the officers' brothels, who are supposedly under orders to wear silk chemises and to bathe themselves before receiving visitors from the rank of captain upwards. The episode of the passionate Lewandowski in hospital has already been mentioned in the context of Remarque's supposed mendacity in relation to life in the military hospital where he was a patient with Peter Kropp; this is described in matter-of-fact terms, as a basic element of life, rather than as an opportunity for obscene allusion or adolescent voyeurism. And the important sequence when some of the comrades cross the canal to visit the three Frenchwomen translates Bäumer's lovemaking with one of the girls into terms of the vague aspirations towards unattainable fulfilment which stalk the pages of his *Jugendstil* works. This comes across most forcibly when the comrades are gazing at a poster advertising an army theatrical performance, which portrays a man in a blue jacket and white trousers, and a girl who fascinates them, clad in a bright summer dress, white stockings and shoes, and holding a straw hat in one hand. They regard the girl as a "miracle", and their immediate reaction is to go off to have themselves deloused in a kind of ritual (as well as actual!) cleansing of their animal natures in response to such perfection and purity. When Bäumer embraces the French girl, he too is in search of a "miracle": "I press myself deeper into the arms which are holding me, perhaps a miracle will happen ..." (*Im Westen*, p. 140) Similarly, Bäumer is reluctant to climb into the bunk on the hospital train which is repatriating him, since it is made up with snow-white sheets.

But the miracle will never come; the comrades are either doomed to die, cut off from their former lives, from reality and even from their own true selves, or doomed to live on in a peacetime environment to which they will never be able properly to adjust, not least on the paradoxical grounds that, once an individual has existed for a period under the immediate threat of death, a return to "normal" life is an impossibility, since the senses have become so accustomed to being sharpened to the keenest edge by the experience of the front line that the comrades will in peacetime be in a constant state of frustration at the very lack of danger. So they and their generation are, in a very real sense of the term, spoiled for all time.

* * *

In all the debates about *Im Westen nichts Neues*, there is one common criticism made by defenders and detractors of the novel alike, from the National Socialists at one extreme, via the liberal pacifists in the middle, to the Marxists at the other end of the spectrum; and that is, that it does not succeed in providing a generally valid overall picture of the war. The novel's opponents argue that this one-sidedness constitutes a serious weakness in a work which has come to be regarded as official war history, its supporters on the other hand congratulate Remarque on refraining from spoon-feeding his readers, but instead assuming that they are sufficiently intelligent to make up their own minds about what happened in the trenches and to the rear. Interestingly, Remarque himself seems to fall into line with this view of *Im Westen nichts Neues*; in the Eggebrecht interview, he admits that he was seeking to do no more than simply put down on paper a "worm's eye view" of the war.[55]

But to argue that Remarque is either a weak-kneed pacifist gnawing away at the nation's vitals, or a mature writer probing fearlessly at the heart of his generation's tragic fate, or again a bourgeois liberal who recognizes the disease and fails to point to a cure, is to miss the point entirely. Nor is it enough to indicate that the limitations of the work are attributable to the fact that Bäumer is a relatively unsophisticated young man who would in any event be incapable of comprehending the wider historical perspective into which his individual life fits. (There is, in any event, no inevitable correlation between the intelligence, insight or whatever of the author's mouthpiece and the quality or complexity of the narrative.)

The truth of the matter is that, in *Im Westen nichts Neues*, Remarque is proposing the view that human existence can no longer be regarded as having any ultimate meaning. Bäumer and his comrades cannot make sense of the world at large for the simple reason that it is no longer possible to do so, not just for this group of ordinary soldiers, but for a substantial proportion of his entire generation. Remarque refuses to lull his reader into a false sense of security, into thinking that God is in his heaven and all is right with the world—all that is amiss is that we as individuals are too limited in vision to be able to recognize the existence of a grand design. On the contrary, he demonstrates that the holocaust of the First World War has destroyed, not only any semblance of meaningfulness that the universe may seem to have possessed in the past, but that even the continuity of the individual existence has been shattered.

The largest unit of significance that remains is the individual life, sustained by the "life force" pulsing within, which holds the individual for the brief span of his existence and then releases him into death.

Philosophers, sociologists and all the rest may argue that this adherence to the notion of the "life principle" is a dangerous aberration and a distortion of all the received dogma of Western civilization; but this is how Remarque experienced life in the Great War with all its contradictions, pleasures and sufferings, and, fortunately for the reader, authors are under no obligation to construct internally consistent philosophical systems which conform to certain predetermined moral and ethical principles. It is for this reason, we would argue, that *Im Westen nichts Neues* captured the imagination of so many millions of readers, and why it continues to be one of the greatest bestsellers of all time. It refuses to inject a consoling but essentially illusory pattern of causality and meaningfulness into human existence.

Not only has the war destroyed any possibility for Bäumer and his like of reaching out beyond his individual existence and grasping at the myth of a meaningful universe, it has also shattered what was formerly a genuine reality, namely, the experience of a human life as a continuous single entity, an onward and upward progression through the years. Now even the individual life has lost its overall significance: it has become alienated from itself, and the knowledge and experiences gained at one stage are demonstrably inapplicable to the next phase. All that can be rescued from the tangle of the lives of Bäumer and his comrades is a profound desire to hold on to life itself, a blind instinct not to let slip the life force, and an equally blind hope for the future. As we have seen, when that hope fades in the closing sequence of the novel, Bäumer's end cannot be far distant. These themes are developed and explored further by Remarque in his subsequent works, especially in the two novels which deal with aspects of the Second World War; *Der Funke Leben* and *Zeit zu leben*, as will be seen when the time comes to discuss them in a later chapter. Nor is it coincidental that the word "Leben" (life) figures prominently in both titles.

Remarque's refusal to simulate meaning where he sees none is probably the cause of so many statements on the part of critics to the effect that *Im Westen nichts Neues* comes close "to being all things to all men"[56]—which it certainly is not, unless "all things" include anathema and "all men" the Nazis. Behind such statements, however, there lies at least a partial recognition of the fact that Remarque has succeeded in distilling the common experience of ordinary individuals in the First World War and beyond, and that he has not set out with any false moralizing or philosophical preconceptions, but has sought honestly to convey his experience of life (and that of countless others), however unpleasant and negative his conclusions may be. Nor is he trying to seek refuge in any new dogma, or sidling towards any existing unorthodoxy, such as existentialism. Remarque is essentially a non-intellectual writer who prefers to express rather than to explain his experience of life, and in *Im Westen nichts Neues* he was able to come to terms with his own full realization of what the experiences of the war meant for him and for so many of his generation; this is why the novel was for him, and for so many others, an "Erlösung", a release.

* * *

In his excellent but solitary study, Claude Cockburn defines as one of the qualities essential to a bestselling novel the presentation in an acceptable fictional form of "certain attitudes, prejudices, aspirations, etc., in the reader's conscious or subconscious mind".[57] In this respect, as we have seen, *Im Westen nichts Neues* is remarkably successful. It is nonsense to assert, as the Marxist critic tends to do, that Remarque has become so totally identified with the "little man", the petty bourgeois, that he is incapable of objectivizing him.[58] Anyone with a nodding acquaintanceship with Remarque's own predilection for the good life would hardly brand him as a defender of drab middle-class mediocrity. Remarque is simply being descriptive rather than prescriptive, to borrow a turn of phrase from the grammarian; and his fictionalized emotional experiences were recognized by millions of people as something with which they had a great deal in common.

If *Im Westen nichts Neues* is regarded in this light, then questions like the accuracy of his presentation of the "lost generation" (the credit goes to Gertrude Stein for inventing the term) cease to seem so vital. It does not really matter that Remarque said that "our generation has grown up differently from any other before or since".[59] Many a critic has pounced gleefully on this assertion with pronouncements like: "Ample evidence shows that the heroes of Remarque are not representative of a whole generation but only of a certain type".[60] Remarque is not so lacking in perception as to be unaware of the truism, and it is disingenuous of his detractors to level this kind of accusation against him. What Remarque is asserting in his novel is that, so extreme were the experiences of Bäumer and his comrades that they were utterly devastated by their recognition of the discontinuity of life, and the absence of any ultimate meaning in the universe. The majority of Remarque's readers, however, have not been eighteen-year-old front-line soldiers in the First World War; but they have, consciously or subconsciously, grown aware of a similar kind of insight in their own lives and experiences. As Cockburn suggests as a principle quality of the best-seller, Remarque has given literary expression to attitudes widely felt by ordinary people at large.

This does not, of course, mean that everyone reads Remarque for the same reasons: just as the pit watched Shakespeare for the farce and the fighting, some of Remarque's readers may have scanned the novel for bloodthirsty battle scenes, the prurient passages (in which they will have been more than a little disappointed), its supposed political and sociological significance, and so on. None of these misreadings should be allowed to be taken as invalidating the novel itself, especially since so many have wilfully distorted it and sought to reduce it to the level of a debating point in some campaign or other.

Cockburn stresses that it is not enough for the writer to touch on a nerve of his time; he must also write with consummate skill. In the words of Meyer:

> It is far more difficult to write a really absorbing book than to concoct a clever experimental one; it is far more difficult to tell a good story or to invent a memorable character that stays for a while in the human brain of millions or even of thousands than to fabricate *Kunstgewerbe* in the medium of words, so clever, so original that it can have any passing meaning we want to find there. This fashion will go, for it has come; and everything that is a fashion comes and goes, but the Odyssey has remained and so has Conan Doyle.[61]

Meyer overstates the case, but that does not impair its validity; as we have seen already, Remarque constructs his novel with considerable skill, employing balanced episodes (happy and tragic alternate with almost excessive inevitability), recurrent motifs and other devices. There is no doubt that the style of *Im Westen nichts Neues* marks a substantial advance on Remarque's previous work, his *Jugendstil* writings as well as the rather indifferent journalism of his Continental days, and indeed it sets the pattern for the rest of his novels. Apart from the major techniques already discussed, there are a number of detailed stylistic devices employed by Remarque which all conspire to enhance the overall impact of the novel. Chief among these are the preference for similes rather than metaphors, which helps to highlight the latter when they appear at key points in the text; the emphatic use of inversion at the beginning of the sentence which, although a not uncommon phenomenon in German, is adopted by Remarque with particular effect at moments of emotional tension; his sparing but striking use of anaphora, which is most impressive in the sequence of short paragraphs each beginning "O mother" in which Bäumer reflects on his leave and his previous life (*Im Westen*, p. 131f); the tendency for concrete substantives to dominate at crisis moments; the occasional very long sentence contrasting strongly with the predominant pattern of short, simple sentences; and so on. In *Im Westen nichts Neues* there is no doubt that Remarque suddenly found his own stylistic voice, so to speak; the language is shorn of all but the occasional trace of his erstwhile sentimentality, and like most of his subsequent writing it is compulsively readable. Remarque owes his success as a writer almost as much to his stylistic craftsmanship as to his ability to express in narrative terms the sentiments of millions of his contemporaries. From both aspects, the novel

> satisfied a need, and expressed and realized emotions and attitudes to life which the buyers and borrowers did not find expressed elsewhere.[62]

One of the worse fates that can befall a writer is to have a runaway bestseller with his first book; everything that follows will be held up against it, and sequels are notoriously disappointing. One critic at least has insisted—quite wrongly—that Remarque is a "one-book" author, despite the more than modest success of others of his works.[63] Remarque did in fact regard *Im Westen nichts Neues* as his "first" novel—*Die Traumbude* he considered as part of his juvenilia and something of an embarrassment, and *Station am Horizont* as a journalistic exercise; in a letter to Rabe, he replies to the latter's invitation to come and give a lecture on his new novel in these terms:

> I have conned your arabesques with much amusement, but you will understand for all that, that at the moment I'd personally prefer to keep myself out of the limelight for a bit. It is only my first book, and one ought really to hide behind one's work for a while and

only come to the surface if and when the second turns out good as well.[64]

Remarque was determined to let *Im Westen nichts Neues* find its own feet; and, in refusing to be dragged into the publicity and controversy which surrounded it, he demonstrated considerable restraint and good sense.

There is no doubt that Remarque was more than a little overwhelmed by the reception accorded to *Im Westen nichts Neues*, and was determined to write a sequel which would not only explore the fate of those returning from the front line in search of a land fit for heroes to live in but which would also be a more substantial literary achievement.

NOTES

1. Quoted by A. Kerker, "*Im Westen nichts Neues*. Die Geschichte eines Bestsellers", broadcast by the Third Programme of the Norddeutscher Rundfunk, 3.4.1973. (Copy in R–S 228a–257).

2. ibid.

3. J. Wulf, *Literatur und Dichtung im Dritten Reich. Eine Dokumentation*, Gütersloh, 1963, p. 46.

4. B.A. Rowley, "Journalism into Fiction. Erich Maria Remarque, *Im Westen nichts Neues*", in H. Klein (ed.), *The First World War in Fiction*, London, 1976, p. 103.

5. "Gespräch mit Remarque", p. 1.

6. C. Riess, *Bestseller. Bücher, die Millionen lesen*. Hamburg, 1960, p. 60.

7. P. de Mendelssohn, *S. Fischer und sein Verlag*, Frankfurt a.M., 1970, p. 1115.

8. ibid, p. 1116.

9. *Frankfurter Allgemeine Zeitung*, 9.7.1962 and 26.7.1962.

10. "*All Quiet on the Western Front*", *Times Literary Supplement*, 8.4.1929, p. 314.

11. E. Childers, *The Riddle of the Sands*, London, 1955, p. 77.

12. "*All Quiet on the Western Front*", *New Statesman*, 25.5.1929, p. 218.

13. K. Kroner, "Ein Arzt über *Im Westen nichts Neues*", *Neue Preussische Kreuz-Zeitung*, 27.6.1929 (Beiblatt).

14. For example, W. Müller Scheld, *Im Westen nichts Neues. Eine Täuschung*, Idstein, 1929, p. 10.

15. P. Kropp, *Endlich Klarheit über Remarque und sein Buch "Im Westen nichts Neues"*, privately printed in Hamm, Westphalia, 1930, p. 10.

16. E. Toller, "*Im Westen nichts Neues*", *Die literarische Welt*, V (1929), no. 8, p. 5.

17. *Der Kampf um Remarque*, Berlin, 1929, unpaginated.

18. See B. Kempf, *Suffragette for Peace. The Life of Bertha von Suttner* (transl. R.W. Last), London, 1972, pp. 23–29 (*Die Waffen nieder!*); pp. 53–63 (Nobel and his Will); pp. 134–63 (extracts from English version of *Die Waffen nieder!* transl. T. Holmes).

19. G.N. Shuster in the Foreword to W.K. Pfeiler, *War and the German Mind. The Testimony of the Men of Fiction who fought at the Front*, New York, 1941, p. 1.

20. H. Heisler, *Krieg oder Frieden. Randbemerkung zu Remarques Buch "Im Westen nichts Neues"*, Stuttgart, 1930, p. 33.

21. G. Lutz, *Die Front-Gemeinschaft. Das Gemeinschaftserlebnis in der Kriegsliteratur*, Greifswald, 1936, p. 71.

22. G. Nickl, "*Im Westen nichts Neues* und sein wahrer Sinn. Ein Betrachtung über den Pazifismus und Antwort an Remarque", *Heimgarten. Monatsschrift für Unterhaltung und Aufklärung*, Sonderheft, 1930, p. 12.

23. ibid, p. 14.

24. Müller Scheld, p. 28.

25. E.M. Requark (pseud.), *Vor Troja nichts Neues*, Berlin, 1930, p. 22.

26. Ibid, p. 7.

27. Ibid, p. 24.

28. Ibid, p. 43.

29. Berlin, 1929.

30. Ibid, p. 11.

31. Ibid, p. 19.

32. See M.S. Jones, *Der Sturm. A Study of an Expressionist Periodical*, German Department, Hull University, 1979: chapter on Friedlaender.

33. A. Soergel and C. Hohoff, *Dichtung und Dichter der Zeit*, vol. 1, Düsseldorf, 1963, p. 349.

34. W. Rothe (ed.), *Die deutsche Literatur in der Weimarer Republik*, Stuttgart, 1974, pp. 204, 206, 208.

35. V. Lange, *Modern German Literature 1870–1940*, New York, 1945, p. 104.

36. J. Rühle, *Literature and Revolution. A critical Study of the Writer and Communism in the twentieth Century*, London, 1969, p. 153.

37. Letter in *Frankfurter Allgemeine Zeitung*, 4.9.1971.

38. H. Liedloff, "Two War Novels: a critical Comparison", *Revue de Littérature Comparée*, XLII (1968), pp. 390–406.

39. H. Swados, "Remarque's Relevance", *Book Week*, 23.10.1966, p. 12.

40. H.M. Klein, "Dazwischen Niemandsland: *Im Westen nichts Neues* and *Her Privates We*", in O. Kuhn (ed.), *Grossbritannien und Deutschland. Festschrift für John W.P. Bourke*, Munich, 1974, pp. 487–512.

41. "Journalism into Fiction", p. 109.

42. Antkowiak, *Ludwig Renn. Erich Maria Remarque*, p. 116.

43. I. Wegner, "Die Problematik der 'verlorenen Generation' und ihre epische Gestaltung im Romanwerk Erich Maria Remarques", Diss., Jena, 1965, p. 32.

44. Liedloff, pp. 391–92.

45. Preface to *The Old Wives' Tale*, London, 1948, p. x.

46. "Remarque und Osnabrück", p. 232.

47. ibid, pp. 199–200.

48. "Gespräch mit Remarque", p. 1.

49. Nickl, p. 38.

50. See Lutz, p. 73.

51. P. Hagbolt, "Ethical and social Problems in the German War Novel", *Journal of English and German Philology*, XXXII, pp. 21–32.

52. Liedloff, p. 391.

53. Letter quoted by C. Day Lewis, "Paul Nash. A private View", in M. Eates, *Paul Nash. The Master of the Image*, London, 1973, p. xii.

54. Ibid.

55. "Gespräch mit Remarque", p. 1.

56. A.F. Bance, "*Im Westen nichts Neues*: A Bestseller in Context", *Modern Language Review*, LXXII (1977), p. 372.

57. C. Cockburn, *Bestseller. The Books that Everyone Read 1900–1939*, London, 1972, p. 11.

58. For example, Wegner, p. 65.

59. "Gespräch mit Remarque", p. 1.

60. W.K. Pfeiler, *War and the German Mind. The Testimony of the Men of Fiction who fought at the Front*, New York, 1941, p. 142.

61. H. Meyer, "Bestseller Research Problems", in D.D. Richards, *The German Bestseller in the Twentieth Century. A Complete Bibliography and Analysis 1915–1940*, unpaginated.

62. Cockburn, p. 3.

63. Obituary in *Daily Telegraph*, 26.9.1970.

64. Letter to Hanns-Gerd Rabe, 12.2.1929. (R-S I, 209).

GEORGE J. MITCHELL

Making All Quiet on the Western Front

ALL QUIET ON THE WESTERN FRONT, produced by Universal Pictures in 1930, is considered today to be a landmark motion picture. It received an Academy Award as the year's best production and ended up on every "10 Best" list that year including the National Board of Review. It was a huge critical and financial success.

Two brilliant film craftsmen were largely responsible for the success of *All Quiet*: Lewis Milestone, the director, and Arthur Edeson, ASC, the cinematographer. Edeson freed the camera from the limitations sound had imposed and Milestone brought back the dynamic style of film editing that reached a zenith with silent pictures but had been absent from the early talkies.

The story of how *All Quiet* reached the screen began when Carl Laemmle, the avuncular head of Universal Studios, bought the screen rights to Erich Maria Remarque's anti-war novel in 1929. Many in Hollywood thought that a movie could not be made from the book. It told of a group of youthful German soldiers thrown into the holocaust of World War I trench warfare. One by one they are either maimed or killed or otherwise destroyed by the war. The author had been a teen-age German infantryman. He wrote out of the anguish of his own experiences with an utter frankness and simplicity that was powerful and compelling.

From *American Cinematographer*, September 1985, vol. 66, no. 9, pp. 34–43. © 1985 ASC Holding Corporation.

Essentially episodic in content, it had no love interest, no suspense and anything but a glorious conclusion. Moreover, it was controversial. The memory of World War I was still vivid. The rampant anti-Germanism that had followed the entrance of the United States into the war was not easily forgotten.

Published in Germany in 1927 under the title *Im Westen Nichts Neues* (Nothing New in the West), it was an instant success selling over a million copies—no mean feat at that time in a Germany still trying to come to grips with her defeat in 1918. The book was translated into English and published in the United States by Little, Brown and Company and was soon on every best seller list.

Uncle Carl Laemmle, as he liked to be called, was certainly one of the most eccentrically lovable of the early movie pioneers. He had come to the United States as a penniless teen-age immigrant from South Germany. Possessed of natural shrewdness, diligence and thrift, Laemmle had prospered. He got into the motion picture business in 1909 at the age of 39 by opening an nickelodeon in Chicago. By 1912 he had formed Universal Film Manufacturing Company, which grew into Universal Pictures. In 1915, he opened Universal City Studios, described at that time as "the world's largest film manufacturing plant." But by 1929, Universal was in dire financial straits. Several expensive pictures had failed at the box office and the coming of sound had produced more problems. Adding to these woes was Uncle Carl's odd-ball, impulsive way of doing business.

Laemmle's helter-skelter *modus operandi* sometimes resulted in lucky decisions. He elevated his 20-year old private secretary, Irving Grant Thalberg, to head production at Universal City. Young Thalberg brought order out of chaos and produced *The Hunchback of Notre Dame* with Lon Chaney in 1923, an enormous critical and box office success. (Thalberg went on to even greater successes at MGM.)

Convinced that his son, Carl Laemmle, Jr., had the same spark of genius, Uncle Carl appointed him to the same post when he had barely turned 21— but Junior was no Thalberg. Junior was not a particularly difficult person. He gave people around him considerable freedom to act on their own. Despite his many detractors, Junior deserves credit for the production of *All Quiet*, and especially for his backing of Milestone and Edeson.

Carl Laemmle was certainly aware of the success of such war pictures as *The Big Parade* (MGM), *What Price Glory?* (Fox) and *Wings* (Paramount). With a proven best seller property like *All Quiet* in his hands, he reasoned there was a good chance for success.

The year 1929 was in many ways a transitional period for the motion picture industry. Two years earlier sound pictures had arrived and struck Hollywood with a vengeance. Filmmakers had a new and powerful tool to work with but they were still struggling with ways to use it. Technical problems were legion.

By 1928, silent pictures had reached heights of artistic perfection in photography and editing. This was set back immeasurably with the arrival of sound. For example, cutting sound to picture had not been mastered. Camera noise was another vexing problem. The ubiquitous microphone picked up the sound of the camera mechanism. The earliest solution was to place the camera and operator inside a small soundproof booth made of celotex. Soon dubbed "sound houses" and "sweat boxes," they effectively shut out camera noise but also rendered the camera virtually stationary.

Herbert Brenon, the first choice to direct *All Quiet*, had directed the highly successful *Beau Geste* in 1927. He wanted a fee of $125,000 which the thrifty Laemmle thought was excessive. Whereupon Agent Myron Selzneck suggested his client, Lewis Milestone, at a fee of $5,000 per week with a ten week guarantee. It was a shrewd move by Selzneck, then just starting a successful career as an agent. It took ten weeks to prepare the script plus 17 weeks to photograph and edit the picture. Milestone's take home pay was $135,000.

Lewis Milestone was born September 30, 1895 in Odessa, the port city on the Black Sea of the Ukraine. His father was a well-to-do man-ufacturer. Young Milestone received his high school education in Russia but in 1913 was sent to Germany to study mechanical engineering. Long interested in the theater, which was looked down upon by his parents, he soon lost interest in his studies. At Christmas time the following year, his father sent him money to come home for the holidays. Instead, Milestone decided to make his move. He and two fellow students visited the United States. His money soon ran out so he wrote his father for more. The elder Milestone answered, "Since you have taken it on yourself to visit the land of opportunity without my permission, suppose you remain and see what opportunity it affords you."

A series of odd jobs followed until he found a job with a theatrical pho-tographer at $7.00 a week. But, for the first time he was interested in what he was doing. He learned developing and printing, helped with the photography and learned to handle film from the standpoint of still photography.

After the United States entered the war against Germany, Milestone enlisted as a private in the Army Signal Corps in September 1917. He was first assigned to the Army's training film unit at Columbia University. After a time there, he was transferred to Washington where he worked in the laboratory and learned to cut film. Victor Fleming, Josef von Stern-berg, Wesley Ruggles, Richard Wallace and Gordon Hollingshead, all well known for their later work in the motion picture industry, served in the same unit with him.

Following his discharge from the Army in December 1918, Milestone headed for Hollywood to work for Jesse D. Hampton, an independent producer he had met while serving in the Signal Corps. He worked in the cutting room assisting the film editor, splicing film, carrying film cans, sweeping the cutting room floor and running errands. An affable, pleasant young man, he was known to all as "Millie"—an affectionate nickname that stuck with him throughout his career.

He was soon noticed by Henry King, then directing a series of H.B. Warner programmers for Hampton, who made Milestone his general assistant and film cutter. This led to an association of several years with William A. Seiter, a popular director of comedies and family oriented program pictures. Milestone became his assistant and film editor as well as the scenario writer on several of Seiter's comedies. The two men became fast friends.

The original screen treatment for *All Quiet* was written by C. Gardner Sullivan, the veteran scenarist of many Thomas H. Ince films and the best of William S. Hart's westerns. Sullivan was a highly skilled scenario constructionist. He was especially noted for his skill at planning and laying out shots in advance of shooting. He became the chief scenario editor of *All Quiet*. Milestone brought in Del Andrews, who had worked with him at the Hughes unit, to help on the script. Andrews had been a film editor and was a sort of jack-of-all-trades. This being an early talking picture, it was thought necessary to bring in someone familiar with the spoken word. Hence, the addition of playwright Maxwell Anderson and Broadway producer George Abbott to the writing team. Milestone holed up with his writers in a house on Catalina Island next door to director John Ford and hammered out a shooting script.

Louis Wolheim, who had worked with Milestone in two pictures, was quickly cast as the front-wise veteran Katczinsky or "Kat." A broken nose gotten on the football field gave Wolheim a face that appealed to D.W. Griffith who cast him as the executioner in *Orphans of the Storm* (1921) and as the renegade Captain Hare in *America* (1924). Wolheim next scored in the successful Maxwell Anderson–Laurence Stallings play, *What Price Glory?* This led to a Hollywood contract and his association with Milestone.

George "Slim" Summerville, a much underrated comedian, was given the part of Tjaden. Summerville added some welcome comedy touches to an otherwise grim story. John Wray, a Broadway actor-playwright, became the sadistic drill sergeant, Himmelstoss.

The roles of the young school-boy soldiers went to William Bakewell as Albert Kropp; Ben Alexander (later Sgt. Friday's *Dragnet* partner) as Franz Kemmerich; Scott Kolk as Leer; Owen Davis, Jr. as Peter; Russell Gleason (replacing Allan Lane) as Müller; and Walter Browne Rogers as Behm. The latter's brooding face was used on all posters and 24-sheets for *All Quiet*.

The pivotal role of Paul Bäumer presented problems. Milestone knew that a great deal of the success—or failure—of *All Quiet* lay in this role of the chief protagonist. Phillips Holmes, a popular juvenile of the day, was considered, as was John Harron, younger brother of the Griffith star, Robert Harron. Both actors had a certain sensitive quality the part demanded but Milestone kept looking.

Paul Bern recommended a young actor who had played the juvenile in Greta Garbo's *The Kiss*, which he had just produced (incidentally, this was MGM and Garbo's last silent picture). He told Lew Ayres, the young man in question, to call Milestone. But somehow things went wrong and the boy could never get Milestone to either give him an appointment or call him back. Disgusted with his efforts to reach Milestone, Ayres joined the other hopefuls being tested in a scene of the men in a chow-line. Ayres stood out and got the part. His sensitive performance as the doomed young private was to skyrocket him to instant stardom.

In a bit of inspired casting, Milestone persuaded his pal, Raymond Griffith, to play the part of the French soldier Paul stabs to death in a shell hole and is forced to watch die. Griffith had been an important comedy star known as the "Silk Hat Comedian" in silent pictures. Unfortunately, he had suffered a vocal affliction as a child and spoke only in a hoarse whisper. With the arrival of talking pictures, Griffith turned to production and was already working as a producer at Warner Bros. when Milestone talked him into playing the part. Griffith delivered a poignant, unforgettable performance. Incidentally, he continued his career as a producer and worked in that capacity for many years at 20th Century-Fox where he was one of Darryl Zanuck's closest associates.

Enter Myron Selzneck again with George Cukor in tow. Cukor had been brought from Broadway where he had been successfully directing plays to work for Paramount as a possible director. He knew nothing about filmmaking but a great deal about acting. Selzneck persuaded Milestone to take on Cukor to help coach the young actors. He became more than just a dialogue director. His work on *All Quiet* has never received the recognition it deserves. He became one of Milestone's most valuable assistants. He immediately took the young actors in hand and began rehearsing them in their roles.

At the same time, the boys were delivered into the hands of Otto Biber, a former German army drill master. Biber instructed them in the art of the goose-step as well as other military exercises. To insure further accuracy, Hans von Morhart and Wilhelm von Brincken, both former German officers, were hired as technical advisers. Outstanding features of *All Quiet* were the authentic German and French uniforms and props Universal purchasing agents brought back from Europe. For example, in the early training scenes the boys are shown in the old Prussian blue uniforms and then later in field gray. Six complete artillery pieces were secured—not to mention machine guns, rifles and all types of military hardware and accoutrements. Such attention to detail helped establish the proper atmosphere.

Tony Gaudio, ASC, was the initial cinematographer considered to handle the cameras on *All Quiet*. Together with Harry Perry, ASC, he had just wrapped up *Hell's Angels* for Howard Hughes. But in Tony's inimical words he'd "had enough of war" so he was not too enthusiastic about doing another war picture. Then Universal executives heard that Arthur Edeson had just finished a Western at Fox Studios and had never gone into a camera booth or sound house as they were sometimes called. The picture was *In Old Arizona*, the first of the Cisco Kid stories to reach the screen. It was "all talking" and was one of the first sound pictures to be made outdoors, a feat some of the early sound engineers said was not feasible.

In 1968 Edeson described how he got the assignment to photograph *All Quiet*. "I had just finished a picture at Fox for Frank Borzage and they had no assignment for me when I received a call from Roy Hunter, head of Universal's lab.

"'Art, are you available,' he asked me."

"I'll have to ask Sheehan (Fox production chief) on that."

"He said we have a picture, *All Quiet on the Western Front*, and they tell me that you never go into a sound house.

"I said that was true. 'I have a very, very quiet camera which is my own.' It was a Mitchell (Standard). I didn't tell him what made it quiet. I told him nothing.

"Actually, I had taken the camera over to Gus, the mechanic at Mitchell's, and he put a micarta gear in the rear of the camera. He took some of the metal parts out and that made the camera 50 percent quieter than other cameras. And I also had a big padded bag we called a "barney" that I put over the camera to quiet it down more. I used this system to photograph *In Old Arizona*. Well, I went over to Universal to see Hunter. Hunter asked me if I would make a test for them. I said yes, 'I'd make a test for you,' one in the sound house and one outside with my Mitchell camera covered with a 'barney' bag.

"I went over to Fox and borrowed one of the 'barneys' we had used on the pictures I had worked on there. Then I took all my gear back over to Universal to do the test. The test was the schoolroom scene where the German boys are lectured by their teacher to join the Army. I remembered it well because I picked out the boy (Lew Ayres) who played the lead. I asked "Millie" Milestone if that was the boy and he said 'yes,' and I think he was pleased with that. He was a very nice guy.

"I shot about 300 feet of film on each take I made both inside and outside the sound house. The little sound man we had there, Bill Hedgecock, never would turn up the gain on his sound panel until the camera got up to speed and the action and dialogue began. He was right alongside me. I told him later, 'you really saved my neck doing what you did.' He said, 'There was need of going ahead and having the noise of the camera come out. I used to hear it there but as soon as the dialogue and action started you couldn't hear the camera. It was very, very quiet.' Well, that was real cooperation because a lot of sound mixers wouldn't do that.

"Incidentally, at that time the camera was turned by a flexible shaft connected to a motor that in turn was interlocked with the sound recorder. We were using the Fox Movietone (Western Electric) sound system, which was the best one.

"The next day all the Universal executives were in the big projection room to see the test I had made. The two Laemmles were there, father and son. So was Martin Murphy, the production manager, Henry Henigson, the studio manager, and, of course, Roy Hunter. The room was crowded with people.

"The picture came on—about 300 feet—of the boys in the school room. There were two takes. Hunter had spliced both scenes together and that's it. When it was over, the lights came on and it was quiet for a few moments. Then someone said, 'Now put on the one that was made without going into the sound house.' 'They are spliced together,' Hunter answered. So they ran it again and when it was over Murphy and Henigson got together with Hunter to talk it over.

"Hunter came over to me and said, 'Arthur, come over to the office with me.' Then he asked me if I'd make the picture and I said 'yes' so we came to an agreement. They paid me $600 a week."

"You couldn't have made a picture like *All Quiet on the Western Front* using those sound houses. I had never gone into one of them. You couldn't get good photography. You couldn't light. Now this picture was at least 50 percent exterior war stuff so my camera could easily handle it. We also shot the battle stuff silent. I often had as many as six cameras turning on those scenes. Sometimes on the interior scenes when the camera moved in close I placed a big piece of plate glass between it and the actors so there were no big problems with camera noise."

"We went on location for about six or eight weeks down in the hills above Laguna Beach. They built roads and a concrete ramp for the big orange colored camera crane that Hal Mohr had built for them a few months before. It ran alongside the trenches they had dug for the battle stuff. It was really a big show."

Edeson laughingly recalled that after working a number of days in a dugout the Orange County Board of Health inspectors shut them down until it was cleaned up. "It was just like a real war except that part of the day the extras which they had gotten from an American Legion post in Santa Ana would change from their German uniforms into French uniforms. They would be fighting themselves. We never had more than a few hundred extras at any one time. Usually, we had about 150 on hand each day.

"I had photographed another war picture for First National, *The Patent Leather Kid*, which Al Santell had directed. It was made at Camp (now Fort) Lewis, Washington a couple of years before *All Quiet on the Western Front*. Without the experience I got on that picture, I don't think I could have done *All Quiet*, which had many of the same problems in the photography of the battle scenes.

"They had gotten some tents from the National Guard for the extras to live in down there on the Irvine Ranch. Except for not using real bullets, we might as well have been in the war. There were some close calls with explosions. Our 'powderman' was working on another picture at night so he didn't get much sleep. He was sometimes a little jittery. Once Millie was hit by some debris from an explosion and was knocked unconscious. He was right by my camera. After that we started wearing those big steel German helmets."

The only fatality was not caused by any of the explosions but took place on the shell torn French village set at Universal City when an extra was thrown off an artillery caisson against the corner of a building.

In addition to the Irvine Ranch and Universal City, other locations used were: Sherwood Forest and Malibu Lakes in the San Fernando Valley, and the so-called "40 acres" backlot of the RKO Pathé Studio in Culver City (where *Gone With the Wind* Atlanta and Tara exteriors were later made). Captain Charles D. Hall, who had served in the Canadian Army during the war, and William R. Schmitt designed the sets. One of the most interesting was the re-creation of a German Army *kaserne* (barracks), complete with a quadrangle for drill, built on the Universal City back lot. This set was further enhanced by a bird's eye view shot created by special photographic effects cinematographer Frank Booth. Some of his other optical work and matte shots are so well executed they pass by virtually unnoticed.

All Quiet on the Western Front opens with the sub-title (taken almost verbatim from the fore-page of the book) that sets the tone for the picture:

"This picture is to be neither an accusation nor a confession, and least of all an adventure, for death is not an adventure to those who stand face to face with it. It will try simply to tell of a generation of men who, even though they may have escaped its shells, were destroyed by the war."

(Unfortunately, Universal deleted this title after the initial release and substituted instead a list of all the awards, including the Academy Oscar, the picture had won.)

The picture then begins somewhat innocuously. An elderly janitor is preparing to unlock a door while talking to the charwoman scrubbing the floor.

"Thirty thousand," he says to her.

"From the Russians?", asks the woman.

"From the French. We capture that many from the Russians every day," he answers as he opens the door revealing marching spiked helmeted German soldiers in 1914 uniforms. A marching military band seems to catch the nationalistic fervor of the crowd as Edeson's camera cranes upward and pulls back through a window. Inside, an elderly schoolmaster (Arnold Lucy) is exhorting his students to enlist. In a series of sharp vignettes, Milestone introduces the young men the picture concentrates on: Kropp, Leer, Kemmerich and the main protagonist, Paul Bäumer.

We follow the boys through their recruit training and see them suffer at the hands of their sadistic drill sergeant Himmelstoss. His particular pleasure is to march his young charges into a muddy, ploughed field and have them "advance and lie down."

Ordered to the front, they pass through a shell torn French village at the railhead and hear the scream of enemy shells for the first time. Inside a deserted factory, beautifully lit by Edeson in deceptive low-key, the boys meet Tjaden, Westhus (Richard Alexander), Detering (Harold Goodwin), and somewhat later the incomparable Kat who arrives with a whole pig they are all soon devouring. That same evening they are ordered front for a wiring fatigue.

They get their first instructions of how to behave under shell-fire from Kat as they pass through a wooded area. Edeson has skilfully lit this sequence day-for-night but it is so convincingly done it seems like actual darkness. His camera trucks along in front of the soldiers, pausing when Kat emphasizes an important point, moving once more when they move. "I'll give you all clean underwear when we get back," Kat tells them.

Edeson lit the scenes of the men putting up barbed wire night-for-night. His lighting of these scenes is very effective. When an enemy bombardment suddenly erupts, the men scatter for cover. In one very effectively lit low-key shot—the light level is *extremely* low but quite visible—a man jumps into a shell hole as an explosion erupts. He screams out in pain, "I'm blind. I can't see," and blindly staggers towards the enemy lines where he is cut down by unseen gunfire. One of the boys runs after him, picks him up and staggers back to cover. Kat severely upbraids him for needlessly exposing himself. "But it's my friend Behm," the boy says. "It's just a corpse now,"

Kat admonishes, "no matter who it is." It is a harrowing scene but sets the tone for what is to follow.

Trapped in a dugout for days by the heavy enemy bombardment, the terrified, shell-shocked boys are somehow held together by the iron will of Kat. Edeson has given these scenes in the dugout an especially realistic look. His low key light level is very effective in catching the claustrophobic effect of the incessant bombardment.

Suddenly the bombardment lifts and the men run outside to man their positions on the trench fire step. Edeson's camera travels over the trenches, easily picks out Paul (whose helmet spike has been shot away—an effective trick Milestone uses to single out his key character). French shock troops are close to the German barbed wire. Machine guns go into action. Now Milestone and Edeson deliver some of the most effective scenes in the picture. Edeson's camera, mounted on the big crane and swung low to the ground, moves rapidly across and in front of the charging French infantry. Milestone intercuts these shots with short cuts of the machine guns firing, French soldiers are mown down by the terrible machine-gun fire as they race toward the German trenches. The tempo and speed of these shots increases. At one point we see a grenade explode in front of a charging French soldier. When the smoke clears only the hands remain suspended on the barbed wire almost as if in prayer. Paul turns his face in horror against his rifle stock.

The French reach the German trenches and leap onto the defenders. Hand to hand combat breaks out. The French are driven out. The Germans counterattack only to be stopped by French machine guns in a series of shots almost identical to what has just transpired. The battle is a stand-off.

This particular sequence has been justly praised for Milestone's mastery of cutting. Trained in the editing tradition of D.W. Griffith and greatly influenced by the so-called "montage" technique of the Soviet directors of the mid-twenties, Milestone and his film cutters (Edgar Adams and Milton Carruth) created some powerful screen imagery. And, Edeson's cameras caught every violent moment of combat. Although Edeson photographed virtually all of these scenes silent, the addition of sound is skilfully and realistically applied so that one is never really conscious of the deception.

According to Milestone, Junior Laemmle complained about the battle footage he was seeing in the dailies back at Universal City. "All I see is guys running to the left and guys running to the right. Where is the battle stuff?" Milestone told him he'd have to wait. "I'm not going to wait. I'm bringing you back to the studio right now."

Milestone went to work virtually around the clock, sleeping in his chauffeur driven car between his home and the studio. Finally, a cut was finished about three o'clock one morning. An exhausted Milestone invited Paul

Whiteman, the band leader, working in an adjoining cutting room on his own film, *King of Jazz*, to see what he and his cutter had wrought. There was a bit over a thousand feet of spliced work-print but with no sound. When it was over, Whiteman was overcome. "If the rest of the picture is anything like this, you've got the winner of all time." (From an interview in 1968 with Kevin Brownlow.)

In another powerful sequence, German infantry are attacking through a church cemetery. They are stopped by heavy artillery fire and take cover in some of the graves that have been opened by exploding shells. A coffin, torn out of one of the graves, is flung over Paul who has been slightly wounded. In a panic he jumps into another shell hole. The enemy counterattacks. Paul crouches in the bottom of the hole, draws his trench knife and feigns death. But the counterattack breaks down and the French retreat. Suddenly a French soldier jumps into the shell hole with Paul. In a panic Paul gags the man with one hand and blindly stabs him in the throat with the other. Unable to leave the shell hole because of heavy fire, Paul is forced to watch the Frenchman die. The ordeal continues through the night. Morning comes. The Frenchman is dead. Paul in remorse begs the dead man's forgiveness. Mercifully, night finally falls and Paul escapes back to his own lines.

Arthur Edeson has treated the passage of day-to-night and from day-back-to-night with a subtle but realistic lighting style. At night flashes of gunfire light up the shell hole. In the morning Edeson's camera catches the dead Frenchman's face in an unforgettable close-up. His dead eyes are open and stare into nothing. A whiff of smoke from the battlefield drifts into the frame. We see Paul's anguished, pleading face. It is terrible moment put on film with great artistry by Edeson.

There is a romantic idyll with three French peasant girls. Paul, Albert and Leer steal over the canal that separates their bivouac from the girls. As an inducement, they have brought along food. We hear—but don't see—Paul and one of the French girls make love. The camera moves slowly about the moonlit room. The lighting is soft and in a low key.

Paul and Albert are both wounded and taken to a hospital behind the lines staffed by Catholic nuns. Edeson uses a higher lighting key for these scenes. Albert's shattered leg is amputated, unknown to him. When he comes out of the anesthetic, he complains of pain in his toes and suddenly remembers the complaint was the same he had heard made by another comrade in the same situation. Edeson's camera adroitly captures the pathetic moment when Albert tilts a small hand mirror in such a way that he sees with horror his leg is gone.

For Paul's convalescent homecoming Edeson has lit the scene in a high key. Bright sunlight streams through the front door as Paul enters his parents' home. His sister runs to embrace him, "Paul's home," she tells the mother, who is bedridden. As Paul realizes that he can no longer fit into life on the home front, the mood of the lighting becomes more subdued.

When Paul returns to his comrades at the front he discovers that only Tjaden and Kat are left. All the others have been either killed or wounded. And on the day of his return, Kat is killed.

Then comes the ending that *All Quiet* audiences long remember.

The author gave few clues concerning Paul's death. Milestone thought of several possible endings but rejected them one by one. The date of the world premiere had been set and the picture had to go in for negative conforming. Pressure from the front office was intense. Junior Laemmle threatened to take the whole thing away from Milestone.

Edeson was committed to another picture and had moved on. Milestone now had the services of Karl Freund, ASC, as cinematographer. Freund had just joined the camera staff at Universal City after distinguished work in Berlin's great Ufa Studios. Freund remembered an earlier scene where Paul pauses by his butterfly collection when he was home on leave. This gave Freund the idea for the ending that he and Milestone shot that afternoon on the back lot at Universal City.

We see soldiers bailing water from a ruined trench. It is a bright day and is quiet on the front. Only the faint sound of a harmonica can be heard. Paul, on guard, is day dreaming in his trench. Suddenly, he sees a lone butterfly land on a shell casing just outside the parapet. He carefully reaches for it, momentarily forgetting the ever present danger. Cut to a shot of a distant French sniper who suddenly emerges from behind a log with a scope-mounted rifle. Back to Paul as he leans outside the trench reaching for the butterfly. The French sniper draws careful aim on Paul. His hand moves closer to the butterfly when suddenly there is the sharp whine of a shot. Paul's hand (actually Milestone's) jerks back, relaxes in death. The harmonica suddenly stops and there is a cut to sunlight streaming through the trees as the music comes up. It is one of the screen's most powerful, well remembered moments.

With such an unforgettable ending one wonders why someone at Universal decided to go one better. In a tear jerking symbolic epilogue, reminiscent of D.W. Griffith at his worst, we see a ghostly file of all of the boys marching obliquely away from the camera and looking back at the audience with a sad, haunting look—the whole scene being superimposed over a sea of white crosses on a shell torn battlefield. Some of the pacifist advertising appearing in magazines at that time probably influenced the addition of this scene.

When *All Quiet* was sneak previewed it unfortunately followed a comedy in which Zazu Pitts appeared. Miss Pitts, a splendid tragedienne as well as a great comedy actress, played Paul's sick mother. Despite her fine, sensitive performance, audiences snickered. It was the unwanted laugh that every

filmmaker fears. Junior Laemmle panicked and despite Milestone's pleas ordered the scenes re-shot with another actress. Beryl Mercer, a plump actress
of that period famous for mother roles, appeared in the re-takes. (Zazu Pitts'
scenes were left in the silent version which Universal had prepared for the-
atres not yet wired for sound and also in some of the prints shipped abroad.)

Despite reports to the contrary, *All Quiet* was well received when it
opened in Germany in 1930. It was denounced by Hitler, then a rapidly ris-
ing leader of the Nazi Party. His SA and SS hooligans released rats, snakes
and stink bombs in theaters showing the picture. When Hitler finally came
to power in 1933, he banned the picture outright. Remarque, who had already
left his native Germany, went on the Gestapo's wanted list.

Over the years, *All Quiet* has been reissued several times. It has suffered
the fate of many fine pictures by having many key scenes deleted. The TV tape
cassettes that are now available appear to have been made from the 1939 reissue and are complete except for a few scenes that were apparently removed
to cut the running time. The mutilated prints that occasionally turn up on
commercial TV are a sad parody of the 14-reel version that stunned audiences
in 1930 and generated world wide praise.

All Quiet on the Western Front is still the yardstick by which all great war
films are measured.

Edeson . . .

Arthur Edeson is one of the small group of cameramen who founded the
American Society of Cinematographers in January of 1919. Over the years
he served on the A.S.C. Board of Governors and was a past president
(1949–50). At the time he photographed *All Quiet* he was one of the top
rated cinematographers in the motion picture industry. It was a position he
consistently maintained until his retirement in the 1950's. A short, handsome man, he was known for his meticulous craftsmanship and his artistic
integrity. His sometimes imperious manner earned him the nickname of
"Little Napoleon."

He was born in New York City, October 24, 1892. After attending the
College of the City of New York, he went to work as a negative retoucher and
platinum printer for various New York portrait photographers. The work was
often seasonal and sporadic so he decided to "try something else." He had
worked as an apprentice portrait photographer so he thought he might land
a job in one of the motion picture studios in nearby Ft. Lee, New Jersey. One
day in 1911, he crossed the Hudson river and applied for a job at the Eclair
Studio hoping for some sort of photographic work. Instead, he was hired as
an extra by director William Haddock at $3.00 a day. This continued for a
short time with Edeson supplementing his income by taking photographs of
some of the actors which they could use in getting other acting jobs. Barbara

Tennant, Robert Warwick and Alec B. Francis were among the players he photographed. This led to a job in the Eclair lab and the additional assignment of still photographer on the Eclair productions.

John van den Broek, Eclair's top cameraman, introduced Edeson to cinematography. "John was a Dutchman and, I think next to Billy Bitzer, was the greatest cameraman in the business," Edeson recalled in 1968. "He was Maurice Tourneur's cameraman, whom I think was next to D.W. Griffith in screen direction. John had a wonderful feel for composition and lighting and in those days the sun was our primary light source. The Eclair Studio was glass enclosed, like a big greenhouse. John used diffusers and soft reflectors to achieve some remarkable effects.

"John took me under his wing and taught me what he did and how he did it. I learned more and more from this wonderfully gifted, warm-hearted man." Tragically Van den Broek was accidentally drowned several years later while filming a Mary Pickford picture for Tourneur.

Director George Sargeant gave Edeson his opportunity as a cameraman in 1914 by assigning him to *A Gentleman From Mississippi* starring Tom Wise, a noted stage actor of the day.

"Eclair was a French company so the cameramen were mainly French. Rene Guissert, Lucien Andriot and George Benoit were three who later became A.S.C. members. I believe I was the first American to become a first cameraman there.

"We went on location to Natchez, Mississippi. It was a wonderful opportunity for me to work on a beautiful Southern estate with great oaks and hanging moss. The photographic opportunities were just there for the taking. I used a Pathé studio model camera with an f/3.5 Hiliar 50mm lens. Prior to and afterward I used an Eclair Gillon which the company built in their shops in France.

"To me the lens is the most important thing about a camera. There are really only three things you need beside a good camera mechanism to photograph a picture: a lens, some good film, and your own ingenuity."

Eclair evolved into World/Peerless Studios, a group put together by J.E. Brulatour, Eastman Kodak's sales representative. Edeson remained there until 1918 when he was drafted into the Army. A bout of pneumonia sent him to California for his health.

"I hated to leave New York and Fort Lee, but it turned out to be a fortunate move for me," he said. His friend, Charles Rosher, ASC, recommended him to Douglas Fairbanks Sr. to photograph *The Three Musketeers* in 1920. Other pictures followed: *Robin Hood* (1922), directed by Allan Dwan, and *The Thief of Bagdad* (1924), directed by Raoul Walsh. *The Bat* (1926), directed by Roland West, was notable for low key effect lighting and Edeson's clever use of low camera angles to enhance dramatic effect. His assistant (and pupil) for several years during this period was the great Gregg Toland, ASC, remembered today for his masterful photography of *Citizen Kane* (1941).

Edeson's name appears on the credits of many famous films made during the 1930's and 1940's: *Frankenstein* (Universal), the original *Mutiny on the Bounty* (MGM), *Sergeant York*, *The Maltese Falcon* and *Casablanca*, all for Warners. He received Academy nominations for *All Quiet* and *Casablanca*. In 1954, he received the George Eastman House Award for his overall contributions during the silent period.

MODRIS EKSTEINS

Memory

We who have known war must never forget war. And that is why I have a
picture of a soldier's corpse nailed to the door of my library.

Harry Crosby

Soyons, à notre tour, le printemps qui reverdit les grises terres de mort, et
de notre sang versé pour la justice, faisons après les veilles d'horreur surgir
des lendemains de beauté.[1]

José Germain, 1923

At school, and in books written for boys, one was so constantly reminded
that we had won the war that my school friends and I found our curiosity
excited by those who had lost it. Losing seemed much more original and
stimulating than winning.

Richard Cobb, 1983

Qui aurait pensé, il y a dix-sept ans, qu'on pourrait louer l'harmonie
du *Sacre*? C'est un fait. On ne songe plus à ses audaces, on admire ses
perfections.[2]

André Rousseau, February 1930

War Boom

Erich Maria Remarque's *Im Westen nichts Neues*, or *All Quiet on the Western Front*, as the English translation would be entitled, was published first in Berlin by the house of Ullstein at the end of January 1929. Twenty months later, in October 30, the *Nouvelles littéraires* in Paris would refer to Remarque as the "author today with the largest audience in the world."[3]

When the book was published, accompanied by an advertising campaign larger than any ever before launched by a German publisher, about ten thousand advance orders had been placed. For weeks Berlin's advertisement pillars had been plastered with posters, each week a different one. First week: "It's coming." Second week: "The great war novel." Third week: "All Quiet on the Western Front." Fourth week: "By Erich Maria Remarque." The novel had by then appeared in serialized form in Ullstein's most distinguished newspaper, the *Vossische Zeitung*, from November 10, the day before the tenth anniversary of the Armistice, to December 9. While the paper's circulation did not skyrocket dramatically, as some have claimed, sales did rise slightly and daily editions usually sold out.

But now, after publication, the rush began. Within three weeks 200,000 copies were sold. The sale of 20,000 copies in one day was not unusual. By early May, 640,000 copies had been sold in Germany. English and French translations were hastily prepared. The English edition appeared in March, the American at the end of May, and the French in June. The American Book-of-the-Month Club selected the novel as its choice for June and ordered 60,000 copies for its 100,000 subscribers. The Book Society, a comparable book club in Great Britain, "recommended" the novel to its members. By the end of the year sales neared a million in Germany, and another million in Britain, France, and the United States together. In Germany the Ullsteins were using six printing and ten bookbinding firms to try to keep abreast of demand. In Britain the Barrow public library announced to its members in November that *All Quiet* had been reserved in advance for two years! Within the year the book had been translated into about twenty languages, including Chinese and Esperanto, and the Ullsteins, in their remarkable promotional effort, even had a German Braille edition prepared and sent without charge to every blind veteran who requested it.[4]

Almost overnight Remarque's novel had become, as one comment put it, "the postwar phenomenon of book-selling." That was an understatement. Remarque's success was unprecedented in the entire history of publishing. In England and Germany the book trade, which had suffered throughout the decade but now was in even worse straits because of the general downturn in the economy in 1928–1929, gave thanks. "Remarque is our daily bread," quipped booksellers in Berlin.[5]

Remarque's spectacular success brought on a flood of war books and other material dealing with the war and ushered in what came to be known as the "war boom" of 1929–1930. War novels and war memoirs suddenly dominated the lists of publishers. Robert Graves, Edmund Blunden, Siegfried Sassoon, Ludwig Renn, Arnold Zweig, and Ernest Hemingway, among others, became familiar names. They were so in demand, as public speakers and radio performers, that they could not cope with the glut of invitations. The sudden public interest in the war meant that moldy manuscripts, previously rejected by wary publishers who thought that the war would not sell, were now rushed into print. New books, too, were quickly commissioned and quickly written.

Translators were in great demand. The stage readily made room for war drama, and R. C. Sherriff's *Journey's End*, in which Laurence Olivier played the lead in the latter part of the London run, became an international hit. By November 1929 it was being staged in twelve foreign countries. The cinema, which had not been quite as reluctant as the publishing industry to deal with war material—Hollywood had started a small wave in 1926 with films like *What Price Glory?*, *The Big Parade*, and *Wings*—the cinema now joined in with a rash of war films. Galleries exhibited paintings and photographs from the war. Newspapers and periodicals gave much space to discussions about war, past and future. What some felt to have been a deliberate silence about the war was now shattered with a vengeance.

What provoked the sudden revival of interest in the war at the end of the twenties? And what did the war boom reveal? A look at the motivations of Remarque in writing his novel may yield some clues.

Life of Death

Until the publication of *All Quiet*, Erich Maria Remarque had led a moderately successful, though unsettled, life as a dilettante intellectual and aspiring author. He was born on June 22, 1898, in Osnabrück, the son of a Catholic bookbinder, Peter Franz Remark, and his wife, Anne Maria. Christened Erich Paul, he adopted a pen name after the war by dropping the Paul—the main character in *All Quiet* is named Paul and dies toward the end of the war—adding his mother's name, and Gallicizing his surname. Remarque did not have a happy childhood. His lower-middle-class milieu apparently depressed him. He was, he said later, deeply moved as a youth by the sorrows of Goethe's sensitive and splenetic Werther; he professed to be a romantic; and he often toyed with the idea of suicide. This mood of existential doubt was never to leave him. It pervades his entire *oeuvre*. In public, though clearly craving recognition, he always assumed the manner of a recluse. Even though he would marry Paulette Goddard, the film star and former wife of Charlie Chaplin, live extravagantly in New York, and surround himself with the trappings of success, he would remain—so it appeared—desperately unhappy, a chain smoker, a heavy drinker, fixated by fast cars, speedboats, and escape.

Remarque's class background bears emphasis. He was the product of a social group strongly affected by technological and social change. John Middleton Murry, who also suffered in his youth from an intense anxiety born, he suspected, of his social background, called the urban lower middle class "the most completely disinherited section of modern society."[6] It was a stratum that the war and especially the economic instability of the twenties would assault with ferocity.

Considerable mystery surrounds Remarque's war experience. Aged sixteen when war broke out, in August 1914, he was conscripted two years later, in November 1916, while training as a teacher, and he first saw front-line action in Flanders in June 1917. At the front he was wounded, according to his own testimony, either four or five times, but according to other evidence, only once seriously. The German army minister, General Groener, was to inform his cabinet colleagues in December 1930 that Remarque had been wounded in the left knee and under one arm on July 31, 1917, and that he had remained in a hospital in Duisburg from August 3, 1917, to October 31, 1918. The minister dismissed as false the reports that Remarque had been either decorated or promoted.[7]

Little else is known about Remarque's days as a soldier. After he was catapulted to international fame, he proved reluctant to give interviews, let alone precise information about his war career. He showed little interest in countering any of the scurrilous rumors that circulated about his earlier life, and many of his critics found his aversion to publicity suspicious. There was a sustained attempt in 1929 and 1930 to uncover the "real" Remarque, especially to disprove the claim of his publisher, Ullstein, that he was a seasoned soldier. A man named Peter Kropp maintained that he had spent a year in a hospital with the author during the war and that one of the characters in *All Quiet*, Albert Kropp, was modeled on him. The leg wound that hospitalized Remarque, Kropp alleged, was self-inflicted, and he insisted that once the wound healed, Remarque had become a clerk in the hospital. In the end, argued Kropp, Remarque had no special qualifications for representing the feelings and behavior of the front soldier.[8] While many of the allegations of Remarque's critics and opponents were malicious and prompted by envy, opportunism, and political intent, there do appear to be grounds for suspecting that Remarque's war experience was not as extensive as his successful novel, and particularly the promotional effort surrounding it, implied.

After the war Remarque returned briefly to the Osnabrück Catholic seminary for teachers, and early in 1919 he became a village schoolmaster. He soon abandoned this occupation and took up freelance journalism and odd jobs to meet financial necessity. He published articles on cars, boats, cocktail recipes; he worked for a while for a tire-manufacturing company in Hanover, writing advertising jingles; and eventually he became a picture editor in Berlin for a publication owned by the right-wing firm Scherl. The glossy, high-society magazine *Sport im Bild* was a German version, despite its misleading title, of *The Tatler*. All the while, he tried to write seriously, working on novels, poetry, and a play. Two of his novels were published, *Die Traumbude*[9] in 1920 and *Station am Horizont*[10] in 1928, but he seems to have derived little satisfaction from them. Trite sentimentality relegated the first work to the rank of pulp fiction. Of *Die Traumbude* Remarque was to say later:

> A truly terrible book. Two years after I had published it, I should have liked to buy it up. Unfortunately I didn't have enough money for that. The Ullsteins did that for me later. If I had not written anything better later on, the book would have been a reason for suicide.[11]

In 1921 he sent a number of poems to Stefan Zweig for comment and attached a letter of near despair: "Remember that this is a matter of life or death for me!" An attempt to write a play left him in deep depression.[12]

The death motif here is striking: thoughts about suicide in his youth and threats of it as an adult. Together with the derivative romanticism and the itinerant existence the motif points to a deeply disconsolate man, searching for an explanation for his dissatisfaction. And in his search Remarque eventually hit upon the *Kriegserleben*, the war experience.

The idea that the war was the source of all ills struck him suddenly, he admitted. "All of us were," he said of himself and his friends in an interview in 1929, "and still are, restless, aimless, sometimes excited, sometimes indifferent, and essentially unhappy." But in a moment of inspiration he had at least found the key to the malaise. The war![13]

That he was not truly interested, after his "discovery," in exploring the variety of war experience, but that his main purpose was simply to describe the terrible effects of the war on the generation that grew up during it, is revealed in a review he wrote of war books by Ernst Jünger, Franz Schauwecker, and Georg von der Vring, among others, for *Sport im Bild* in June 1928. It is even possible that these books were the source of his inspiration. Jünger's exuberant, intoxicating vitalism and brutal grandeur, Schauwecker's breathless, mystical nationalism, and von der Vring's lyrical simplicity were lumped together in a rather bland discussion that displayed little appreciation for these distinctive interpretations of the war experience.[14] Remarque was, one must conclude, more interested in explaining away the emotional imbalance of a generation than in a comprehensive or even accurate account of the experience and feelings of men in the trenches. Many of the metaphors and images that Remarque used in his book are strikingly similar to those used by the authors he had discussed, Jünger in particular, and it is not unreasonable to suggest that he took many of his ideas from these sources.

In July 1928 Remarque published another article in *Sport im Bild* that throws more light on his frame of mind at the time. This was a short, rather ingenuous piece about modern photography, in which he regretted the injustice that most professional photographers did to reality. By isolating their subjects from a wider context, by turning the world into a neat and rosy "9 x 12 or 10 x 15 format," photographers created an illusionary world.[15] The point was a simple and honest one, but coming from a picture editor of a snobbish and expensive magazine, it had a pathetic poignancy; it indicated how unhappy the author was in his work and environment.

Having fixed upon the "war experience," Remarque sat down in mid 1928 to write. Working in the evenings and on weekends, he completed his book, so he claimed, in six weeks. The suddenness of the inspiration, the speed of composition, and the simplicity of the theme all indicate that Remarque's book was not the product of years of reflection and digestion but of impulse born of personal exasperation.

Remarque stated the purpose of *All Quiet* in a brief and forceful prefatory comment:

> This book is to be neither an accusation nor a confession, and least of all an adventure ... It will try simply to tell of a generation of men who, even though they may have escaped its shells, were destroyed by the war.[16]

The story then recounts the experiences of Paul Bäumer and his schoolmates, who move from the classroom to the trenches, bursting with energy and conviction, enthusiastic knights of a personal and national cause. One by one they are ripped apart at the front, not only by enemy fire but also by a growing sense of futility. The war is transformed from a cause into an inexorable, insatiable Moloch. The soldiers have no escape from the routinized slaughter; they are condemned men. They die screaming but unheard; they die resigned but in vain. The world beyond the guns does not know them; it cannot know them. "I believe we are lost," says Paul.

Only the fraternity of death remains, the comradeship of the fated. At the end Paul dies, forlorn yet strangely at peace with his destiny. Peace has become possible only in death. The final scene of the American film version of the novel was to be a masterly evocation of the mood of Remarque's work: a sniper's bullet finds its mark as Paul is reaching from the trench to touch what the war had rendered untouchable, a butterfly. All the shibboleths lose their meaning as the men die violent deaths—patriotism, national duty, honor, glory, heroism, valor. The external world consists only of brutality, hypocrisy, illusion. Even the intimate bonds to family have been sundered. Man remains alone, without a foothold in the real world.

The simplicity and power of the theme—war as a demeaning and wholly destructive, indeed nihilistic, force—are made starkly effective by a style that is basic, even brutal. Brief scenes and short crisp sentences, in the first person and in the present tense, create an inescapable and gripping immediacy. There is no delicacy. The language is frequently rough, the images often gruesome. The novel has a consistency of style and purpose that Remarque's earlier work had lacked and that little of his subsequent work would achieve.

Despite Remarque's introductory comment and his reiteration of the point in later statements, very few contemporary reviewers noted, and later critics have generally ignored, that *All Quiet* was not a book about the events of the war—it was not a memoir, much less a diary[17]—but an angry declaration about the effects of the war on the young generation that lived through it. Scenes, incidents, and images were chosen to illustrate how the war had destroyed the ties, psychological, moral, and real, between the generation at the front and society at home. "If we go back," says Paul, "we will be weary, broken, burnt out, rootless, and without hope. We will not be able to find our way any more." The war, Remarque was asserting in 1928, had shattered the possibility of pursuing what society would consider a normal existence.

Hence, *All Quiet* is more a comment on the postwar mind, on the postwar view of the war, than an attempt to reconstruct the reality of the trench experience. In fact that reality is distorted, as many critics insisted—though with little effect on the initial acclaim for the novel. Remarque's critics said that at the very least he misrepresented the physical reality of the war: a man with his legs or his head blown off could not continue to run, they protested vehemently, referring to two of the images Remarque had used. But far more serious than such shoddiness, they claimed, was his lack of understanding of the moral aspects of soldiers' behavior. Soldiers were not robots, devoid of a sense of purpose. They were sustained by a broad spectrum of firmly established values.[18]

Although his publisher did not like such admissions, because they undermined the credibility of the novel, Remarque was prepared to say that his book was primarily about the postwar generation. In an exchange in 1929 with General Sir Ian Hamilton, the British commander at Gallipoli in 1915 and now head of the British Legion, Remarque expressed his "amazement" and "admiration" that Hamilton for one had understood his intentions in writing *All Quiet*:

> I merely wanted to awaken understanding for a generation that more than all others has found it difficult to make its way back

from four years of death, struggle, and terror, to the peaceful fields
of work and progress.[19]

It was in part the misinterpretation of his purpose that led Remarque to
write a sequel to *All Quiet*. *Der Weg zurück* (*The Road Back*), a novel published in 1931, explicitly argued the case of the "lost generation."

All Quiet can be seen not as an explanation but as a symptom of the
confusion and disorientation of the postwar world, particularly of the generation that reached maturity during the war. The novel was an emotional condemnation, an assertion of instinct, a *cri d'angoisse* from a malcontent, a man
who could not find his niche in society. That the war contributed enormously
to the shiftlessness of much of the postwar generation is undeniable; that the
war was the root cause of this social derangement is at least debatable; but
Remarque never took part in the debate directly. For Remarque the war had
become a vehicle of escape. Remarque and his book were, to borrow from
Karl Kraus, symptoms of the disease they claimed to diagnose.

Notwithstanding Remarque's opening declaration of impartiality—that
his book was "neither an accusation nor a confession"—it was in fact both.
And it was more. It was a confession of personal despair, but it was also an
indignant denunciation of an insensate social and political order, inevitably of
that order which had produced the horror and destruction of the war but particularly of the one that could not settle the war and deal with the aspirations
of veterans. Through characters identifiable with the state—the schoolmaster
with his unalterable fantasies about patriotism and valor, the former postman
who functions like an unfeeling robot in his new role as drill sergeant, the
hospital orderlies and doctors who deal not with human suffering, only bodies—Remarque accused. He accused a mechanistic civilization of destroying
humane values, of negating charity, love, humor, beauty, and individuality.
Yet Remarque offered no alternatives. The characters of his *generazione bru-
ciata*—the Italian notion of a "burned generation" is apt—do not act; they
are merely victims. Of all the war books of the late twenties—the novels of
Arnold Zweig, Renn, R. H. Mottram, H. M. Tomlinson, Richard Aldington,
Hemingway, and the memoirs of Graves, Blunden, Sassoon, to name but a
few of the more important works—Remarque's made its point, that his was a
truly lost generation, most directly and emotionally, even stridently, and this
directness and passion lay at the heart of its popular appeal.

But there was more. The "romantic agony" was a wild cry of revolt and
despair—and a cry of exhilaration. In perversion there could be pleasure. In
darkness, light. The relation of Remarque and his generation to death and
destruction is not as straightforward as it appears. In his personal life and in
his reflections on the war Remarque seemed fascinated by death. All of his
subsequent work exudes this fascination. As one critic put it later, Remarque

"probably made more out of death than the most fashionable undertakers."[20] Like the Dadaists, he was spellbound by war and its horror, by the act of destruction, to the point where death becomes not the antithesis of life but the ultimate expression of life, where death becomes a creative force, a source of art and vitality. A young Michel Tournier, on meeting Remarque, noted the paradoxical nature of this modern author-hero: world famous for his antimilitarism, Remarque, "with his stiff posture, his severe and rectangular face, and his inseparable monocle," looked like a larger-than-life Prussian officer.[21]

Many of Remarque's generation shared his apocalyptic post-Christian vision of life, peace, and happiness in death. George Antheil would, when appearing in concert to play his own music, carry a pistol in his evening jacket. As he sat down to play, he would take out the pistol and place it on the piano. The .25 caliber Belgian revolver that Harry Crosby used in December 1929 to kill himself and his mistress had a sun symbol engraved on its side. A year earlier while saluting Dido, Cleopatra, Socrates, Modigliani, and Van Gogh among others, he had promised soon "to enjoy an orgasm with the sombre Slave-Girl of Death, in order to be reborn." He yearned to "explode . . . into the frenzied fury of the Sun, into the madness of the Sun into the hot gold arms and hot gold eyes of the Goddess of the Sun!"[22]

Success would not mellow Remarque or still his chronic anxiety. The very vital Countess Waldeck, née Rosie Gräfenberg, who in 1929–1930 was the wife of Franz Ullstein, later had this to say of the young author at the height of his success:

> Remarque was in his thirties. He had a pretty boy's face with a defiant soft mouth. The Ullsteins thought him a little difficult. But that was merely the result of Remarque's having almost rejected the motor-car with which the grateful firm presented him, because it lacked the travelling luggage which, in his opinion, belonged on the luggage rack. I myself thought this and other traits charmingly childlike in Remarque; he wanted his toy to be exactly as he had imagined it. He was a hard worker. Often he would shut himself up for seventeen hours at a stretch in a room where not even a chaise-lounge was permitted, because it might possibly be a temptation to laziness. He was immensely sorry for himself because he worked so hard—was Remarque.[23]

Fame

According to Remarque, his completed manuscript lay in a drawer for six months. In fact it was probably only a couple of months. His employer, the Scherl firm, an important part of Alfred Hugenberg's right-wing nationalist press empire, could not even be considered a potential publisher of the work.

Finally Remarque approached the S. Fischer Verlag, the most reputable literary publisher in Germany, but Samuel Fischer was still convinced that the war would not sell. He turned the manuscript down.

Through an acquaintance word reached Remarque that Franz Ullstein, by contrast, did feel that it was time to publish books on the war. Remarque tried the Ullstein Verlag. There the manuscript was passed around to various editors. Max Krell was "gripped by the unusual tone"; Cyril Soschka, head of the production department and a war veteran, was convinced that it would be a great success because it told "the truth about the war"—a phrase on which the controversy about the book would turn; Monty Jacobs, *feuilleton* editor of Ullstein's *Vossische Zeitung*, accepted the novel for serialization. The Ullsteins developed great confidence in the book, and, led by Franz Ullstein, one of the five brothers who ran the large newspaper- and book-publishing operation, they proceeded to launch their flamboyant and expensive advertising campaign.[24]

The initial critical response to Remarque's novel was very enthusiastic, not only in Germany, where the playwright Carl Zuckmayer wrote the first review for the Ullsteins' large-circulation *Berliner Illustrirte Zeitung* and called *All Quiet* a "war diary," but also when it appeared in English and French translations. Remarque's supposedly frank portrayal of human responses to war and the depiction of a pitiful dignity under suffering were praised with gusto. "The greatest of war novels" was a phrase that appeared over and over again in the reviews. Its "holy sobriety" would bring about "the rehabilitation of our generation," predicted Axel Eggebrecht, a well-known and respected German critic. Herbert Read, veteran, poet, and art historian, heralded Remarque's account as "the Bible of the common soldier" and struck, thereby, a religious note that would recur frequently in the commentary. "It has swept like a gospel over Germany," wrote Read, "and must sweep over the whole world, because it is the first completely satisfying expression in literature of the greatest event of our time." He added that he had by then read the book "six or seven times." An American rhapsodized about "its blasting simplicity" and called it the "Book of the Decade": "I should like to see it sell a million copies," concluded Christopher Morley. Daniel-Rops, philosopher, theologian, and historian, shared such sentiments in Switzerland: it was "the book we waited for" for ten years, he said. Bruno Frank, Bernhard Kellermann, G. Lowes Dickinson, and Henry Seidel Canby were other eminent literary figures among the early enthusiasts. Several people suggested that Remarque be awarded the Nobel Prize for literature.[25]

In the initial reviews, then, there was rarely a note of vigorous criticism, and there was near unanimity in the belief that the book presented "the truth about the war," or, as the London *Sunday Chronicle* put it, "the true story of the world's greatest nightmare."[26] The exuberance, especially the extravagant use of superlatives and absolutes, and the shrill insistence that this book told "the truth," indicated how sensitive a nerve Remarque had touched and how completely many people shared his frustration—his postwar frustration. The tone of the novel and, the tone of the early reviews were very similar.

But what was this "truth" to which almost all referred? That the war had been a nihilistic slaughter without rationale? That its front-line protagonists and chief victims had no sense of purpose? That, in short, the war had been in vain? Few said so outright, but the liberal left and moderate socialists throughout Europe, and even here and there in America and the dominions, were now inclined to view the war as, in the end, a tragic and futile civil conflict in Europe, one that need not have occurred.

However, as sales mounted through the spring and summer of 1929, an opposition began to organize and to voice its opinions as shrilly as the early supporters. The communist left derided the novel as an example of the sterility of bourgeois intelligence: the bourgeois mind, incapable of locating the real source of social disorder, resorted, in its treatment of the war, to tearful sentimentality and regret. The book was seen as a fine illustration of the "decline of the west" mentality.[27] To those at the other end of the political spectrum, the conservative right, Remarque's work was pernicious because it threatened the entire meaning of postwar conservatism, the idea of regeneration based on traditional values. In the eyes of conservatives in all belligerent countries the war had been a necessity, tragic of course, but nonetheless unavoidable. If the war was now found to have been an absurdity, then conservatism as a set of beliefs was an absurdity. Consequently, *All Quiet* had to be rejected—as deliberately "commercialized horror and filth" and as the outgrowth of a degenerate mind that could not rise above the inevitable horror of war to see "the eternal issues involved," the grandeur of an idea, the beauty of sacrifice, and the nobility of collective purpose.[28]

The fascist opposition to the novel blended often with that of the conservatives and presented many of the same arguments, but there was an essential difference in the reasoning. The fascists sanctified not so much the purpose of the war as the "experience" of the war, the very essence of the war, its immediacy, its tragedy, its exhilaration, its ultimate ineffability in anything but mystical and spiritual terms. The war, as we shall see, gave meaning to fascism. Thus, any suggestion that the war had been purposeless was a slur against the very existence of this form of extremism. It is here, on the extreme right, that the most active opposition to Remarque, and to the whole wave of so-called negative war books, films, and other artifacts, assembled.

Both traditionalists and right-wing extremists were incensed by what they saw as a completely one-sided portrait of the war experience. They objected to the language in the novel, to the horrifying images, to the frequent references to bodily functions, and, especially, to a scene involving a jovial group perched on field latrines. Little, Brown and Company of Boston, the American publisher, actually deleted the latrine scene at the insistence of the Book-of-the-Month Club, cut an episode concerning a sexual encounter in a hospital, and softened certain words and phrases in A. W. Wheen's British translation.[29] The latrine passage, retained in the British edition, was harped on by a large number of British critics, who began to refer to Remarque as the high priest of the "lavatory school" of war novelists. In November 1929, *The London Mercury* felt the need to editorialize on this school.

> "Criticism," wrote Anatole France, "is the adventure of the soul among masterpieces." The adventure of the soul among lavatories is not inviting: but this, roughly, is what criticism of recent translated German novels must be. . . . The modern Germans . . . suppose that lavatories are intensely interesting. They are obsessed by this dreary subject, and they are obsessed by brutality.[30]

An Australian, writing in *The Army Quarterly*, asked how British firms could publish "unclean war books"; in his view the translation and publication of "filthy foreign books" was an act of treason.[31]

The denunciation of the book as a piece of propaganda—pacifist, Allied, or German, depending on the critic—was the other main form of attack on the right. Franz von Lilienthal noted in the conservative financial daily, *Berliner Börsen-Zeitung*, that if Remarque did in fact receive the Nobel Prize, Lord Northcliffe, the press baron, would have to be applauded as well, because Remarque had nothing to say that Northcliffe, master propagandist that he was, had not said earlier. To the German military the novel was "a singularly monstrous slander of the German army" and thus a piece of "refined pacifist propaganda." The military everywhere for that matter was inclined to support such a view. In November 1929, the Czechoslovak War Department banned *All Quiet* from military libraries. Outside Germany many conservative critics looked on the novel as part of a clever German campaign of cultural dissimulation. In a speech at Armistice celebrations at Folkestone in 1929, a Baptist minister deplored the tenor of the popular novels and plays on the subject of the war. He certainly had *All Quiet* in mind, as well as Robert Graves's recently published *Goodbye to All That* and R. C. Sherriff's *Journey's End* when he said, "I did not think I should ever live to read books written by my own countrymen which are like the dirty work done by enemy propagandists."[32]

Earlier in the year G. Lowes Dickinson, Cambridge humanist and ardent promoter of the League of Nations, had sensed that Remarque's book might be subjected to this type of attack. Urging all those to read the book "who have the courage and honesty to desire to know what modern war is really like," he added, "They need not fear German propaganda. The book is far above all that. It is the truth, told by a man with the power of a great artist, who is hardly aware what an artist he is."[33]

But J. C. Squire and *The London Mercury* would have none of this. "This is not the truth," they retorted, referring to the work of Remarque and other German war novelists, and warned against the apparent tendency among the British public "to sentimentalize over the Germans" and to neglect the French. Then, with a stunning burst of ferocity, reminiscent of the war itself, they continued:

> We repeat . . . (being cosmopolitans and pacifists, but facers of facts) that the Germans (many of whom were not even Christianized until the sixteenth century) have contributed very little indeed to European culture . . . In war we exaggerated the defects of the enemy; do not let us, in peace, exaggerate his merits; above all, do not let us, in a wanton reaction, take more interest in the enemy than in the friend. The cold truth is that the Russians, who are still largely barbaric, contributed far more, in music and literature, to culture in the nineteenth century than the Germans, let alone the square-head Prussians, have contributed in hundreds of years. . . . Peace with the Germans, by all means; understanding with the Germans, if possible; but let us not, out of mere sentimentality, concentrate our gaze upon the Germans at the expense of more cultivated, productive and civilized peoples. Let us welcome, by all means, whatever good may come from Germany; but the present tendency is to think that anything that comes out of Germany must be good. "Omne Teutonicum pro magnifico" seems the motto of the publishers and the press: it is a grotesque motto.[34]

Paradoxically, when in February 1930 Wilhelm Frick, the newly appointed Nazi minister of the interior in the state government of Thuringia, banned *All Quiet* from schools in that state, a Nazi paper, announcing the decree, commented, "it is time to stop the infection of the schools with pacifist Marxist propaganda."[35]

Both the critical praise and the scurrility that *All Quiet* provoked had, in the end, little to do with the substance of the novel. As *All Quiet* was a reflection more of the postwar than of the wartime mind, so the commentary, too, was a reflection of postwar political and emotional investments. Yet everyone pretended to be arguing objectively about the essence of the war experience. The critical dialogue was worthy of characters in a Chekhov play. They talked past each other. The wider public response was similar.

Remarque's success came at what we now see was a crossroads in the interwar era: the intersection of two moods, one of vague, imploring hope and the other of coagulating fear; "the Locarno spirit" and a fling with apparent prosperity intersecting with incipient economic crisis and mounting national introspection.

Accompanying the efforts at international détente after 1925 was a wave of humanism that swept the west. A wishful rather than assertive humanism this was, however. In 1927 Thornton Wilder ended his Pulitzer Prize–winning novel, *The Bridge of San Luis Rey*, with the sentence: "There is a land of the living and a land of the dead and the bridge is love, the only survival, the only meaning." Melancholy, sentimentality, and wish constitute the dominant mood here. Two years later, in 1929, the disastrous economic slump brought the underlying doubt starkly to the surface. The popular cultural activities of the twenties as a whole were, more or less, a bewildered salute to a bygone age when the individual had had a recognized social purpose.

The war boom of the late twenties and early thirties was a product of this mixture of aspiration, anxiety, and doubt. All the successful war books were written from the point of view of the individual, not the unit or the nation. Remarque's book, written in the first person, personalized for everyone the fate of the unknown soldier. Paul Bäumer became Everyman. On this level only could the war have any meaning, on the level of individual suffering. The war was a matter of individual experience rather than collective interpretation. It had become a matter of art, not history.

Art had become more important than history. History belonged to an age of rationalism, to the eighteenth and particularly the nineteenth century. The latter century had shown great respect for its historians. The Guizots, Michelets, Rankes, Macaulays, and Actons were read and appreciated, especially by a bourgeoisie bent on expansion and integration. Our century has, by contrast, been an antihistorical age, in part because historians have failed to adapt to the sentiments of their century but even more so because this century has been one of disintegration rather than integration. The psychologist has, as a result, been more in demand than the historian. And the artist has received more respect than either.

It is noteworthy that among the mountains of writing built up on the subject of the Great War, a good many of the more satisfying attempts to deal with its meaning have come from the pens of poets, novelists, and even literary critics, and that professional historians have produced, by and large, specialized and limited accounts, most of which pale in evocative and explanatory power before those of the *littérateurs*. Historians have failed to find explanations to the war that correspond to the horrendous realities, to the actual experience of the war. The spate of official and unofficial histories that issued forth in the twenties was largely ignored by the public. By contrast, Remarque's *All Quiet* became, virtually overnight, the best seller of all previous time. Imaginative, not historical, literature it was that sparked the intense reconsideration of the meaning of the war at the end of the twenties. The historical imagination, like so much of the intellectual effort of the nineteenth century, had been sorely challenged by the events of the war; and it was consistent with the subsequent self-doubt of the discipline that H. A. L. Fisher's 1934 lament, in the preface to his *History of Europe*, should have become one of the most frequently quoted theoretical statements by a historian of our century:

> Men wiser and more learned than I have discerned in history a plot, a rhythm, a predetermined pattern. These harmonies are concealed from me. I can see only one emergency following upon another as wave follows upon wave.[36]

Whether the poems, novels, and other imaginative efforts provoked by the war stand as "great" art is a debatable matter. William Butler Yeats, in his idiosyncratic 1936 edition of *The Oxford Book of Modern Verse*, omitted Wilfred Owen, Siegfried Sassoon, Ivor Gurney, Isaac Rosenberg, Robert Graves, Herbert Read, and others, on the grounds that passive suffering could not be the stuff of great poetry, which had to have a moral vision. But he was imposing his critical vision on a public that felt otherwise. Ten years after the war, amidst the glut of war novels that appeared during the war boom, the *Morning Post* bemoaned in an editorial that "the great novel of the Great War, which will show all things in a true perspective, has yet to be written."[37] The great war novel, explaining all, was a constant vision among intellectuals in the twenties and even the thirties. Mottram's *Spanish Farm* trilogy, Tomlinson's *All Our Yesterdays*, Aldington's *Death of a Hero*, and, in a different vein but with similar intent, Renn's *Krieg* and Remarque's *All Quiet*, to cite but a few, were motivated by this challenge and quest. "The witness of a hundred thousand nobodies," wrote André Thérive in *Le Temps* in December 1929, "isn't worth the semifiction conceived by a great man."[38] This attitude, that art might be truer to life than history, was hardly a new notion, but never before had it been so widespread, in fact so dominant.

Ironically, during the war French and British soldiers had become the "frontier" personalities identified with the avant-garde and with German *Kultur* as a whole before the war; they were the men who had experienced the very limits of existence, who had seen no man's land, who had witnessed horror and agony, and who, because of the very experience that made them heroes, lived on the edge of respectability and morality. Given the failure of the postwar era to produce the apocalyptic resolution promised by wartime propaganda, the whole social purpose of the war—the content of duty and *devoir*—began to ring hollow. Since the tangible results of the war could never justify its cost, especially its emotional toll, disillusionment was inevitable, and soldiers in the postwar world withdrew from social activity and commitment. Only a minority bothered even to join veterans' organizations. Relatively few were able to articulate their alienation, but the statistics speak loudly: of those unemployed between the ages of thirty and thirty-four in Britain at the end of the twenties, 80 percent were ex-servicemen. The incidence of mental illness among veterans was also staggering. "The worst thing about the war generation of introspects," said T. E. Lawrence, "is that they can't keep off their blooming selves." Aldington talked about the "self-prisons" in which former soldiers had become trapped, and Graves wrote about his "cage-mates."[39]

Yet, while former soldiers suffered from a high incidence of neurasthenia and sexual impotence, they realized that the war, in the words of José Germain, was "the quivering axis of all human history."[40] If the war as a whole had no objective meaning, then invariably all human history was telescoped into each man's experience; every person was the sum total of history. Rather than being a social experience, a matter of documentable reality, history was individual nightmare, or even, as the Dadaists insisted, madness. One is again reminded of Nietzsche's statement, on the very edge of his complete mental collapse, that he was "every name in history."

The burden of having been in the eye of the storm and yet, in the end, of having resolved nothing, was excruciating. The result often was the rejection of social and political reality and at the same time the rejection even of the perceptual self—only dream and neurosis remained, a world of illusions characterized by a pervasive negativism. Fantasy became the mainspring of action, and melancholy the general mood. *Nous vivons une triste époque ... Tout est foutu—Quoi? Tout un monde ... Il fait beau, allons au cimetière.*[41] Carroll Carstairs ended his book *A Generation Missing* in 1930 with the words "It's a weary world and the raspberry jam sent me from Paris is all finished now."[42]

What was true of the soldiers was true with somewhat less immediacy and poignancy of civilians. The crowded nightclubs, the frenzied dancing, the striking upsurge of gambling, alcoholism, and suicide, the obsession with flight, with moving pictures, and with film stars evinced on a popular level these same tendencies, a drift toward irrationalism. Of course bourgeois Europe tried to "recast" itself, but it was capable of doing so only superficially. The modern temper had been forged; the avant-garde had won. The "adversary culture" had become the dominant culture; irony and anxiety, the mode and the mood. "The war is breaking us but is also reshaping us," Marc Boasson had written in July 1915. Fifteen years later Egon Friedell, the cultural historian, asserted emphatically, "History does not exist."[43]

All Quiet captured for the popular mind some of the same instincts that were being expressed in "high art." Proust and Joyce, too, telescoped history into the individual. There is no collective reality, only individual response, only dreams and myths, which have lost their nexus with social convention.

In the tormented and degraded German front soldier depicted in *All Quiet*—and he could just as easily have been a Tommy, *poilu*, or doughboy—the public saw its own shadow and sensed its own anonymity and yearning for security. A small number of critics perceived this at the time. "The effect of the book springs in fact," wrote a German commentator,

> from the terrible disillusionment of the German people with the state in which they find themselves, and the reader tends to feel that this book has located the source of all our difficulties.[44]

An American noted, "In Remarque the sentiment of the epoch comes to bloom."[45] *All Quiet* seemed to encapsulate the whole modern impulse as it manifested itself in the postwar world: the amalgamation of prayer and desperation, dream and chaos, wish and desolation.

In each country there was a specific variation on this general theme. In Germany after 1925 one noticed a distinct relaxation of political tension, evidenced by the lowest turnout at the polls in the whole of the Weimar period in the national elections of May 1928, the first since December 1924. The government that was formed in June 1928 was appropriately a "grand coalition," ranging from Social Democrats on the left, who led the government, to the moderate right-wing People's Party of Gustav Stresemann. The government began its life in a conciliatory mood. However, in May 1930 it fell, the victim of revived nationalist and conservative sentiment.

Nineteen twenty-nine was the critical year. That the economic situation deteriorated drastically in a year that marked the tenth anniversary of the Treaty of Versailles was an unfortunate coincidence. Reparations were on the public mind. Alfred Hugenberg, press lord and leader of the right-wing Nationalist People's Party, campaigned for his referendum against the Young Plan, the new Allied proposal for reparations, and accepted Adolf Hitler into his camp. The right, in its spirited new offensive against the republic, blamed Germany's renewed economic difficulties on the draconic peace settlement and on the blood lust of the Allies. Public demonstrations against the "war guilt lie" grew in number and frenzy through the early part of 1929 and climaxed in a flood of meetings in June. The government declared June 28, the anniversary of the treaty, a day of national mourning. Remarque was able to capitalize on both the remnants of political moderation and the heightened sensitivity to the question of the war.

Remarque blamed the war for his personal disorientation; the German public, too, assumed that its suffering was a direct legacy of the war. *All Quiet* actually raised the consciousness of Germans on the issue of the war as the source of their difficulties.

In Britain, where the economy took a very bad turn in late 1928 and where unemployment dominated the election campaign in the spring of 1929, Remarque's portrayal of the German front-line soldier as a miserable, downtrodden pawn, striving to retain some dignity and humanity, met with sympathy. By the late twenties much of British opinion had become favorable toward Germany. French pettiness and obstreperousness earlier in the decade and then "the Locarno, spirit" had drawn the British away from the French and closer to the Germans. "In foreign affairs the psychological drama of British politics is precisely that we like the Germans more, and the French less," *The Fortnightly Review* mused, "but with the first we fall out and the latter we are obliged to accept as partners." However, even this partnership with France was under question in some quarters. J. C. C. Davidson, confidant of the conservative leader, Stanley Baldwin, spoke about the advantages of loosening the tie with France, a "parochial and highly cynical" nation "whose population is declining and whose methods are so little in harmony with our own." Douglas Goldring, who described himself as a "crusted libertarian and little Englander of ingrained Tory instincts," suggested that some terrible errors had been made by British statesmen: "Any intelligent undergraduate, interpreting the past in the light of recent happenings, would probably arrive at the conclusion that our entry into the war was a blunder ... My generation," he concluded, "was betrayed, swindled, exploited and decimated by its elders in 1914." And Robert Graves, in his memoir, *Goodbye to All That*, which he wrote in the spring and summer of 1929, thought it fit to quote Edmund Blunden: "No more wars for me at any price! Except against the French. If there's ever a war with them, I'll go like a shot."[46]

The undercurrent of suspicion and scorn in the Anglo-French alliance naturally did not flow only in one direction. In the twenties Frenchmen were convinced that it was mainly they who had won the war; the British contribution had never been equal to the French. How could it have been? The French had held three quarters of the line on the Western Front. British concerns, moreover, had always been overseas and not in Europe. Even during the war the French were prone to accuse the British of fighting to the last drop of other people's blood. Joffre said of the British in 1915: "I'd never let them hold the line on their own—they'd be broken through. I trust them only when they are held up by us." During the mutinies of June 1917 a French soldier was heard to say, "We have to have the Boches on our side within a month to help us kick out the British." By 1922, even before the Ruhr crisis, when the British failed to back French and Belgian punitive measures against the Germans over reparations, General Huguet, the former French attaché to the British armies, could describe Britain as an "adversary."[47] As the decade wore on the relationship deteriorated further. So Frenchmen, while generally calmer in their response to Remarque's novel, were nevertheless drawn to a book that portrayed the mutual hell through which the principal combatants, French and German soldiers, had gone. Perhaps the *poilu* and the *boche* were not irreconcilable. The success of *À l'ouest rien de nouveau* brought a flood of French translations of German works on the war, and, appropriately, in the initial phases of the war boom at least, British war books were neglected by French publishers.[48]

The great discovery that foreign readers said they made through *All Quiet* was that the German soldier's experience of the war had been, in its essentials, no different from that of soldiers of other nations. The German soldier, it seemed, had not wanted to fight either, once the emotional decoration put on the war by the home front had been shattered. Remarque's novel did a great deal to undermine the view that Germans were "peculiar" and not to be trusted. Furthermore, *All Quiet* promoted at a popular level what historical revisionism was achieving at an academic and political level: the erosion of the idea of a collective German war guilt. But on this score too "art" was clearly more effective than "history." Remarque alone accomplished much more than all the revisionist historians in America and Europe put together.

Who read *All Quiet* with most interest? Veterans and young people appear to have been the most avid readers of war books as a whole. By the end of the decade the disillusionment of former servicemen with postwar society had matured into vituperative scorn for the so-called peace, not only in the defeated countries but also in the victor states. *All Quiet* and other war books of "disenchantment," as C. E. Montague's early venture in this genre was actually entitled, elicited many a "bravo" from embittered and saddened veterans. Yet there were also frequent denunciations from veterans who regarded the spirit and success of *All Quiet* as a manifestation of the malaise that had engulfed the postwar world, as a symptom of the spirit that had betrayed a generation and its hopes. Where exactly the balance lay is difficult to ascertain. What is clear, however, is that the interest of veterans in the literary protest was based largely on their postwar experience. They were reacting to the disappearance, in the course of the decade, of the vision the war had promised.

Youths who had matured after the war were naturally curious about the war. Many commentators noted that fathers who had survived the front were reluctant to talk about their experience even with their families, which is why young people, wishing to penetrate the silence, constituted a sizable part of the readership. And having grown up in the shadow of the hero-father, they were also fascinated by the "negative" portrayal of the war. The literature of disenchantment offered a less ascetic, more humane, and hence more interesting portrait of the warrior-father.[49] In a straw vote among senior

Gymnasium, or secondary school, students in Düsseldorf in January 1930 on favorite authors, Remarque topped the poll, outstripping Goethe, Schiller, Galsworthy, Dreiser, and Edgar Wallace. It is worth noting, however, that alongside war diaries and memoirs, works on economics elicited most interest among the students polled.[50] Obviously the economic insecurity felt by students in depression-ridden Germany and the fascination with accounts of horror and death in the trenches were linked. Youth, too, was prone to blame uncertain employment prospects on the war.

The "real war" had ceased to exist in 1918. Thereafter it was swallowed by imagination in the guise of memory. For many the war became absurd in retrospect, not because of the war experience in itself but because of the failure of the postwar experience to justify the war. For others the same logic turned the war into ultimate experience, again in retrospect. William Faulkner was hinting at this process of metamorphosis when he wrote, in 1931, "America has been conquered not by the German soldiers that died in French and Flemish trenches, but by the German soldiers that died in German books."[51] The journey inward that the war had initiated for masses of men was accelerated by the aftermath of the war.

All Quiet, contrary to the claims of many of its enthusiastic readers, was not "the truth about the war"; it was, first and foremost, the truth about Erich Maria Remarque in 1928. But equally, most of his critics were no nearer "the truth" of which they too spoke. They expressed merely the tenor of their own endeavors. Remarque used the war; his critics and the public did the same. Hitler and National Socialism were to be, in the end, the most obsessive and successful exploiters of the war. The war boom of the late twenties reflected less a genuine interest in the war than a perplexed international self-commiseration.

Cloud Juggler

Hart Crane's elegy for Harry Crosby was called "The Cloud Juggler." The title would have suited Erich Maria Remarque as well. Crosby put a pistol to his head, literally, and pulled the trigger. Remarque did so figuratively, again and again. The paradoxical figure of the vital victim—squirming, twitching, pleading, cursing in the face of annihilation—preoccupied both. For both, art had become superior to life. In art resided life.

Virtually everything Remarque wrote after *All Quiet* was concerned with disintegration and death. Yet virtually everything he wrote was an international success.

The film version of *All Quiet* was a fine effort, directed by Lewis Milestone for Universal Studios, and released in May 1930. It met rave reviews and played to crowded cinemas in New York, Paris, and London and was accorded Hollywood's highest accolade, the Academy Award for best picture of

1930. In Berlin, however, after several performances were disrupted by Nazi hooligans led by Joseph Goebbels, it was banned in December, ostensibly because it slandered the German image but actually because it was a threat to internal security and order owing to the controversy it provoked.[52]

On May 11, 1933, after Hitler's takeover in Germany, Remarque's books were among those burned symbolically at the University of Berlin as "politically and morally un-German." "Down with the literary betrayal of the soldiers of the world war!" chanted a Nazi student. "In the name of educating our people in the spirit of valor, I commit the writings of Erich Maria Remarque to the flames."[53]

On November 20, 1933, 3411 copies of *All Quiet* were seized at the Ullstein publishing house by the Berlin police, on the basis of the presidential decree of February 4, which was drawn up "for the protection of the German people." In December the Gestapo instructed that these copies be destroyed.[54] On May 15 Goebbels, who had been a mere stripling during the war, had told representatives of the German book trade that the *Volk*, the German people, were not supposed to serve books, but books were to serve the *Volk*; and he had concluded, *Denn es wird am deutschen Wesen noch einmal die Welt genesen.*"[55]

Erich Maria Remarque had sought refuge in Switzerland in 1930. After a long journey to New York, Hollywood, and back, he would die there in his mountain retreat in 1970, still handsome and still unhappy.

Notes

1. Let us in turn be the spring, which brings green new life to the gray terrain of death, and with the blood we gave for justice let us, after sleepless nights full of horror, give rise to new days of beauty.

2. Who, seventeen years ago, would have ever thought that you could praise the harmony of *Le Sacre*? But that's the case. One no longer thinks of its presumption; one admires its perfection.

3. *Nouvelles littéraires*, October 25, 1930.

4. *Börsenblatt für den deutschen Buchhandel*, June 10, 1930, 540; *Die Literatur*, 31 (1928–29), 657; *Publisher's Weekly*, September 21, 1929, 1332; *Daily Herald*, November 23, 1929.

5. Friedrich Fuchs in *Das Hochland*, 2 (1929), 217.

6. John Middleton Murry, *Between Two Worlds* (London, 1935), 65.

7. Cabinet minutes, December 19, 1930, Reichskanzlei files, R431/1447, 383, Bundesarchiv Koblenz (hereafter BAK).

8. Peter Kropp, *Endlich Klarheit über Remarque und sein Buch "Im Westen nichts Neues"* (Hamm i. W., 1930), 9–14.

9. *Dream Lodgings*.

10. *Horizon Station*.

11. *Der Spiegel*, January 9, 1952, 25.

12. In D. A. Prater, *European of Yesterday: A Biography of Stefan Zweig* (Oxford, 1972), 140.

13. Interview with Axel Eggebrecht, *Die Literarische Welt*, June 14, 1929.

14. *Sport im Bild*, June 8, 1928.

15. Ibid., July 20, 1928.

16. I have used the A. W. Wheen translation (London, 1929) for quotations. Wheen was himself a veteran of the war; see R. Church, *The Spectator*, 142 (April 20, 1929), 624.

17. Hanna Hafkesbrink, for instance, called *All Quiet* a "genuine memoir of the war"; see *Unknown Germany: An Inner Chronicle of the First World War Based on Letters and Diaries* (New Haven, Conn., 1948), ix.

18. For examples of the criticism see Jean Norton Cru, *Témoins*, 80; and Cyril Falls, *War Books* (London, 1930), x–xi, 294.

19. E. M. Remarque and Gen. Sir Ian Hamilton, "The End Of War?" *Life and Letters*, 3 (1929), 405–406.

20. *Time*, March 24, 1961, in its review of *Heaven Has No Favorites*.

21. Michel Tournier, *Le vent Paraclet* (Paris, 1977), 166.

22. Harry Crosby, "Hail: Death!" *Transition*, 14 (1928), 169–70.

23. R[osie] G[räfenberg], *Prelude to the Past* (New York, 1934), 320–21.

24. The legends about Remarque and *All Quiet* are many. One is that he offered his manuscript to forty-eight publishers. See the obituary in *Der Spiegel*, September 2–8, 1970. For accounts of the publication see Peter de Mendelssohn, *S. Fischer und sein Verlag* (Frankfurt am Main, 1970), 1114–18; Max Krell, *Das gab es alles einmal* (Frankfurt am Main, 1961), 159–60; Heinz Ullstein's version in a *dpa* release, June 15, 1962, as well as his letter to the *Frankfurter Allgemeine Zeitung*, July 9, 1962; and the remarks of Carl Jödicke, an Ullstein employee, in his unpublished "Dokumente und Aufzeichnungen" (F501), 40, Institut für Zeitgeschichte, Munich.

25. Carl Zuckmayer, *Als wär's ein Stück von mir*, 359–60; Axel Eggebrecht, *Die Weltbühne*, February 5, 1929, 212; Herbert Read, "A Lost Generation," *The Nation & Athenaeum*, April 27, 1929, 116; Christopher Morley, *The Saturday Review*, April 20, 1929, 909; Daniel-Rops, *Bibliothèque universelle et Revue de Genève*, 1929, II, 510–11.

26. The *Sunday Chronicle* is cited in *The Saturday Review*, June 1, 1929, 1075.

27. See Antkowiak's survey of the communist reviews in Pawel Toper and Alfred Antkowiak, *Ludwig Renn, Erich Maria Remarque: Leben und Werk* ([East] Berlin, 1965).

28. Freiherr von der Goltz, *Deutsche Wehr*, October 10, 1929, 270; Valentine Williams, *Morning Post*, February 11, 1930; *The London Mercury*, 21 (January 1930), 238; and *Deutschlands Erneuerung*, 13 (1929), 230.

29. See the reports in the *New York Times*, May 31, June 1, July 14, July 29, 1929.

30. *The London Mercury*, 21 (November 1929), 1.

31. *The Army Quarterly*, 20 (July 1930), 373–75.

32. *Berliner Börsen-Zeitung*, June 9, 1929; *New York Times*, November 17, 1929; *Daily Herald*, November 12, 1929.

33. *The Cambridge Review*, May 3, 1929, 412.

34. *The London Mercury*, 21 (January 1930), 194–95.

35. Reported in the *New York Times*, February 9, 1930.

36. H. A. L. Fisher, *A History of Europe*, 3 vols. (London, 1935), I:vii.

37. "War Novels," *Morning Post*, April 8, 1930.

38. André Thérive, "Les Livres," *Le Temps*, December 27, 1929.

39. Robert Wohl, *The Generation of 1914* (Cambridge, Mass., 1979), 120; A. C. Ward, *The Nineteen-Twenties* (London, 1930), xii; Robert Graves, "The Marmosite's Miscellany," *Poems (1914–26)* (London, 1927), 191.

40. José Germain, in his preface to Maurice d'Hartoy, *La Génération du feu* (Paris, 1923), xi.

41. We live a melancholy era . . . Everything is screwed up. What? A whole world . . . It's nice out. Let's go to the cemetery.

42. Carroll Carstairs, *A Generation Missing* (London, 1930), 208.

43. Letter, July 2, 1915, Boasson, *Au Soir*, 12; Egon Friedell, *A Cultural History of the Modern Age*, trans. C. F. Atkinson (New York, 1954), III:467.

44. W. Müller Scheid, *Im Westen nichts Neues—eine Täuschung* (Idstein, 1929), 6.

45. *Commonweal*, May 27, 1931, 90.

46. *The Fortnightly Review*, October 1, 1930, 527; Davidson, in John C. Cairns, "A Nation of Shopkeepers in Search of a Suitable France: 1919–40," *The American Historical Review*, 79 (1974), 728; Douglas Goldring, *Pacifists in Peace and War* (London, 1932), 12, 18; Graves, *Goodbye*, 240.

47. Joffre, in Marc Ferro, *La Grande Guerre 1914–1918* (Paris, 1969), 239; Pedroncini, *Les Mutineries*, 177; General Huguet, *L'Intervention militaire britannique en 1914* (Paris, 1928), 231.

48. See the introductory remarks by René Lalou to R. H. Mottram's *La Ferme espagnole*, trans. M. Dou-Desportes (Paris, 1930), i–iv.

49. Isherwood, *Lions and Shadows*, 73–76, and also his *Kathleen and Frank*, 356–63; and Jean Dutourd, *Les Taxis de la Marne* (Paris, 1956), 189–93.

50. *New York Times*, January 18, 1930.

51. William Faulkner, *The New Republic*, May 20, 1931, 23–24.

52. See my "War, Memory, and Politics: The Fate of the Film *All Quiet on the Western Front*," *Central European History*, 13/1 (March 1980), 60–82.

53. In Henry C. Meyer (ed.), *The Long Generation* (New York, 1973), 221.

54. See the correspondence between the Polizeipräsident in Berlin and the Geheime Staatspolizeiamt, December 4 and 16, 1933, Reichssicherheitshauptamt files, R58/933, 198–99, BAK.

55. See page 80. Wolff'sche Telegraphen Büro report, May 15, 1933, in the Neue Reichskanzlei files, R43II/479, 4–5, BAK.

HANS WAGENER

All Quiet on the Western Front

In 1928 Remarque felt depressed in his situation as the editor of *Sport im Bild*. As he stated in an interview, he realized that the reason for this depression and feeling of desperation was his war experience, and he observed similar feelings in his friends and acquaintances.[1] He thus sat down and wrote *All Quiet on the Western Front* as a therapeutic attempt to rid himself of these feelings. He began writing after returning home from his office one evening, and finished the book within a period of six weeks.

It is difficult to summarize the plot of *All Quiet on the Western Front* in terms of one logical story line, since Remarque intends to describe neither a linearly developing action nor a psychological development. He wishes instead to characterize the condition of being at war. He also describes the state of being estranged from everything that one's former life and home represented. Consequently this novel consists of a number of short episodes that describe typical war experiences such as food disbursements, artillery barrages, gas attacks, furloughs, watch guards, patrols, visits to a comrade in the army hospital, rats, latrines, and so on. The story is told in the first person except for the final paragraph, where an anonymous narrator is introduced who reports Paul Bäumer's death. The novel in its original version is only 288 pages long and consists of twelve relatively short chapters, each containing several episodes.

From *Understanding Erich Maria Remarque* by Hans Wagener, pp. 9–36. © 1991 University of South Carolina.

Influenced by their patriotic teacher, Kantorek, who during drill time gave the class long lectures, asking the young students in a moving voice: "Won't you join up, Comrades?" (AQ 9), the young Paul Bäumer and his classmates volunteer to join the army during World War I. Their military boot camp training, headed by the vicious sergeant Himmelstoss, is a rude awakening. They are soon sent to the front, where they experience the gruesome reality of a war in the trenches with several somewhat older soldiers, including Bäumer's mentor Katczinsky (Kat). When Bäumer returns home during leave, he is unable to identify with the memories of his youth. Nor can he understand the patriotic enthusiasm of the older generation, including his father who wants proudly to show off his son as a hero. Consequently he is happy to go back to this comrades where he feels he belongs. During a patrol Bäumer stabs a Frenchman who jumps into the same shell crater where he is hiding, and he witnesses the Frenchman's slow, painful death. Later he is himself wounded and experiences the horrors of war in an army hospital. Back at the front, he sees his comrades die one by one, until he too is finally killed.

In *All Quiet on the Western Front* Remarque deals with the last two years of World War I from the perspective of the common soldier in the trenches. Although it is not a historical novel, does not mention battles by name or give their exact dates or geographical places, a knowledge of the political background of World War I and the postwar years is nevertheless essential for understanding the novel and its reception in Germany.

Germany had gone to war in 1914 on the side of Austria against Russia in the east and against France and England in the west. Germany's hope for a quick victory in France by marching through Belgium, thus violating its neutrality, had crumbled as early as 1914. The unsuccessful attacks of German volunteers in Flanders, particularly at Langemarck in the fall of 1914, had claimed many lives and brought the German advance to a halt. The war in the trenches had begun. Large offensives mounted in the following years had failed—the Germans could not break through the French lines, nor could the French and British troops break through the German lines. 1916 marked the year of two great battles—the Verdun offensive and the battle of the Somme. Both battles resulted in hundreds of thousands of casualties on both sides. In the latter battle, for instance, some fifty thousand English troops were killed or wounded in the first three days of battle. As a result, the German armies were severely depleted and ever younger recruits were drafted. Due to a British blockade the German people were starving. In order to break the blockade Germany escalated its submarine warfare. This in turn led, after the sinking of the *Lusitania*, which carried some American passengers but also war munitions, to the United States' intervention on April 2, 1917, on the side of the Allied Powers. From that point on, Germany had to fight against not only armies with superior manpower, including the fresh American troops that arrived in Europe, but also against an overwhelming advantage in the quantity and quality of war materials, medical and food supplies. An armistice between Germany/Austria and Russia was declared after the czar and his government were toppled in the 1917 Russian Revolution. This event ultimately resulted in the separate Peace of Brest-Litowsk (March 3, 1918).

The military relief gained from this peace at the eastern front came too late for Germany. Several German offensives in 1918 were to a large extent unsuccessful because temporary gains could not be exploited due to lack of reserves. Tanks, used by the Allied Powers since November 1917, were a modern weapon rare in the German army. After several successful French offensives the German front gave way. Germany had gone on the defensive, and it became clear that Germany could not win the war. Negotiations for an armistice resulted in the Allied insistence on terms Germany considered insulting, and as a result the German fleet was ordered to resume fighting. This order provoked a sailors' revolt on October 28, 1918, which quickly spread all over Germany. Workers' and soldiers' councils were elected locally and took power. The Bavarian king was forced to flee; Emperor William II abdicated and went into exile in the Netherlands. On November 11, 1918, an armistice was concluded and the Peace of Versailles was signed on June 18, 1919.

This summarizes the historical framework of *All Quiet on the Western Front*. However, Remarque rarely mentions any specific historical facts or geographical locations, thus making it easy for millions of readers to identify with the characters of the novel. At the same time, Remarque's vagueness makes it impossible to localize the events in any specific time or place. Remarque recounts only subjective individual experience, that is, those experiences that are generally excluded from official historiographies. Only in the second half of the novel does he allude to the fact that the war is coming to an end, and he specifically mentions that Bäumer "fell in October 1918" (AQ 291), so that we roughly know that we are dealing with 1917–18.

Remarque prefaces his book with the following:

> This book is to be neither an accusation nor a confession, and least of all an adventure, for death is not an adventure to those who stand face to face with it. It will try simply to tell of a generation of men who, even though they may have escaped its shells, were destroyed by the war.

This statement is a key to understanding the author's intention in writing his book and to the novel's "message." Since the book is not intended to be an accusation, the author clearly states that he did not consciously wish to make any political statement, not even one advocating pacifism. The phrase "simply to tell" implies on the one hand that the book is going to relate mere facts. On the other hand, however, this phrase denies the wish to "confess." This denial can also be interpreted as Remarque's own denial that this novel is an exact autobiographical account of his war experiences. Although written as a first-person narrative, the book is a fictional work and not an autobiography. Paul Bäumer should not be confused with Remarque. Indeed, Remarque has stated in an interview that he himself experienced most of the things he is reporting here, but it is also true that many things he just heard from others, especially from his time in the Duisburg hospital, and through letters from his friends. Working as a sapper, Remarque was in an area that was exposed to enemy shelling—otherwise he could not have been wounded. However, we must not forget that he did not actually serve on the front line, nor did he ever participate in hand-to-hand combat or direct attacks and counterattacks. Thus, Remarque himself had experienced the war only from the perspective of a sapper and as a patient in an army hospital. Many other aspects of the book are in fact autobiographical, particularly the scenes about boot camp in the barracks, the camp on the moors, furlough, work as a sapper, getting wounded, and being in the army hospital. However, these autobiographical elements are carefully interwoven into a work of fiction. It is unfair to take the author to task for having deviated from his own biography, as many of his contemporary critics have done.

The second aspect of the statement that prefaces the novel is that he is reporting about a generation of men who were destroyed by the war even though they escaped its shells. What he is thus saying is that his report has a general application and validity; that he wants to report not about an individual but about a collective fate. Furthermore, he implies that he does not want to tell us about the war experiences of young people, at least not solely, but rather wishes to justify the inability of young people to successfully cope with life after war, that is, life during the Weimar Republic. Such an interpretation focuses not on the war itself but on the year 1928, the very year when Remarque was writing his novel. One may very well argue that he uses his war experience to justify his own lack of professional success after the war, his inability to choose a solid career, and particularly his initial lack of success as a writer immediately following the war years.[2] There is no doubt that the notion of an entire generation ruined by war and unable to function contributed decisively to the book's success. Many readers were readily able to identify with the novel's heroes and found a ready-made justification for their own inability to cope with life during the Weimar years. The "lost generation" theme, coined by American writer Gertrude Stein, also plays an important role in the work of Ernest Hemingway, as can be seen in the epigraph for *The Sun Also Rises* (1928).

A third theme of the novel is also alluded to; namely, that of survival in war. Remarque claims that any war survival will at best be a physical survival and can never be an emotional or psychological one.

In his very first chapter Remarque jumps into the war action: "We were at rest five miles behind the front" (AQ 3), he states. Throughout the novel it is not always apparent from the immediate context whether "we" refers to the entire military unit or only to the narrator, Paul Bäumer, and his immediate group of friends—here the latter is more probable. His immediate friends include his former classmates from high school, Albert Kropp, Müller, and Leer, as well as some more mature friends—Tjaden, a locksmith; Haie Westhus, a peat cutter; Detering, a farmer; and the forty-year-old Stanislaus Katczinsky, called Kat. Remarque does not present these soldiers as complete, psychologically developed characters. In fact, each is merely characterized as having universal human qualities that appear as leitmotifs in the text: Tjaden is the biggest eater of the company; Kat has a sixth sense for danger, good food, and soft jobs; Haie Westhus continually has women on his mind; and Detering longs for his farm. Thus, these soldiers actually can be placed into two distinct groups: the former students and the somewhat older generation who had already had a job and usually a wife. When Remarque refers to the lost generation, he does not mean the older comrades who were already rooted in a profession or family of their own, but the students whose youth was cut short and ruined by the war. These students never had a career or wife, and have nothing to come back to after the war, nothing that would provide a secure place for them in society. Later, the term "generation" also applies to a broader group of all young people whose life was ruined by the war.

The group of friends presented by no means includes representatives of the entire society. Workers and representatives of the upper strata of society are missing. Sociologically speaking, the friends thus represent a homogenous group of members of the lower middle class, the class to which Remarque himself belonged.

In chapter 1, only 80 out of 150 men in the "Second Company" return back to the camp from the front lines. The remaining 80 soldiers are happy to receive food for 150 men. "Stomach" and "digestion" are repeatedly mentioned and become the two most important themes for the soldiers. One scene—left out of the earlier American editions—describes a soldier sitting in a latrine for two hours. This event is described as a recreational idyll where soldiers can talk and rest.

In a flashback Kantorek, the class's former teacher, is introduced. Kantorek had so indoctrinated the boys with his patriotic speeches that the entire class consequently volunteered to join the army. (Remarque himself was drafted and had not volunteered.) For Remarque, Kantorek is a representative of the thousands of well-meaning but misguided teachers in pre–World War

I Germany who sent young men into the war while themselves staying home. In Remarque's opinion this is a clear indication of the shortcomings of the older generation. Educators who were supposed to guide the younger generation into the world of adulthood, into the world of work, duty, culture, and progress, have failed. The youth's belief that their elders have greater insight and wisdom was shattered by their sight of the first war casualties. All that these teachers had taught them—their entire world—view crumbled during the first artillery barrage. Remarque stresses the fact that these young soldiers were not cowards. They are described as courageously advancing in each attack. They love their country, but have begun to see how they have been betrayed. They now see the old world as a façade, that their education had no practical application. They are not provided with the necessary spiritual, intellectual, and psychological tools to deal with the experience of war. Remarque's statements resound as a reproach to the older generation. It is important to note that Remarque also underscores the conservative virtues of soldierly courage and love for one's homeland. This resulted in some initial positive reviews of *All Quiet on the Western Front* in right-wing newspapers and magazines.

The small group of former students visit their former classmate Kemmerich in the field hospital. He has had one leg amputated and is dying. Müller is interested in a pair of soft leather British pilot's boots that Kemmerich will never be able to wear again. Kemmerich first refuses, but during a second visit, described in chapter 2, he asks the narrator to take the boots along for Müller. Already before the second visit the narrator interjects an extensive passage pointing out that simply because Müller wants to have Kemmerich's boots does not mean that he has less compassion for him than someone who does not dare think of it. If the boots would be of any use to Kemmerich, Müller would do anything to get hold of them for Kemmerich, but it is clear that Kemmerich will die soon. At the front line only the facts count. In this way Remarque demonstrates how conventional modes of behavior and thinking have been turned upside down by the war. Being a soldier means to forget about conventional emotions and behavior. These must be superseded by a pragmatic analysis of the situation at hand. The boots themselves also have symbolic significance. Müller, who now has the boots, is killed. They are then passed on to Tjaden, and after Tjaden is killed, to the narrator, Paul Bäumer, thus foreshadowing his death.

At the end of chapter 1 the narrator laments the loss of his youth: "Youth! We are none of us more than twenty years old. But young? Youth? That is long ago. We are old folk" (AQ 17). The war has aged them before their time; it has deprived them of their youth.

The motif reappears at the beginning of chapter 2. The narrator points out that these soldiers have been cut off from their youth by underscoring the difference between the former students and the older soldiers. Because of their interests, professions, and families of their own, these older soldiers are more firmly rooted in their former lives and are able to return to and continue their lives. For them the war is just an interruption of their activities during times of peace. The students, on the other hand, do not know what the future will hold for them. A touch of pathos and sentimentality marks this section of the novel, a trait that unfortunately became much more pronounced in several of Remarque's later works.

After the scene with Kemmerich's boots, the narrator recalls the time when he and his classmates volunteered for the army full of idealized and romantic feelings about the war. He then bemoans their tough boot camp training, which required the denial of all idealistic values of their former education. However, he also admits that giving up their individual personalities was necessary to survive. The narrator thus indirectly supports the necessity of carrying out seemingly sadistic behavior in a wartime situation. After describing in detail the deliberate harassment by Sergeant Himmelstoss, he concludes: "We became hard, suspicious, pitiless, vicious, tough—and that was good; for these attributes had been entirely lacking in us. Had we gone into the trenches without this period of training most of us would certainly have gone mad. Only thus were we prepared for what awaited us" (AQ 25). The sergeant's dehumanizing and depersonalizing viciousness may be described as a necessary element of survival in war, but the statement made remains an indirect comment on the nature of war itself.

The friends do not break apart; they "adapt," and a feeling of togetherness awakes in them. Remarque feels that this comradeship is the only positive thing that the war has produced. It is again something found in many war novels or, to be precise, in many novels about the front lines written by politically right-wing authors. However, closer analysis reveals that this comradeship also includes a readiness to help one's fellow comrade. This readiness to help, however, is deeply rooted in the will to survive, which is only possible with the reciprocated help of the other comrade.

After Kemmerich dies and Paul Bäumer leaves the hospital, a great, joyful feeling at simply being alive fills him. A feeling of lust for life overcomes him, and he seems to be getting this inner strength from the earth through the soles of his shoes: "The earth is streaming with forces which pour into me through the soles of my feet. . . . My limbs move supple, I feel my joints strong, I breathe the air deeply" (AQ 32). Remarque often uses such contrasts; and here when describing this rapturous state, this frenzy of life that seizes the narrator, he describes a kind of biological vitalism typical of his time. This kind of life-cult permeates all of his work from the first to the very last.

In chapter 3 ever younger recruits are brought in to replenish the company and fill in the gaps created by the mounting number of casualties. The detested Himmelstoss comes to the front, and Paul Bäumer's friends take their revenge by beating him up one night. Marxist critics have often interpreted this as Remarque's own private revenge on the older generation.[3] Many of Remarque's statements about war support this claim. Here in chapter 3 Kropp suggests that wars really ought to be fought by the state secretaries and generals dressed in swim trunks and armed only with sticks. Clearly Remarque is not a political person. There are no detailed plans for organized resistance, nor does he advocate a utopian socialist state.

The tendency to mythologize is also apparent in chapter 4, where the group is brought to the front to dig new trenches. The noises heard from the front awaken the soldiers' senses, electrifying them, and making them more alert. The front has an incredible power of attraction. The earth is envisioned as the protective force which gives the soldier shelter, taking him in and protecting him. The influence of the front forces the soldiers to regress by many thousands of years. They become animals with bestial instincts that are the sole means for survival. This too is testimony to the dehumanizing effect of war. However, it also becomes clear in the following that even Remarque is not insensitive to an aesthetic appreciation of war, as he describes the shining backs of the horses in the moonlight, the beauty of their movements, and the sparkling of their eyes. The horsemen with their steel helmets look to the narrator like knights from a time long past, a scene that appears somehow beautiful and touching to him:

> The backs of the horses shine in the moonlight, their movements are beautiful, they toss their heads, and their eyes gleam. The guns and the wagons float before the dim background of the moonlit landscape, the riders in their steel helmets resemble knights of a forgotten time; it is strangely beautiful and arresting (AQ 56–57).

Such passages are not very different from right-wing war novels. Such heroic descriptions of war are reminiscent of the German writer Ernst Jünger, who considered war a steel bath, a storm of steel that tests character and forges a new man.

Suddenly a massive artillery barrage not only scares the young recruits but also kills and injures many "screaming" horses in a horrifying scene. At the end of the episode the farmer Detering asks a rhetorical question about the horses' guilt and considers it the most horrible aspect of war that innocent animals are involved. This argument is designed to make the reader question the soldiers' own guilt and the reasons they "deserve" to be in the war. After another surprise attack, including a gas attack, the same argumentation is transferred to the young recruits and at the end Kat shakes his head saying: "Young innocents——" (AQ 73).

In chapter 5, after discussing the news that Himmelstoss has been sent to the front line, the friends discuss life after the war. Although Haie Westhus first thinks about catching up on his sex life, he would ultimately like to stay in the army. The life of a sergeant seems more attractive to him than the hard life of a poor peat cutter. Army life in times of peace is described in almost idyllic terms. Tjaden insults Himmelstoss verbally, which results in several days' confinement for him. In this scene Remarque demonstrates that the rules governing the front line are very different from those governing the camp. In one conversation the friends mock the lessons they were taught in school, assignments that have no practical application in war. Connections to cultural values and traditions have disintegrated. They can no longer communicate with those who stayed at home, and the continuity of development from their childhood to their current stage in life has been lost. These former students do not know how they can possibly continue when the war is over. After their experience it is inconceivable to them that they could get accustomed to a professional career. This inability to imagine any meaningful future after the bigger-than-life experience of war is seen by Remarque as the experience of an entire generation represented by Paul Bäumer and his friends. They have been spoiled by war, he maintains, spoiled for everything in life. They have nothing to believe in any more except war, and they feel lost. This is the main theme of the novel. It clarifies the perspective from which it is written, although its logic is not completely consistent. Neither Paul Bäumer nor any of his friends have been psychologically shattered by the war. They are now able to see all the patriotic phrases of their teachers in perspective, and they realize that their book knowledge has no apparent application. However, they are not broken; they do not get the opportunity to prove that they are part of the lost generation because they are killed one by one. Instead, Remarque demonstrates a kind of quiet heroism, a heroism that was created perhaps for the wrong reasons. But it is nevertheless a kind of heroism through which these young men are proving themselves.

Although Remarque condemns Himmelstoss and his methods of preparing the recruits for war, he also points out the usefulness of his hard, repetitious drills. The company leader, Lieutenant Bertinck, is presented as a reasonable human being ("He is a decent fellow" [AQ 91]) who gives Tjaden only the minimum punishment for insubordination. "They used to tie us to a tree," Remarque comments, "but that is forbidden now. In many ways we are treated quite like men" (AQ 91). This is perhaps one of the strongest indictments of the spirit of Prussian militarism. Here it is not the war that makes the soldiers regress by thousands of years, turning them into animals, but the militaristic spirit of those who do not consider soldiers human beings.

It is interesting to see that every time he describes an intense war scene, Remarque interjects scenes of soldiers resting in the camp, thus skillfully interspersing his novel with action and rest. In this case he even paints an idyllic picture of the soldiers in a manner reminiscent of picaresque novels. The soldiers are described stealing and frying a goose, eating it in a deserted shack, and sitting together surrounded by death. The final words of the chapter describe an emotional celebration of comradeship: "but by my side, stooping and angular, goes Kat, my comrade" (AQ 97).

In chapter 6 the sight of coffins piled high announces a new offensive. Paul Bäumer philosophizes about the importance of coincidence as the sole reason for a soldier to survive. Such arguments, of course, nullify much of the rightist notions of manhood and bravery. If a soldier stays alive in a modern war only as the result of a coincidence, all personal bravery and heroism is for naught in the battle for survival. Remarque goes on to describe the effects of continued heavy artillery barrages, the crumbling trenches, young recruits going berserk, and the sequence of attack and counterattack. He describes how the soldiers turn into animals without personal enemies. It is death itself that they fight against full of rage. Fighting is not done out of patriotism or heroism, but purely out of a feeling of instinctive survival:

> We have become wild beasts. We do not fight, we defend ourselves against annihilation. It is not against men that we fling our bombs, what do we know of men in this moment when Death with hands and helmets is hunting us down. . . . We feel a mad anger. No longer do we lie helpless, waiting on the scaffold, we can destroy and kill, to save ourselves, to save ourselves and be revenged (AQ 113).

In sharp contrast to this desperate description is an idyllic vision of the hometown, as idealized by childhood memories. Remarque describes an alley of poplar trees and a brook which he recalls from his own town, Osnabrück. These poplar trees and the brook often appear in his novels. They signify the innocence and peace of a lost youth. Remarque again laments the impossibility to connect with the past after the experiencing of war and concludes: "I believe we are lost" (AQ 123). Thus, the soldiers' situation is described as a life with no link to the innocence of youth. Their ability to conform to a regular, bourgeois life after the war has been destroyed by the war as well.

The fighting continues. It is disheartening to see the ill-trained recruits get wounded and killed because of their lack of experience. The lamentation about the lost youth is transferred directly to the front line in this passage by describing how the youth is now killed before the eyes of the "lost generation." In the course of these war activities Haie Westhus is killed. The mention of the trees changing color marks the passage of time: It is fall now, no year is given. This time the company of 150 has been reduced to a total of 32, thus indicating the severity of the losses in this advanced stage of the war.

Chapter 7 finds the rest of the company in the camp again. Food and rest are the two basic needs of a soldier. He can bear the horrors of war only when he does not think about them. And it is this condition of not thinking that also prevents reflection about the causes of war. Humor and obscenities, one might add, are weapons for survival. Remarque postpones the great discussions and arguments about the fundamental issues until after the war. To be sure, his remarks have a threatening tone, but he is so unclear, so uncertain about what he says, that his words admit his (or rather Paul Bäumer's) inability to clearly visualize the coming revolution, as he concludes this pensive interjection by declaring: "We shall have a purpose, and so we shall march, our dead comrades beside us, the years at the Front behind us:—against whom, against whom?" (AQ 141).

Remarque provides variety in this otherwise unrelievedly grim story by introducing women. First he describes friends discussing a poster with a picture of a pretty, clean girl which is in stark contrast to the soldiers' dirty condition. The poster depicts a kind of utopian dream. Consequently they decide to get rid of their lice. But reality is different from the pictured dream. They cross a canal and meet for several nights with some French girls who feel sorry for the German boys and make love with them in return for army bread. This is an attempt to try to forget the reality of war, although Paul Bäumer comments that "a man dreams of a miracle and wakes up to loaves of bread" (AQ 154). In war, Remarque is bitterly saying, even love is reduced to pragmatism. Love is something that belongs to the private sphere. Thus the uniforms and boots, the symbols of anything soldierly and thus also the war, must remain outside when they enter the French girls' house.

Then Bäumer is given seventeen days' leave, including three days for travel, and he uses them to return home. Many aspects of this visit home are clearly autobiographical. The town described resembles Remarque's hometown, Osnabrück. A glass box with butterflies Bäumer had collected as a boy hangs on the wall—just as in Remarque's own home. Bäumer has a close relationship with his mother in the text, while that to his father is more distanced, just like Remarque's own. Moreover, his father is identified as a bookbinder by trade and his mother is described as seriously ill, dying of cancer, just as in Remarque's case. During his military training Remarque himself received time off to visit his sick mother.

Bäumer's furlough is marked by unhappy personal experiences. When he fails to see an old major on the street, he is forced to go back and salute him according to military etiquette. Remarque tells his reader that at home the old traditions are still—for now—strictly adhered to, whereas the realities of war force different rules at the front. For a front-line soldier such formalities are petty harassment. The reality of the front and the dream world of those who have stayed at home are contrasted time and again. For Bäumer it is already an embarrassment that his father would prefer him to wear a uniform so that he could proudly present his heroic son to his acquaintances. For Bäumer such a demonstration would constitute a misrepresentation of the reality of war. His father would like him to relate his front-line experiences. Bäumer considers it dangerous to put his experiences into words for fear that they will take on a kind of reality with which he would be unable to cope. At this point, as elsewhere in the novel, he is afraid to acknowledge what is happening "out there" at the front. The experience of realization is simply too frightening and would itself threaten his life since it would take away from the act of mere survival.

His father also takes him aside and leads him to a table in the inn reserved for regular guests. Here the old generation still clings to patriotic phrases and unrealistic territorial claims in a war they expect Germany to win. The contrast between the military stalemate and the reality of dying at the front, on the one hand, and the official patriotic optimism of 1914 which has been preserved at home, on the other hand, once again becomes clear.

Bäumer must realize that he has changed under the impact of the war experience and that the world at home—once so familiar—now alienates him. It is this feeling of strangeness, a feeling of not belonging, an inability to connect with the past, be it with his mother's nave concerns or the schoolboy's world, that prevails in this entire important episode. This feeling is most clearly symbolized by the old books Bäumer peruses on his bookshelf. These books represent the lost youth he mourns, the old quiet passions and wishes, the impatience of the future, and the lofty joy of the world of thought. They describe the spiritual and intellectual world which he has created for himself outside of school. However, the books are unable to bring back his youth or to melt the heavy, dead block of lead which has formed deep inside him. It is here that Bäumer realizes that his youth is past, that memories have been reduced to shadows, and that the presence of war has erased all that he considered beautiful.

Remarque has presented this experience of estrangement and loss with a certain quiet pathos and sentimentality. We must ask ourselves whether it is justified to blame this supposed loss of youth only on the war and whether the realization of these hard realities is not something every young person has to endure at the end of his teen-age life. Rather than allowing the individual to develop in the process of growing up, to allow him to slowly become conscious of the new reality of adulthood and the impossibility of realizing the dreams of puberty, the war accomplishes this through a kind of shock therapy. The maturing process is shown as a necessary development that everyone must go through, one that war does not allow.

A lighthearted picaresque interlude follows this reflective scene, as is often the case in the novel. While visiting his old classmate Mittelstaedt in the local army barracks, Bäumer sees at first hand how his old patriotic teacher Kantorek is being drilled for active duty. A friend of Bäumer's, also a former student, takes revenge on the teacher for former humiliations in the classroom. But serious overtones appear as well. Kantorek had coerced a student by the name of Joseph Behm to volunteer and this boy was consequently killed three months before he would have been drafted. Thus Remarque underscores the guilt of the older generation symbolized by the patriotic teacher Kantorek. Bäumer visits Behm's mother, assuring her that her son was indeed killed instantly, and when she insists, Bäumer even swears an oath that he died without suffering. Bäumer maintains that he himself would not come back from war if it were not true, which clearly foreshadows his ultimate death.

Before Bäumer goes back to the front, he must attend a military training course in the camp on the moors. Remarque interrupts the novel here with this chapter in order to present a new, more human picture of the enemy. Here it is the Russian prisoners of war who are housed in an adjacent camp with very little to eat. Remarque characterizes them positively by describing them as having the faces of "meek, scolded St. Bernard dogs" (AQ 191) or as having good farmers' faces. This description also implies that they should be threshing, reaping, and picking apples. In other words, by making these people soldiers, Remarque not only describes them as having been estranged from their usual surroundings, but he also juxtaposes their natural calling, which is producing food, killing and being killed. Nature and nurturing are overcome by death and murder. Bäumer does not see enemies in them, only human suffering. These human beings have been transformed into enemies by the signing of a document by some unknown persons. Remarque's statement delineates a theory about the origin of wars as being simply a bureaucratic act that makes people into enemies who are not, thus emphasizing the idiocy of all wars. However, Bäumer does not want to think this thought through as yet; he saves it until the end of the war. The senselessness of war seems to him to be the invitation to a new life after the war, a task worthy of the many years of horror:

> I am frightened: I dare think this way no more. This way lies the abyss. It is not now the time; but I will not lose these thoughts, I will keep them, shut them away until the war is ended. My heart beats fast: this is the aim, the great, the sole aim, that I have thought of in the trenches; that I have looked for as the only possibility of existence after this annihilation of all human feeling; this is a task that will make life afterward worthy of these hideous years. (AQ 196).

Unfortunately, Remarque once again fails to clearly formulate his idea. The reader must complete the notion himself in his own fight against the possibility of such wars occurring again. A clear pacifist statement is lacking, but it may easily be inferred by the reader. Still, this is one of the clearest statements in the book indicating that it was intended to be a pacifist novel.

Back at the front in chapter 9, Bäumer confesses that "this is where I belong" (AQ 203), with his comrades. The emperor arrives to inspect the troops. New, better uniforms are temporarily handed out, and a discussion within the group about the origins of war follows. Although extremely simplistic—after all, the speakers are simple people—Remarque again underscores the insanity of war without, however, coming to any conclusions about its causes. The emperor supposedly did not really want war. Moreover, it is impossible to tell which side is justified. The Germans and French, it is said in the text, both believe that they are only defending their homeland, a view that is confirmed by the intellectuals on both sides. Wars originate because one country insults another (but then, how can one mountain insult another one?). During this war Germans fight against French whom they have never seen before: workers, artisans, and petty civil servants. The implication of these statements is that war does not make any logical sense. Detering comes to the conclusion: "There are other people back behind who profit by the war, that's certain" (AQ 208). With these words Remarque seems to allude to a—very debatable—Marxist explanation that wars are waged for the benefit of the big industrialists. However, Remarque does not pursue this idea. Instead, he describes other possible reasons for war: the prestige and glory for the emperor and the generals, and the war as a kind of fever or disease.

The conclusion is, of course, that there is no such thing as a "better" or "worse" kind of war. Even more important is Remarque's statement: "The national feeling of the soldier resolves itself into this—here [i.e. at the front] he is. But that is the end of it; everything else from joining up onwards he criticizes from a practical point of view" (AQ 209). The mere fact that Remarque does not have his characters realize any "good" reasons for a war also makes the book a pacifist one. The fact that the soldiers are not depicted as fighting from some patriotic feeling, but have been simply drafted and are fulfilling their duty without thinking, was to make the novel appear insulting to the political right wing of the late Weimar Republic. That Remarque does not pursue the potential Marxist argument about the causes of war similarly provoked criticism from the political left wing. Remarque cuts off the discussion by interjecting a statement by Albert: "The best thing is not to talk about the rotten business" (AQ 209). Remarque was reproached by Marxists for not providing a positive perspective. His "heroes" do not want to think, nor do they wish to talk, about war. Perhaps to simple soldiers in their situation that is the way it was, but the fact is that Remarque sees war as accidental, not conditioned by conflicts and constellations of economic interest.

When Bäumer is sent out on patrol, he has an anxiety attack. Only the awareness that he is out there for his comrades whose voices he hears from afar in the trenches fills him with a feeling of warmth and tears him out of his deadly fear. It becomes clear again that he feels close to them because they suffer the same fears and they fear for their lives just as he does. Comradeship as described here then is not so much a love for individual persons as a feeling of community with those who are daily threatened by death.

Bäumer is surprised by a French attack. In a kind of reflex action he stabs the Frenchman who jumps into the shell crater in which he is hiding and witnesses the dying of the man whose death he is personally responsible for. This Frenchman too is addressed as comrade, as a human being, and Bäumer understands that he is just as much a poor devil as he and his comrades are. Bäumer must feel all the more akin to the Frenchman since the latter is a printer, closely related to his own father's profession. And he vows more clearly than anywhere else in the novel to fight "against this, that has struck us both down; from you, taken life—and from me—? Life also. I promise you, comrade. It shall never happen again" (AQ 229). Remarque thus unequivocally confirms the pacifist message of his novel. But we must use caution. The wording is extremely imprecise; the statement is emotional. Bäumer wants to fight against "this." He has never directly or clearly thought about the origins of the war, and he can therefore only advocate a fight without direction and clear goal. Back with his friends, the experience is treated as less important than it was. They tell him that he was just together with the Frenchman for such a long time that the experience had such an enormous effect on him. This does not mean, however, that Remarque wants to discount Bäumer's previous feelings. Rather, he wants to demonstrate the numbing effect that war has—"After all, war is war" (AQ 232). Even feelings of human compassion are annulled by the fight for survival.

After this high point in the action Remarque adds another idyllic scene, which he expressly terms "an idyll of eating and sleeping" (AQ 234). Placed in charge of guarding a food supply depot, the comrades prepare an opulent meal, including roast suckling piglets. Several days later they must vacate the village, and Albert and Bäumer are wounded by shell fragments. The doctor in the field hospital who operates on Bäumer is described as sadistic; and after a train takes Bäumer to an army hospital, another doctor appears who uses the simple soldiers as guinea pigs to operate on their flat feet. Even here the simple soldiers are characterized as dependent and unable to resist the superior powers, in the same way they must obey their superiors at the front.

The suffering that Bäumer witnesses in the army hospital is another occasion for him to reflect on the nature of the war and its consequences.

He thinks how senseless everything is that has ever been written, done, and thought if something as horrible as war is possible. Everything in the world must be a lie and without consequence if thousands of years of culture could not prevent these torrents of blood being spilled, could not prevent hundreds of thousands of these dungeons of torture (hospitals) to exist:

> I am young, I am twenty years old; yet I know nothing of life but despair, death, fear, and fatuous superficiality cast over an abyss of sorrow. I see how peoples are set against one another, and in silence, unknowingly, foolishly, obediently, innocently slay one another. I see that the keenest brains of the world invent weapons and words to make it yet more refined and enduring. And all men of my age, here and over there, throughout the world, see these things; all my generation is experiencing these things with me. What would our fathers do if we suddenly stood up and came before them and proffered our account? What do they expect of us if a time ever comes when the war is over? Through the years our business has been killing;—it was our first calling in life. Our knowledge of life is limited to death. What will happen afterwards? And what shall come out of us? (AQ 266–67).

All the main themes of the novel may be summarized as follows: the senselessness of war; the collapse of the old value system of Western culture and its inability to prevent war; the involvement of the older generation in allowing the war to happen and driving the younger generation into war; the young draftees' lack of roots in society; the soldiers' fear with regard to the time spent in the war since they do not know what will become of them later; their fear of not being able to adjust to a normal life, to find their place in society in times of peace since all they know is death and killing. The themes of pacifism, of the senselessness of all wars, and of the lost generation are thus combined without any clear transition. In Remarque/Bäumer's mind one conditions the other.

As is often the case, this scene of serious reflection is followed by a humorous scene in which the severely wounded Lewandowski makes love to his visiting wife in the hospital bed while the others play a game of skat, a German card game, making sure that the nurses do not interrupt the lovemaking. It is not surprising that this scene was excluded in older American editions.

The end of the war is near. New transports arrive every day with the wounded from the front line; the makeshift dressings are made out of crepe paper: the German army is failing. Germany cannot even properly care for its wounded and dying soldiers any more. In a short monologue Bäumer relates events of the last few months. After a convalescent leave he is sent back to the front. The fact that his mother does not want to let him return foreshadows his impending death.

Chapter 11 continues the account of events in order to indicate that nothing has changed—the front always remains the same. The soldiers are not counting the weeks any more. It was winter when Bäumer returned to the front line. Now the trees are green, marking the advent of spring, symbolizing hope for a new life. War has become a routine of going back and forth between the front line and the barracks. The soldiers have become dull in their acceptance of war, which now appears to them to be just another cause of death, like cancer or tuberculosis, flu or dysentery. The only difference is that here death occurs more frequently, in a greater number of ways, and in more horrible fashion.

The soldiers feel that together they have formed a brotherhood of comrades trying to survive in an arena of death. Each activity is reduced to a mere act of survival and is therefore restricted to that which is absolutely necessary. Anything else would be a waste of energy. This primitiveness, this regression to bestial behavior, also provides the means for survival, including emotional survival. Entirely in conformity with contemporary vitalism, Bäumer/Remarque then demonstrates the existence of an active life force that has adapted even to this form of reductionism. All other expressions of human emotions are dormant, as the only concern is that life is on a constant watch against the threat of death. Men have turned into animals in order to give them an instinctual weapon; they have become dull in order to prevent a breakdown in face of horrors. If they would give in to clear, conscious thinking, they would surely be unable to face their lives right now. And life has given them the sense of comradeship so that they can escape the abyss of loneliness and abandonment. Thus, once again Remarque emphasizes comradeship as a significant weapon in the soldiers' fight for survival.

This support system is, however, so fragile that it slowly begins to break down. Detering, the farmer, sees the twigs of a cherry tree in bloom and thinks of his farm at home. Without thinking, he deserts right into the arms of the military police. But what would court-martial judges know about his motivations? Detering is never heard of again. The old contrast between front-line experience and the barracks or back home is thus alluded to again. Berger is killed next while trying to save a messenger dog, another example of a lack of logical thinking as the breakdown of inner defenses begins. Müller is killed and Bäumer inherits his boots, although Tjaden was supposed to get them, which clearly indicates Bäumer's impending death.

At this point it has become abundantly clear that Germany cannot win the war. There are too many fresh English and American regiments on the other side, too much corned beef and white flour, and too many new cannons, too many airplanes. The new, ever younger German recruits are dying by the thousands because of lack of military training and experience.

Remarque stresses the heroism of the German soldiers in light of these problems, soldiers who attack time and again in spite of the fact that their front is falling apart: "Is it nothing that regiment after regiment returns again and again to the ever more hopeless struggle, that attack follows attack along the weakening, retreating, crumbling line?" (AQ 279). This is one of the instances in which one could defend Remarque's position against the charges of defeatism and of having smeared the memory of the German soldier. The company leader, Lieutenant Bertinck, who is killed, is described as "one of those superb front-line officers who are in every hot place" (AQ 280). Although Remarque takes great care to show that not all officers are bureaucratic and uncaring about their men, it is interesting that he chooses only the lieutenant, a front-line officer of the lowest rank, as deserving of this praise.

High-ranking officers do not appear in Remarque's novel. Therefore, no reasons for military actions are given or questioned in any way. The group surrounding Bäumer is not a military unit but a unit of friends who simply carry out orders. Seemingly ordered around by anonymous forces, the soldiers have no clear aim. Since the military activities take place without any defined rhyme or reason, their motives themselves are also not questioned or criticized in any way. War is just a dirty, destructive, life-threatening force caused by negligent and stupid politicians. The mechanisms of war cannot be understood by the simple soldier. War is only experienced as a gigantic destructive force against which the soldier fights for survival. He is thus not so much fighting against an enemy as against the anonymous power of war itself—against death. Equating war with death becomes a most pronounced theme in the final section of the novel as the friends die one by one.

Remarque emphasizes that the German soldiers were "not beaten, because as soldiers we are better and more experienced; we are simply crushed and driven back by overwhelmingly superior forces" (AQ 283). He thereby justifies the German defeat and exonerates the soldiers, many of whom, to be sure, would be among his readers. However, this justification does not mean that he subscribes to the right-wing argument that the German army had been stabbed in the back by politicians at home.

Kat is wounded, and Bäumer carries him back to the barracks. When he arrives at the field hospital, Bäumer discovers that Kat is dead, having been hit by a shell splinter in the head while Bäumer was carrying him.

The final chapter is only a little over two pages long. The theme of the lost generation, of the lost youth, and the somewhat pathetic conviction that they will perish, resounds again: "We will be superfluous even to ourselves, we will grow older, a few will adapt themselves, some others will merely submit, and most will be bewildered;—the years will pass by and in the end we shall fall into ruin" (AQ 290). How can it be that youth is gone? Youth is something that Bäumer/Remarque describes as something soft that made their blood restless; it is something uncertain, bewildering, and yet to come; it represents a thousand faces of the future, the melody of dreams and books, the rustling and inkling of what women are all about. Remarque/Bäumer does not want to believe that all of this has been destroyed by artillery barrages, despair, and enlisted men's brothels. Life is still in his own hands and in his eyes.

Looking closely at this description of what lost youth represents, we find that on the one hand it is a yearning for things romantic, for something still to be found in books and thus not real but ideal; on the other hand it constitutes unrealistic expectations with regard to the future, a kind of fulfillment to be derived from a relationship with a woman, presupposing a romantic picture of women which is just as unrealistic. Remarque deplores the loss of innocence that he finds in youth, just as many other writers envision children as symbols for innocence. Clinging to such visions would mean clinging to illusions. To be sure, Remarque makes the aspect of inner destruction more profound by not giving his protagonist the ability to develop more specific ideas about the future and instead having him escape from reality into childhood dreams. On the other hand, we might argue that according to his own biography Remarque himself did not have any more precise ideas. We might also argue that it is not natural for this kind of dreaming to be cut short by the horrors of war. The natural growing process should have been allowed to be more gradual and kinder. However, it is logically just as unjustified to make the war responsible for a necessary maturing process. In his next novel Remarque was to say that education has a similarly negative effect on people. This opinion stems from a romantic notion of what man is supposed to be, a pathetic denial of the necessity of growing up, of adjusting to the realities of adulthood.

In the final two short paragraphs of the book a new narrator is introduced who reports Bäumer's death in a few words. Bäumer was killed in October 1918, on a day that was so quiet on the entire front line that the report in the daily war bulletin was reduced to a single sentence: "All quiet on the Western front." The irony is, of course, that if Bäumer was killed, it was not all quiet on the western front. Thus, Remarque stresses the impersonal character of the killing, the discrepancy between a military point of view and the actual suffering and dying of millions of soldiers, of individual human beings. The title of the book itself thus becomes an accusation, and the entire novel refutes the callous statement of its title: it is not true that it was all quiet on the western front (the literal translation of the German text is "nothing new in the west"). It is incidentally not true that Remarque used a standard phrase of the German army high command. But he did choose a phrase that summarized the cold exigencies of the military value system. This is, also incidentally, the first time in the book that a precise date is given, by reference to the historical daily war bulletin. By taking the change of seasons into consideration, it is possible thus to conclude that the action took place roughly between the summer of 1917 and October 1918.

Remarque does not reveal the identity of the new narrator who gives a seemingly objective report and thus creates a distance between Bäumer and the reader. Yet he does describe the expression on Bäumer's face when he was turned over—a tranquil expression of being almost satisfied that it turned out that way, which makes us believe that this narrator is really one of Bäumer's comrades.

Since the entire preceding narration was first-person narrative, and since Bäumer nowhere in his story explicitly implies that he is writing a diary, this conclusion of the novel does not logically follow from the lost-generation theme. Although Bäumer's death was foreshadowed in numerous ways, it occurs in contrast to the theme of the lost generation, that is, those soldiers, who had escaped the physical destruction of war and remained consequently lost in the society. Thus, the initial statement of the novel can not refer to Bäumer but only to Remarque himself who made himself a spokesperson for the majority of his intended readers, former soldiers of World War I. Given Remarque's tremendous success as a writer, it seems almost ironic that this success is based on the prediction that war destroyed the generation he writes about and made it impossible for them to succeed in real life.

As is obvious from the above quotations, Remarque has tried to write in a simple nonliterary language.[4] He is trying to imitate the normal spoken language of the German front-line soldier with all its repetitive formulas and filler expressions that often say very little, its drastic slang, metaphors and comparisons that often derive their crude humor from references to digestive bodily functions. He thus writes in a style that is the opposite of the Neo-romantic style he used in *Die Traumbude*; indeed, he consciously avoided the somewhat stilted and sophisticated language of literature and used expressions that at the time were considered not acceptable for a literary work of art. The fact that the text is replete with soldiers' jargon identifies the narrator as a simple soldier who speaks the language of the majority of the front-line soldiers. This language, which was so familiar to the majority of the novel's readers, comes across as honest because it does not have the ring of "literature." Remarque thus wants to create the impression that a simple soldier and not a professional writer is giving a truthful report about the war. Through his language the narrator clearly appears as the mouthpiece of millions of soldiers.

This realistic language, however, is often interrupted by soft, lyrical passages which are emotionally charged and which at the same time are reminiscent of the "old," Neo-romantic Remarque of *Die Traumbude* and his early poetry. The following passage may serve as an example:

> The parachute-lights shoot upwards—and I see a picture, a summer evening, I am in the cathedral cloister and look at the tall rose trees that bloom in the middle of the little cloister garden where the monks lie buried. Around the walls are the stone carvings of the Stations of the Cross. No one is there. A great quietness rules in this blossoming quadrangle, the sun lies warm on the heavy grey stones, I place my hand upon them and feel the warmth. At the right-hand corner the green cathedral spire ascends into the pale blue sky of the evening. Between the glowing columns of the cloister is the cool darkness that only churches have, and I stand there and wonder whether, when I am twenty, I shall have experienced the bewildering emotions of love (AQ 119).

The images conjured up in this passage are in stark contrast to the war environment which surrounds Bäumer at that time. At other times, however, similar imagery even serves to romanticize scenes of war. In the above passage it is designed to idealize the memories of early youth and peace in order to underscore the loss of youth brought about by the horrors of war. One might be tempted to criticize Remarque for shifting from one stylistic mode into another, but passages such as the above can easily be explained by attributing them to the former student Bäumer, who had literary ambitions and who was taken directly out of school to be trained as a murderer. Bäumer's education has not endowed him with the ability to rationally question the origin or purpose of war; it is rather the reason for his heightened sensibility.

Other passages that contain strong emotional outbursts and a pathos that seems to contradict the matter-of-factness of a soldier's life with its concentration on survival are like Expressionist prose poems with all their pathetic questioning—for example, the following, which is taken from one of the last pages of the book:

> Summer of 1918—Never has life in its niggardliness seemed to us so desirable as now;—the red poppies in the meadows round our billets, the smooth beetles on the blades of grass, the warm evenings in the cool, dim rooms, the black, mysterious trees of the twilight, the stars and the flowing waters, dreams and long sleep——. O Life, life, life!
>
> Summer of 1918—Never was so much silently suffered as in the moment when we depart once again for the front-line. Wild,

tormenting rumours of an armistice and peace are in the air, they lay hold on our hearts and make the return to the front harder than ever.

Summer of 1918—Never was life in the line more bitter and full of horror in the hours of the bombardment, when the blanched faces lie in the dirt and the hands clutch at the one thought: No! No! Not now! Not now at the last moment!

Summer of 1918—Breath of hope that sweeps over the scorched fields, raging fever of impatience, of disappointment, of the most agonizing terror of death, insensate question: Why? Why do they not make an end? And why do these rumors of an end fly about? (AQ 282–83).

The repetition of the phrase "Summer of 1918" marks the individual paragraphs off like stanzas of a poem. The repeated exclamations or rhetorical questions are just as characteristic for Expressionist poetry as its life pathos is for German literature at the turn of the century.

The fact that Remarque presents his novel in small episodes, also typical of all his future novels, made it particularly suitable for serialization. It was easily possible to interrupt the reading and pick it up again with another episode without losing track of the action. The individual episodes can be compared to sequences of a movie, and they considerably facilitated turning Remarque's novels into movies. The episodes that immediately follow each other are often in sharp contrast to each other. Action contrasts with episodes of rest and calm, surprising the reader, creating suspense and at the same time corresponding to the experience of war itself. They are like stones in a mosaic, which only taken together form a whole picture of war. They enable Remarque to highlight only a few experiences, the way they assume importance in the eyes of Bäumer, rather than painting a complete picture in long strokes. The fact that these episodes are only loosely connected or starkly contrasted underscores the fact that Remarque describes only the condition of being at war and not the personal development of his hero.

It is a myth that twelve to fifteen publishers rejected *All Quiet on the Western Front* before it was finally accepted by the publishing house of Ullstein. In point of fact the manuscript was first rejected by Samuel Fischer, the legendary head of Fischer Publishers, because he believed that nobody wanted to read about the war any more; Fischer thought the war experience was something the German nation wanted to forget. Ullstein took a different view; the book was printed in the daily newspaper *Vossische Zeitung* as a serial. Ullstein kept another manuscript ready to substitute for it in case they had to stop printing the novel because of readers' reactions. The opposite happened. During the serialization, from November 10 through

December 9, 1928, the *Vossische Zeitung* more than doubled its circulation. With the help of a skillfully launched advertising campaign the book became one of the greatest international successes in publishing history when it appeared in book form on January 31, 1929, under the imprint of the Ullstein Propyläen Verlag. The first edition of 30,000 copies had been printed in advance, and within two months 300,000 had been sold. On May 7, a half million, and after sixteen months a total of one million, copies were sold in Germany alone. For quite some time the publishing firm received orders for 6,000 to 7,000 copies daily. Within a short period of time the novel also became a best-seller abroad. By the end of 1929 it had been translated into twelve languages and a million and a half copies were sold. In the summer of 1930 approximately three million were sold. It is impossible to determine the total number of copies sold worldwide, but in 1952 the author estimated the number to be six million. Others estimated the total number to be twenty to thirty million copies in forty-five to fifty different languages, though more conservative estimates place the number at eight million copies in forty-five languages.

Apart from the publisher's advertising campaign the flood of letters received and published by newspapers and magazines, and the many reviews and articles which ranged from enthusiastic acceptance to total rejection, also contributed to the novel's commercial success. Especially outraged were many conservative groups who claimed that Remarque's characterization of the war was unpatriotic and defeatist. The author himself was also severely attacked. Remarque was said to be not thirty but fifty-five years old. Some claimed that his name was not Remarque but Kramer, Remark read backward and that he was not German but a French Jew, and had never served in the war—and certainly not on the front. In fascist Italy the book was forbidden as early as 1929, and in Germany it was publicly burned in 1933.

Why such uproar about one book? By writing *All Quiet on the Western Front*, Remarque had taken up events and issues the repercussions of which were still decisive in the political situation in Germany. Millions of people could identify with the soldiers' experiences in the novel and saw themselves as one of the characters. Millions were able to use the war as a scapegoat for their own lack of success, their inability to succeed in life. They could blame not their own shortcomings or the political and social situation of contemporary Germany, but the war. For others the war was a high point in their lives, and to see it described as a horrible fight for survival seemed to betray all their youthful patriotic ideals and the ideals of manhood and bravery to which they were clinging in the present. Right-wing political groups such as the Nazis had mythologized World War I and made it the cradle of the spirit of the new Germany which they were envisioning. For them any other view was abhorrent—an insult to the fearless, undefeated German soldier who had been stabbed in the back by his homeland, by those who had started the November 1918 revolution.

Remarque remained rather quiet in all of the public discussions about his book. He gave only a few interviews, in which he claimed that he never intended to write a political book nor one which claimed to make any social or religious statements. He only wanted to report about the individual feelings of a small group of soldiers, mostly former students, during the last two years of the war. Remarque's intention to remain neutral was to no avail. His book had become a political issue, against his will, immediately following its publication. As evidenced by the many different and at times even contradictory political statements in the book and by the superficiality of its argumentation, Remarque was surely not a politically minded person in 1928, and he had no idea that his novel would have such political implications. His protest against war was diffuse and unclear in the text; the war served only as a literary backdrop to the fight for survival of the group of former students and their friends. However, the novel became the testing ground for conflicting political forces within the late phase of the Weimar Republic. In their fight against the novel and particularly its tremendous success, the various groups of the nationalistic political Right had found a common enemy and were thus able to unite.

In contrast to the reception in Germany, the American reviews of *All Quiet on the Western Front* were all positive. The American reviewers did not have an ax to grind with an author who inherently pleaded for peace, equality, and brotherhood, and as a result they did not attack the author as a pacifist or a traitor to the German cause. This is why they dwelt less on the implied pacifist message of the book, concentrating more on its credibility and ability to convince on a purely human level. It seems as if the description of suffering had completely dominated all political and, to a certain extent, aesthetic considerations. The reviewers praised time and again the book's sincerity, simplicity, honesty, its lack of sentimentality, its realism and economy of style. They overlooked the redolent sentimentality and pathos in the theme of lost youth, and particularly in the scenes involving Paul Bäumer's furlough back home. Also typical of the American reviews were references to other war novels, including Henri Barbusse's *Le Feu* (*Under Fire*, 1916).

Although the American translation of *All Quiet on the Western Front* is no better or worse than most translations, *The New York Times* immediately raised the question of censorship.[5] The president of Little, Brown, and Company, Alfred R. MacIntyre, gave the following explanation in a letter to the *New Republic*:

When we read the English translation we knew that the book as it stood would offend some people by its frankness, and that under the Massachusetts law, which judges a book not as a whole but by as little as a single phrase, its sale would probably be stopped in Boston.... We decided, however, to take this risk, and did no more than delete three words having to do with the bodily functions. We then offered the book to the Book-of-the-Month-Club.[6]

In addition to this minor change, however, three additional passages were left out in the American edition, two of which have been briefly mentioned above: first, several lines referring to the supposed obligation of girls in officers' brothels to wear silk blouses and to take a bath before entertaining guests from a captain upward (AQ 5; first German edition 9); second, one dealing with the German soldiers enjoying sitting on latrines in a meadow and playing a game of cards (almost 3-1/2 pages, AQ 9; first German edition 12–16); third, a scene in the army hospital in Duisburg where a convalescing soldier is having sex with his visiting wife (almost 3-1/2 pages, AQ 267; first German edition 261–64). No censorship had taken place in the British hardcover edition published by Putnam's in 1929. It was not until 1975 that Little, Brown published a new edition based on the complete British edition of 1929.[7] One must add, however, that a letter from Putnam's to Little, Brown and Company of March 21, 1929, had conveyed Remarque's permission "to do what, in your judgement, is in the best interest of the book."[8] It is certain that had Little, Brown not agreed to the cuts, the important advance sale to the Book-of-the-Month-Club would not have materialized.

Remarque was not the first to write a novel about World War I. As is clear from a review that he had written about a number of other war novels, he was intimately familiar with the genre. He simply continued an existing literary trend and gave it a new direction. In doing so, he together with another German writer, Ludwig Renn, whose antiwar novel *Krieg* (War) had appeared in 1928, established a new type of war novel which was later to become popular: The events are reported consistently from the perspective of the simple soldier, and the focus of the action is the events that take place on the front line. All other elements connect directly to these events. Thus, the war novel was changed into a front-line novel, which during the following years was a style adopted by politically right-wing authors.[9]

With regard to Remarque's own literary development *All Quiet* marks a turning point: With *All Quiet on the Western Front* he had found the basic theme for all his later literary works—life threatened by large, overbearing situations, whether they be political forces or deadly diseases. In all his future works the backgrounds change, but the basic underlying principle remains the same.

NOTES

1. "Gespräch mil Remarque," interview with Axel Eggebrecht, *Die literarische Welt* June 14, 1929: 1–2.

2. This is the main argument put forth in a somewhat exaggerated mariner by Hans-Harald Müller, *Der Krieg und die Schriftsteller: Der Kriegsroman der Weimarer Republik* (Stuttgart: J. B. Metzler, 1986) 36 ff. The most balanced evaluation of the novel is given in the definitive study by Hubert Rüter: *Erich Maria Remarque: Im Westen nichts Neues. Ein Bestseller der Kriegsliteratur im Kontext* (Paderborn: Schöningh, 1980).

3. See, e.g., Alfred Antkowiak, *Erich Maria Remarque: Leben und Werk* (Berlin: Volk und Wissen, 1980).

4. In the following discussion of style and structure I am largely following the analysis of Rüter, 74ff.

5. See Richard Arthur Firda, *Erich Maria Remarque. A Thematic Analysis of His Novels* (New York: Peter Lang, 1988) 58–59.

6. Quoted Firda 59.

7. According to Firda, "a popular Grosset and Dunlap rpt. (New York) published in 1930 was 'complete' and appears to have been based on the London edition" (64).

8. Quoted Firda 59.

9. Rüter 23.

ARIELA HALKIN

The Flood

The recent flood of the "literature of disillusionment" or of "war books"—
a phrase which has just acquired this special significance—differs from
what has gone before only in that it is a flood in place of a trickle and that
the water has grown decidedly muddier.

TLS, June 12, 1930

Beginning in 1929, German and English war novels swamped the
English book market. As Robert Wohl graphically describes: "Then
manuscripts were fetched from trunks and the presses began to groan
with dozens and eventually hundreds of war books, until the critics cried
out for mercy and respite."[1] Sales were unprecedented. *All Quiet on the
Western Front* sold 250,000 copies in its first year. In the same year, the
Barrow public library announced that readers had reserved the book for
the coming two years and no further orders could be taken. The war book
boom became, in itself, a subject of countless articles and commentar-
ies. How long would it last? Which of the mass of books would survive
the ravages of time to become classics? Had The Great Novel of the war
already been written, or would that take another generation? Why had
this genre suddenly become so popular? How was it that books which a
year earlier no publisher could have hoped to sell were now being read
eagerly by hundreds of thousands? What did the date of the beginning

From *The Enemy Reviewed: German Popular Literature Through British Eyes Between the
Two World Wars* by Ariela Halkin, pp. 53–69, 179–181. © 1995 by Ariela Halkin.

of the outpour signify? Would 1929 really be remembered, as Desmond MacCarthy claimed, as the year "in which men's emotions first began to turn against the idea of war?"[2] Did Remarque's *All Quiet on the Western Front* start the rage, or was it triggered by R. C. Sherriff's international stage hit *Journey's End*? And last but not least, how long would it last? In 1930, Arnold Bennett predicted in the *Evening Standard* that the stream of war novels would continue to flow despite the glut.[3] *The Daily Herald* disagreed informing its readers that the undiscerning fashion for war books would end in June 1930, "when a novel will no longer be sure to sell on the mere virtue of its relation to the war."[4] When voices complaining of the surfeit of war books began to be heard, Arnold Bennett indignantly countered that he felt inclined to answer anyone who said they were tired of war books with a dagger. He insisted that nobody, except those who had fought in the war, had the right to be bored by good books about it.[5] The subject seemed inexhaustible.

On one issue the critics were agreed—that publishers had apparently decided that German war novels were superior to English ones. Many lamented this trend, complaining of the thinness of English output in both quality and quantity. Some accused their colleagues of having lost their heads over German war novels, but they were forced, nonetheless, to concede that most of the outstanding war novels of the day had indeed originated in Germany. Germany had a monopoly on memorable war novels, Arnold Bennett believed, because the finest war novels were the product of defeat, not of triumph: "Sadness, not exhilaration, brings beauty."[6]

Robert Graves even credited German war novels with paving the way for the public's positive reception of the English ones, maintaining that after *All Quiet and Sergeant Grischa*, the public was now ready to read the same sort of story from the British point of view and to see it dramatized on stage.[7]

Although publishers were understandably engaged in lavishing praise on their German authors and in claiming immortality for their novels, by the end of the 1920s reviewers were splitting into two opposed camps in what became known as the War Books Controversy. At the center of the debate was the meaning of the war experience and its artistic expression. Traditional moral standards and modes of expression were confronted by new values couched in rebellious language. The controversy was heated to a degree quite exceptional in the annals of English literary criticism. It encompassed both the British and the German war novels, but it was the German that bore the brunt of the attack, drawing the greatest accolades as well. Each new German novel provoked fresh tirades of abuse as well as impossibly exaggerated praise and, as the flow of books from Germany continued, both sides became more firmly entrenched in their positions.

Code, Counter Code

Ostensibly, the core of the War Books Controversy was whether the novels adequately depicted the war experience. The debate extended to issues covering both the content and language of the books. But the violence of emotions unleashed derived from the challenge that most of the books posed to deeply entrenched British values and assumptions that were already under attack from many quarters. The celebrated code of the officer and gentleman, by which every boy at public school was required to abide, called for certain idealized standards of conduct: restraint and self-control; dignity and the ability not to betray emotion; chivalry toward ladies and defeated foes; ungrudging acceptance of service, duty, and sacrifice for one's country; loyalty to the team, the school, the nation, and only lastly to oneself.[8] O. F. Christie reverently described this ideal in his popular book *Clifton School Days* (1935): "To be all things decent, orderly, self mastering; in action to follow up the coolest common sense with the most unflinching endurance; in public affairs to be devoted as a matter of course, self sacrificing without any appearance of enthusiasm . . . making a fine art of stoicism."[9] That often quoted bible of "muscular Christianity" *Tom Brown's Schooldays*, condenses the three seminal elements of the code—medieval chivalry, Christian values, and patriotism—into one short sentence in Squire Brown's soliloquy on the eve of his son's first day at school: "If he'll only turn out a brave, helpful, truth-telling Englishman, and a gentleman, and a Christian, that's all I want."[10]

The "gentleman," however, was also a potential "officer" and had to be well versed in the art of fighting. Sport was, of course, an integral part of the public school ethos and was meant to instill an honorable fighting spirit among the boys. "What would life be like without fighting?" asks Hughes, "Fighting, rightly understood, is the business, the real highest, honestest business of every son of man."[11] Fighting with fists, says the revered school captain, is the natural and English way for English boys to settle their quarrels. A fight must be avoided if possible, but if not: "don't say 'No' because you fear a licking, and say or think it's because you fear God, for that's neither Christian nor honest. And if you do fight, fight it out; and don't give in while you can stand and see."[12]

Sir Henry Newbolt's famous poem *Vitai Lampada* directly linked public school playing fields with the battlefield by applying the same set of values and rules of conduct to both:

There's a breathless hush in the Close tonight
Ten to make and the match to win
A bumping pitch and a blinding light,
An hour to play and the last man in.
And it's not for the sake of a ribboned coat,

Or the selfish hope of a season's fame,
But his Captain's hand on his shoulder smote
'Play up! play up! and play the game!'

The sand of the desert is sodden red,
Red with the wreck of a square that broke;
The Gatling's jammed and the Colonel dead,
And the regiment blind with dust and smoke.
The river of death has brimmed its banks,
And England's far, and Honour a name,
But the voice of a schoolboy rallies the ranks:
'Play up! play up! and play the game!'

In many ways, the code was already archaic by the time the war was over. Trench warfare and new weapons of mass destruction had stripped the war of romance even for those who had not actively participated in the fighting. The proverbial stiff upper lip and the ability to bear pain unflinchingly were described as nothing less than barbaric by writer and ex-soldier H. M. Tomlinson, who pointed out that the Red Indians had considered it a point of honor to keep a straight face when being flayed alive and that the more barbaric they were, the less they cried out. "The reproval of articulate pain, forced from torn bodies and lacerated minds by the cruelty of the machine made horror of modern war, is itself a sign of timid barbarism,"[13] he asserted in a stark and uncompromising declaration of war on the code.

The war novels led the attack. Even if gutting the code was not their authors' intent, these books inevitably subverted it, or at least raised troublesome questions about it. Of all the novels of the period, Erich Maria Remarque's *All Quiet* presented the most powerful affront to the code. Although Remarque denied any intentional political message, his novel attacked all traditional values and assumptions about war. It depicts war not as a natural phenomenon, but as an incomprehensible aberration, which, once begun, proceeds automatically with machinelike efficiency until it is completely out of control, leaving in its berserk trail a generation of damaged and lost men unable to adjust to the postwar world. It shows war as dehumanizing and haphazard, without rhyme or reason, and the soldier as a wretched victim with no say in his destiny save to try to survive. The major motivating force is shown to be nothing higher than the effort to survive. Heroism, the conventional value associated with war, is reduced to a desperate determination to stay alive. Soldiers do not risk their lives for patriotism or adventure or even duty, but only for comradeship and even that is divested of its conventionally positive connotations, and is exposed as a form of group solidarity crucial for survival.

Of the English war books, it was Robert Graves's *Goodbye to All That* (1929) that seemed to present the strongest challenge. In his autobiographically styled novel, Graves described the horrifying experiences of a young English soldier at the front, and bitterly attacked the sacred values in the name of which Englishmen were traditionally thought to have fought and died. Like Remarque, he categorically denied the validity of patriotism as a reason for fighting, claiming that patriotism was nothing but a "big" word, utterly rejected by the troops "as fit only for civilians or prisoners." Everyone agreed, according to Graves, that the only thing that kept the troops going as effective fighting units was regimental pride. This, he claimed, was the strongest moral force in times of war, especially when contrasted with other moral forces like patriotism and religion.[14] The book unleashed an uproar. Treating its contents as unadulterated facts, the socialist *Daily Herald* chose to splash the "news" of its publication over the entire width of its front page. In sensational lettering, it announced: "Soldier-Poet's Amazing Allegations," "Privates Who Shot a Sergeant Major," "Declaration That Officers Were Frequently Drunk," "Candid Narrative of Heroism and Dissipation," "Suicide Cases," "Shot At Dawn."[15] Angry letters from readers for and against Graves, denials, recriminations, and threats filled the pages of the *Daily Herald* in the coming weeks. The book was accepted as a full-fledged historical document and was used to prove that old conservative traditions were crumbling and that only a massive turn to the left could save England from the perils to which its enfeebled Establishment had led it. Although Graves adamantly denied the pacifistic and revolutionary intentions that the paper attributed to him, claiming that he had simply described events as they had happened, the message struck home and the *Herald*'s inevitable comparison to Remarque stuck.[16]

Needless to say, the assault on the code was vehemently countered. Valentine Williams, of the conservative daily newspaper the *Morning Post*, promptly rose to the defense of the public school spirit under attack by the "morbid-sordid school of war books." Everyone who was out in France, Williams asserted, knew that "it was this spirit in its most ideal form which was the leaven leavening the whole lump of our fighting forces." He angrily contrasted the "unhappy warriors" with their spirited public school counterparts: "The one was an individualist, the other worked for the side; the one was a pessimist, the victim of his emotion, the other was philosophical and, where his fellow saw merely a muddy shell hole, was apt to catch sight of a star shining in it."[17] Douglas Jerrold, a war veteran himself, agreed: "Any fool and any knave can attack patriotism. But it takes something exceptional among fools and something utterly contemptible among knaves to argue that the individual in a world at war has no obligations at all."[18] Jerrold launched a tirade against those arrogant enough to set themselves up in judgment against their country. He claimed that the German war writers showed themselves incapable of understanding the deep patriotism displayed by their own troops during the war. In propagating the idea that war was futile and meaningless, German writers were deliberately ignoring the tenacity of resistance and strength of morale that the German army had exhibited throughout the war and the stupendous military feats it had achieved: "Such feats, surpassing in sheer courage anything in ancient history, are simply not consistent with the psychological reconstructions of our sensitive novelists. Not only was the war neither futile nor avoidable but it was not believed to be either by the men who fought."[19] In Jerrold's eyes, a just war did indeed arouse in men patriotic emotions that gave them the strength to withstand the risks and hardships involved. Moreover, it was inconceivable to him that the terrible sacrifice had been made for anything less than a great and universal cause. This cause, never clearly defined in the pamphlet, hovers behind his whole argument, ghostlike, but with unshakable certainty.

It is against the backdrop of this particularly English cultural struggle that the War Books Controversy must be viewed. The German war novels afforded both camps the opportunity to wage battle for and against the remnants of the code. It was apparently easier for Englishmen to project the cultural battle onto foreign ground. Measuring German books by English code criteria, loyal Englishmen flayed the German texts for transgressing English taboos. J. C. Squire, editor of the *London Mercury*, led the battle against the German war novels, to which he repeatedly referred as the "lavatory school of literature." He condemned their scatological elements, their lack of manly patriotism, their disjointed, unreadable language, their political bias, their untruthfulness, and their hysteria and exaggeration. If a great book is to be written about the war "it will not come from a German," categorically stated the *London Mercury*.[20] Squire's ferocious assault on German war authors degenerated into a vituperative attack on the German people: "The facts are that the German nation is more permeated by all the perversions in the text-books than any other race on earth."[21] Both conservative and liberal literary critics joined the attack on so-called German coarseness, lack of subtlety, inability to see beyond the immediate surroundings, and selfishness. Some libraries banned German war books as obscene and unfit for their readers. Military historian Cyril Falls published an annotated bibliography of war books which the *TLS* recommended to its readers as "a signpost pointing, for the benefit of the bewildered, to where the healthy spots may be found and the paths that avoid the unhealthy."[22] The German war books, to judge by the low ratings Falls accorded them, were definitely among the "unhealthy spots."

The other side, convinced that the war had effectively destroyed all existing beliefs and had made a mockery of the public school ethos, praised the German war novels for their sincere and unsentimental presentation of the war, free of ready-made attitudes, of the false jolly spirit of adventure, and of misleading terms such as glory, sacrifice, heroism, patriotism, nationalism, and courage. For these reviewers the German novels served as a model for realistic representation of war unspoiled by high rhetoric and elevated cliché-ridden language.

Herbert Read was among those who led the fight for recognition of the German war novels' superbly honest portrayal of the war. Those who joined him were most often war veterans who agreed with him that England must be shaken from its sleep to face new realities. Many of the celebrated English war novelists were themselves advocates of the new literature, and, like the German authors, they attempted to divest themselves of the shackles of old literary traditions.

The literary representation of the war experience unleashed an emotionally charged controversy. Subject matter, style, language, and structure were all issues in a heated debate that centered once again on the Truth. Almost every war novel in the interwar period was perceived as an historical document and its intrinsic worth judged on the basis of its veracity. Reviewers disregarded poetic license, becoming embroiled in questions that are meaningful when asked about histories but irrelevant to novels. Was the novelist not misleading his reading public in describing the capture of a machine gun whose make the enemy did not possess? Was the reader to trust an author whose characters used expressions not yet coined, or wore uniforms and carried equipment not yet in use at the date in question? Was the war novelist entitled to present his readers with a supposedly true war diary that he had, in fact, invented? Had Erich Maria Remarque actually experienced all the horrors described in his book, or had he, in fact, invented them from a safe distance at the rear?

Remarque's supporters never attempted to argue that *All Quiet* was fiction, rendering the truth or falsity of the author's own wartime experiences irrelevant. On the contrary, they rushed into the fray to insist that every word of the book was factually and historically accurate. Similarly, when Ludwig Renn's *War* appeared in England, both supporters and opponents refused to realize that its chronicle form was nothing but a literary stratagem. The style of the books, too, did a good deal to foster the illusion. In Renn's *War*, realistic descriptions of battles, information on the seasons and weather conditions, minute details of the landscape—all strengthened the realism, creating an illusion of truth and obscuring the fact of its being a wholly private vision. Hans Carossa achieved a realistic effect in his diary-novel *Rumanian Diary* (1929) by prefacing each entry with precise dates and locations. Ernst Jünger wrote his tale of adventure, *Storm of Steel* (1929) as though it were an eyewitness account of life at the front. Rudolph Binding, among others, used the diary form as a powerful tool to criticize both the German High Command

and the common German soldier. Binding further strengthened the illusion of objectivity and truth by employing a seemingly detached style.

It is obvious today that the novels were intended to convey images of the truth as seen by the individual writers, at times ten years after the event. The war writers were not trying to portray the absolute truth about any particular event in the war, but rather their own physical or mental experiences. Even in the midst of the fray, Robert Graves soberly reflected that "the memoirs of a man who went through some of the worst experiences of trench warfare are not truthful if they do not contain a high proportion of falsity."[23]

Needless to say, reviewers in the opposing camps in the War Books Controversy perceived the Truth differently. In his pamphlet *The Lie about the War* (1930), Douglas Jerrold sought to expose the unrepresentativeness and untruthfulness of most of the war books: "I indict a class of book, a kind of critical attitude and a kind of publicity which is sufficiently notorious today to be described and accepted as fact."[24] Jerrold's famous pamphlet offers a representative definition of both the Lie and the Truth as perceived by the opponents of the antiwar books. The Lie lay in the statistical falsity presented in these books. There may have been men shot for cowardice, but these were few and far between. There may have been drunken officers, but most were responsible, brave, and showed exemplary behavior under stress. Some members of the General Staff may have been misguided, negligent, or callous, but for the most part they were dedicated, loyal, and good men. Some soldiers may have lost their faith in the meaningfulness of the war, but for the most part they believed in the causes for which they were fighting and knew them to be just. As for the horrors described in the books, these were telescoped into a picture of the war "which bears no more relation to the reality of war than Remarque's picture of the ex-soldiers of all nations as men who are 'weary, broken, burnt out.'"[25] The Lie, then, lay in the disproportionate representation of the negative side of the war. The Truth, as Jerrold saw it, was that the war was a great tragedy because it was a great historical event. It was a great drama because "neither in its origins, its actions or its results was there any element fundamentally accidental or ultimately without meaning ... To deny the dignity of tragic drama to the war in the interests of propaganda is not only unworthy but damnably silly and incredibly dangerous."[26]

British reviewers opposing the antiwar novels attacked German writers not only for what they represented as the realities of war but also for how they represented them. To some extent, these issues are inevitably intertwined. Reviewers who cast doubt on the accuracy of the horrors depicted in the German war books also complained that the language and style in which these unpleasant details were rendered reduced the novels to cheap "commercialized filth."[27]

German authors developed a new style to convey what they obviously considered a totally new experience. The war was often presented in the first-person narrative mode based on the responses and language of the ordinary infantry soldier. Many of these authors had, in fact, been officers. Some, like Renn, were aristocrats who had served as company and battalion commanders. Nonetheless, they chose this mode of narration to facilitate direct, unsophisticated, immediate, and realistic impact on their readers. This often entailed the use of coarse army language to describe frankly and in great detail the horrors of the war, including the unsavory details of the bodily activities of the men in the field. Bowel movements and lice picking were favorites. The *TLS* warned its readers that in reading German war novels they must be prepared for coarseness of a type not usually found in English novels: "We do not mean merely insistence upon the realities of war—for a war novel would not be of much value without that—but a constant preoccupation with the bodily functions."[28] The German novelists, according to the *London Mercury*, had committed the unforgivable sin of deliberately and intentionally piling on the agony in order to sell their books. Their descriptions were grotesque and thoroughly untruthful: "They are mostly sensational, and exploit blood, mud, and other substances for commercial purposes."[29] Cyril Falls agreed, expanding his criticism of German literary scatology to encompass the nature of the German soldier in general: "We must recall that the latrine has always had a fascination for the German soldier, and that during the War one used to find on postcards in prisoners' pockets pictures of this necessity of nature in use."[30] The *TLS* predicted that the "twist of perversion so common in German books on the war" would undoubtedly alienate British sympathy.

Books such as Ernst Glaeser's *Class 1902* (1929) proved beyond a doubt that the "disgusting" and "repellent" descriptions proliferating in German war novels were not a truthful reflection of the real horrors of the front but simply a reflection of German fascination with the darker and seamier side of life. For here was a book without battlefields, yet containing scenes that were as disgusting as the German novelists' supposed realistic descriptions of the battlefields. The same reviewer, viewing *Zero Hour* (1929) by Georg Grabenhorst more positively, observed with relief that the squalid had been kept down to its true proportions. Nonetheless, here too there were "hints of sexual perversion."[31] The anonymous *Schlump* (1929) was "so coarse that it sometimes seems to aim deliberately at shocking the average reader."[32] Other German war books, such as Fritz von Unruh's *Way of Sacrifice* (1928), Karl Bröger's *Pillbox 17* (1930), Georg Bucher's *In the Line* (1932), Theodor Plievier's *The Kaiser's Coolies* (1931), and Franz Schauwecker's *The Fiery Way* (1929) were described as hysterical. Although hysteria was perhaps understandable in the aftermath of war trauma, it was, in the opinion of many English reviewers, a particularly German vice that was unsuitable in art:

"To understand the reason for a defect of temper is not to accept its artistic expression."[33] The vices of German war fiction were succinctly summed up in a review of Ernst Johannsen's *Four Infantrymen of the Western Front, 1918* (1930):

> Frankly, this book has every vice which German war fiction has displayed in the last two years. It is wordy, brutal, hysterical, and at times improbable. It is full of philosophical discussions of which the basis seems to be that "mankind is garbage." It is kept at one emotional pitch—the highest—from first to last, so that, after a little, the author is unable to move one in the slightest, despite his industry in piling up of superlatives and his undaunted search for more and more horrors.[34]

Reviewers in the other camp had a diametrically opposed notion of the truth of the war novels, German and English alike. Of *All Quiet*, Herbert Read wrote: "It is not a pacifist book; it is not a humanitarian book; it is the truth, and to read it is to become filled with a passion for universal goodwill." He praised *Private Suhren* by Georg von Der Vring for its remarkable objectivity, *A Fatalist at War* by Rudolph Binding for its acuteness of observation, *Sergeant Grischa* by Arnold Zweig for its detached, wide vision, and *Four Infantrymen on the Western Front* by Ernst Johannsen for communicating reality. So much truth could not be let loose on the world in such a short period, observed Read, without creating a strong opposition; for after all "the truth always affects some established interests."[35]

It was mainly the English war writers themselves, in their capacity of literary reviewers in the press, who enthusiastically embraced the German war novels, praising not only their content but also their language and style. Edmund Blunden, Siegfried Sassoon, Robert Graves, R. H. Mottram, Henry Williamson, H. M. Tomlinson, and Richard Aldington applauded German novelists for breaking with previous literary traditions, praising them for inventing a new language to fit the new realities of modern war. Communicating the incommunicable, in Richard Aldington's words, was possible only when the obstacle of obsolete literary tradition was removed. It was ludicrous to write about war with the same technique that one would use to write about the English countryside, stated Herbert Read. "The war demands its own style. It breaks all preconceived moulds. It was no pastoral."[36] H. M. Tomlinson mocked Churchillian bombastic prose as wholly inappropriate to the new reality of modern war: "It is a sad mistake to suppose you may reproduce the sound of drum-fire by words resembling the rolling of the drums.... It seems indeed that if we want the truth at any time we shall have to surprise her.... She is shy. Words rolling like drum-fire scare her clean out of sight."[37] German authors were demonstrating their distrust of coherent language and conventional rhetoric by fragmenting narrative sequence, using plain words, and breaking up historical continuity, thereby disconnecting their war experiences from the past. Favorable reviews often described their style as futuristic, modernistic, and cinematographic. Unlike their English counterparts, most of these books were written in a language consciously cut loose from any previously existing literary styles. Short sentences and paragraphs mostly divested of qualifying adverbs and adjectives followed each other in thudding staccato rhythm, making for a tense, journalistic style. Unrelated subjects, presented in harsh and powerful narration, were often juxtaposed to achieve maximum shock effect reminiscent of an expressionist style of painting tempered by realism.

The English war novels seem to have been less abrasive in tone than their German counterparts, evoking milder and less emotional responses among the critics. Both criticism and praise were more tempered. Reviewers found their language and style more palatable and were readier to accept their truth. Although no less critical of the war than the German writers, English authors remained anchored in their past traditions, literary style, and historical associations. As Paul Fussell has shown in *The Great War and Modern Memory* (1977), English war novels were suffused with references to the classical world and to British literary traditions. Shakespeare obsessively permeated the consciousness of many of these writers who seem to have regarded the war as one more link in a long chain of wars fought by England over the centuries. The seamless transition from Agincourt to the Somme, from Henry V to the soldier poets of the trenches, powerfully reinforced the sense of continuity of the British fighting tradition.

English war novels were also saturated with associations drawn from the public school world. Graves, for example, rebelled against the public school tradition, exposing it mercilessly as a hypocritical and soulless system whose sole concern was to instill a herdlike loyalty in its pupils so that they could die bravely and unquestioningly on the battlefields. Nonetheless, *Goodbye to All That* is permeated with public school terms, images, and associations. Comparing it to Remarque's *All Quiet*, one is immediately struck by the different worlds of English and German war writers. Both focus on the *fronterlebnis*, yet Remarque's book begins and ends at the front. The trauma of the *fronterlebnis* dominates everything past, present, and future, and nothing exists nor, indeed, can exist outside it. Graves, on the other hand, devotes a third of his book to his prewar years, mainly public school memories. The transition in the book from public school life to life at the front is so smooth and natural that it almost goes unnoticed. It is as though both are ordained by custom and tradition and, although rebelled against, cannot be broken away from totally. When his friend Sassoon tries to make a real break with the code by publicly declaring his refusal to continue fighting, Graves brings him back to "reason" and reality by arranging for his transfer to a military psychiatric rehabilitation center. The language and terminology in both parts of the book are interchangeable, just as they are in Sassoon's *Memoirs of an Infantry Officer* and his *Memoirs of a Fox-Hunting Man*. Words such as ripping, topping, good show, good sport, and good fun are used to describe both school activities and forays into No Man's Land. Public school values, traditions, and pride of achievement reverberate throughout. In both public school and army, sportsmanship was regarded as an entry pass to social acceptance, and Graves is obviously proud of his boxing prowess, just as Sassoon is proud of his riding and hunting skills. Although Graves ostensibly satirizes both his public school and his regiment, he devotes much space to detailed description of the history of both institutions, the underlying note remaining demonstratively one of pride. As he himself reflected in his old age: "a conditioning in the Protestant morality of the English governing classes, though qualified by mixed blood, a rebellious nature, and an overriding poetic obsession, is not easily outgrown."[38] Despite his ardent desire to shock and to rebel, *Goodbye to All That* is permeated with elements of the stiff upper lip tradition and of English calm and humor.

Reviewers found the close intertwining of war and public school perfectly natural. The *Spectator*, in reviewing *Goodbye to All That*, took this juxtaposition for granted: "The major part of this book is concerned with the worlds of school and war. They are written vividly, truthfully, and utterly without mercy either for the subjects of discussion or for the reader."[39] English war books are framed by a setting that existed before the war and would continue to exist after it. The war constituted only a temporary, if terrible, interlude. The majority of German books are frameless in this sense. The war occupies the entire stage with neither past to nostalgically recollect nor future to look forward to with hope. English writers mostly invoked nature and pastoral imagery to offset the horrors of the killing fields, inserting pastoral passages in between scenes of death and destruction. Malcolm Muggeridge tartly described those strange creatures—the English soldier-poets: "The fashion was for the soldier poet, agonized at having to shed blood, listening to birds singing when the guns paused, with his Keats or Shakespeare's Sonnets in the pocket of his tunic; yet not less courageous and effective in action for that; if anything, more."[40] Indeed, the wartime literary output of soldier-poets like Graves, Sassoon, Blunden, Wilfred Owen, and Isaac Rosenberg reflects this unlikely trench preoccupation. The same cannot be said of any of the German war novels. Remarque specifically emphasized the break from all prewar life in an unforgettable scene in which Paul Bäumer, the narrator in *All Quiet*, returns home on leave and attempts to find some peace of mind by rereading his old books. Sitting in his old room, surrounded by books that he cannot read, he realizes the futility of the attempt. Books are no longer a part of his life. His existence is war and war alone. The other world is dead forever.

Reviewers found the conscious artistry of English writers more familiar and agreeable than the expressionistic mode of the German war novelists. They tended to refer to English war writing as solid, objective, sane, balanced, fair, truthful, steadfast, and above all quiet and serene. The following extracts from a few reviews of English war books should be sufficient to illustrate the different critical approach. Of Sassoon's *The Memoirs of an Infantry Officer*, Ivor Brown of the *Listener* said: "How quiet is his verbal attack; how little he shatters our eardrums. . . . This book is a triumph of tranquility. Its modesty of mood finds perfect expression in its modesty of phrase. There is no effort to make words roar like a cannon."[41] Of Robert Graves's *Goodbye to All That*, the *Spectator* wrote: "Yet it is good, objective writing. There are no harangues, but solid quoting of incidents which are allowed to speak for themselves."[42] Of Henry Williamson's *A Soldier's Diary of the Great War*, the *Daily News* wrote: "Throughout he is beautifully sane, steadfast, unselfish, and brave. . . . Yet so quietly does this officer tell his story, that the brutality and waste that he records are dominated by the serenity of the recorder's spirit."[43] Arnold Bennett of the *Evening Standard* assured his readers that Edmund Blunden's *Undertones of War* had nothing of Arnold Zweig's "big bow-wow manner." On the contrary: "It is quiet, restrained, unpretentious, subtle. He paints no large, comprehensive pictures. . . . The intimate horror of war has never been, and never will be, more movingly and modestly rendered than he renders it."[44]

Major-General Sir Ernest Swinton praised Charles Douie, author of *The Weary Road*, for his balance and sanity in not severing ties with the past: "In amplifying and illustrating what he wishes to express by numerous quotations from some of the finest things already written on the subject in the English language, he leads us on and upward."[45] These extracts indicate that reviewers revered what they perceived as English restraint, historical continuity of style, familiar language and tone, moderation, serenity, and sanity.

The picture that has so far emerged is one of two opposing teams of reviewers—the one for, the other against the influx of German war novels. Superficially, this is correct. Upon close examination, however, a more complex picture emerges, and it becomes clear that both the defense of the code and the attack on it posed a dilemma for the critics. The war writers themselves, both English and German, were often ambivalent about their experience. Manning spoke of the mystery that encompassed every man in the trenches, a mystery that they could neither identify with nor cut themselves off from. Sassoon, Graves, Renn, Remarque, and countless other war writers were, by their own admission, powerfully attracted to the front and did not manage to cut loose from it for the rest of their lives. George Orwell, too young to fight in the war, spent the first postwar years in the company of men a little older than himself, who had fought. In his essay, "My Country Right or Left," he described their incessant talk of war with horror, but also with steadily growing nostalgia. The Englishman "is trained for war from the cradle onwards, not technically but morally," claimed Orwell; and this training he saw as part of the explanation for the national fascination with war.[46] In her autobiography *Testament of Youth* (1933), Vera Brittain lamented the terrible decimation of her generation, yet at the same time spoke of the delirious glamor and magic of war: "the challenge to spiritual endurance, the intense sharpening of all the senses, the vitalising consciousness of common peril for a common end." She admitted that the fever subsided as soon as the war was over, but while it lasted "no emotion known to man seems as yet to have quite the compelling power of this enlarged vitality."[47] As the years passed some veterans, like Charles Douie, came to look back nostalgically on the war as the moment of supreme manhood: "We can look back almost with longing on days which, however tragic, at least gave us the honour and dignity of being men. We may perhaps realise how rare is the privilege of dying well, and feel a trace of envy at the thought of those who will never grow old, whom 'age shall not weary nor the years contemn'."[48]

Those very English writers who expressed their disgust with the deeply ingrained Hotspurian ideal of war were often unable to shake off romantic notions of war. Although they would undoubtedly have been disgusted with Newbolt's *Vitai Lampada*, they themselves constantly drew analogies between the world of the trenches and that of the public schools where readiness to fight was an integral part of the value system. Despite their obvious attempts to invent new forms, they were firmly anchored in the classical world. Rebecca West, astutely noticing this strange gap between the aim and the end result, spoke of the "precipitation of a class bred from its beginnings to eschew profundity into an experience which only the profoundest thinking could render tolerable, with no words to express the agony but the insipid vocabulary of their education, no gods to guide them save the unhelpful gods of Puritan athleticism."[49] Here she was speaking of Siegfried Sassoon and R. C. Sherriff, both of whom were in the forefront of the English war book rebellion. George Orwell, too, admitted that it was impossible to shed one's upbringing completely. Comparing John Cornford's poem *Before the Storming of Huesca* with Newbolt's *Vitai Lampada*, Orwell pointed out that the emotional content of both poems was almost identical: "The young communist who died heroically in the International Brigade was public school to the core. He had changed his allegiance but not his emotions."[50]

Almost all reviewers spoke of peace, yet the responses of the opponents of the antiwar books were fiercely antagonistic. Some claimed that far from being a deterrent, the antiwar books, especially the German ones, provoked a fascination with war in the younger generation who had not fought in it. War was being romanticized inversely. The very horror and violence fascinated. Yet to judge from the vehemence of the passages that have been quoted in this chapter, it would seem that the reviewers themselves were no less fascinated by the violence than their readers. Almost every review delved gleefully into the horrors described in the books under review, often quoting liberally and at length.

The dilemma that the war books—and the war—posed for the reviewers is aptly illustrated by the response to the war diary *Storm of Steel* (1929) by Ernst Jünger, a highly decorated German officer who served on the Western Front throughout the war, sustaining multiple wounds on fourteen separate occasions. The book is unusual in that it is virtually the only war book of the period that unabashedly glorified the battle. Unlike the antiwar authors who formed the German mainstream, Jünger elevated war to a mystical experience. For him war was sublime, lifting man out of his humdrum existence to join the gods. Jünger was unconcerned with the causes of the war, never questioned its legitimacy, and never tried to justify it. He simply saw the war as a great adventure affording man the supreme opportunity to prove himself on the field of Mars. Like the knights of old, whenever Jünger and his men grew bored with a lull in the fighting, they crossed into enemy lines hoping to find action. They killed without compunction and yet harbored no resentment or hatred for the enemy. On the contrary, much in the spirit of a jousting match in King Arthur's Court, Jünger respected the courage of his foes, especially the English, and praised them warmly. For him, war was simply a law of nature, as much a feature of human life as the sexual urge—to live was to kill.

English reviewers reacted ambivalently. Jünger represented the German barbarian they both feared and admired. J. Knight Bostock could not endorse his extreme view of war as a positive force, but his admiration for this flamboyant and dashing fighter is evident: "Jünger is a handsome, energetic and capable young man," he wrote, "who would be warmly welcomed by an aristocratic tribe of headhunters desirous to remodel their methods on modern West European lines, but his philosophy is of little practical value to civilized people."[51] At first glance, it would appear that the civilized Westerner was merely chastising the barbarous Hun. Closer examination of the passage, however, reveals undertones of admiration and sympathy for the "barbarian." Bostock enthusiastically applauded Jünger's thrilling accounts of trench warfare and lamented the fact that there were few young men as bold and courageous. The Oxford don was consistently transmitting a double message. On the one hand, perceiving himself to be a supremely civilized Englishman, Bostock condemned Jünger for his unrestrained, barbaric, almost Dionysian joy in war. On the other hand, he could not help but admire this free spirit, who so clearly embodied the virtues of courage, fortitude, patriotism, chivalry, loyalty, and comradeship—in fact, those very values of the code that the war writers were, at that moment, challenging.

Similar ambivalence can be detected in the responses of other Englishmen. R. H. Mottram's introduction to *Storm of Steel* reveals disgust with Jünger's love of war alongside a strong fascination with his daring and dynamism. Cyril Falls admits that Jünger is a danger to society but cannot resist liking and admiring his courage and vitality. A *TLS* reviewer comparing Renn's *War* with Jünger's *Storm of Steel* declared Renn's by far the better book, yet upon completing his review was astonished to discover his own unconscious bias toward Jünger: "We discover that, after declaring *War* to be the better written of the two books, we have here devoted most attention to *Storm of Steel.*"[52] A *Daily News* reviewer wrote candidly that he detested Jünger's pitiless Nietzschean philosophy, but commended his courage, as did Vita Sackville-West in her weekly BBC talk. Jünger might not be very attractive in everyday life, she said, but one would forgive him much for the sake of his youth and his extraordinary courage. The *Spectator* echoed the BBC: "We may be horrified, perhaps disgusted, but we cannot but admit that the author has an ideal here, even if he is sometimes misguided. Courage itself is never misguided."[53] Jünger's book was an extreme case. Not only was it a pro- rather than anti-war book but its author positively revelled in war and frankly extolled killing. It was a book that presented the horrors of war not only without revulsion, but also without guilt, without shame, and without apology. It is hardly remarkable that English critics and reviewers all rejected the book's message out of hand. But the fact that the book drew the attention it did and provoked grudging admiration points to the ambivalence that infused the English reception of the war books, both positive and negative. It was perhaps Clennel Wilkinson who best encapsulated the British attitude: "We are all of us aware that while the war plumbed the depths of human misery, it also scaled the very heights of human happiness."[54]

The ambivalent response of British reviewers to the German war books reflected a deep anxiety about the future of the political, moral, and cultural order in England. Ostensibly, reviewers were concerned with such stylistic issues as truth or fiction, realism or romance, obscenity or modesty, pastoral or purgatory, but it seems evident that the interest charging these reviews stemmed from nothing less than the threat posed by the books under review to deeply ingrained moral, social, and political stances.

Critics generally evaluated the war books in accordance with their political and moral beliefs and assumptions. Conservatives (and most older people) tended to review the antiwar books negatively, defending themselves against the books' implied charges that they were responsible for a meaningless war and for its horrendous casualties. Liberals and socialists and, on the whole, younger people striving for radical change, reviewed the same books positively. The German war novels, which repeatedly and passionately demonstrated that the war had created a new reality, rendering the old values and institutions obsolete, provided these critics with a way of attacking the established political system at home. Pacifists also naturally found much to praise in these novels and hoped that they would serve as effective rallying cries for peace. The pacifists adopted as their slogan Paul Bäumer's "never again" oath in *All Quiet*, sworn after a night spent in a ditch in the company of a dead Frenchman whom he had killed. Those who opposed pacifism, on the other hand, feared that the books would undermine the will of English soldiers to fight in a future war. In later years, some even blamed the books for England's political passivity in the 1930s and refusal to see that Germany was preparing for a "new barbarism."[55] Avant-garde critics saw in these German books an opportunity to encourage the breakup of traditional structures in favor of new values and new literary forms. Traditionalists, on the other hand, perceived these books with their fragmented, obscure style and coarse language as promoting literary and, hence, moral anarchy. Those who had not fought in the war generally displayed more hostility, prejudice, and anti-German stereotypes than veterans, who tended to respect the honesty and courage of the German writers.

The lines of division, however, were not always clearly drawn. There were soldiers, young and old, on both sides, as well as avant-garde alongside establishment figures. Many embittered ex-soldiers applauded the books of "disenchantment," while just as many veterans denounced them as demeaning and disrespectful to those who had died for their country. Charles Edmonds recorded his experiences in the trenches in *A Subaltern's War* (1929) in the hope that his book would "strike a responsive chord in the hearts of some old soldiers who are tired of the uniform disillusion of most authors of war-books."[56] He charged the "authors of disenchantment" with "souring the milk of human kindness" by dwelling disproportionately on the indecencies of war. Charles Douie, another subaltern of infantry who recorded his recollections of the war, avowed in his book *The Weary Road* (1929) that his service in the Great War had been in defense of the ideal of liberty and justice not only for his own countrymen but also for all peoples of the world. In Douie's view, the new war books spoke only of the degradation and disillusion of war but did not portray "the dominance of the spirit of man over things material, the resolution which met and mastered demands unparalleled before, the courage which triumphed over pain and death."[57]

What does emerge, however, from the heated, one might almost say frenzied, tones of the so-called literary debate is fear of being overwhelmed by the German barbarian, not only or even primarily militarily, but also culturally and more than that, morally. The unusually fierce and passionate tone of the discourse suggests that the critics were engaged in a struggle to preserve those bastions of the code which they feared were disintegrating. This conclusion is reinforced by the consistent strident note of superiority in the reviews. It seems that English reviewers bore out Tomlinson's claim that when people were afraid they greatly disliked having the cause of their fear indicated to them: "They will not look at it and get angry when invited to do so. They assert roundly that they are superior to whatever may be disturbing their minds."[58]

More often than not, reviewers displayed tolerance and understanding for English war books which they simply refused to accord the German books. For the most part, they treated English war writers as equals but talked down to German writers. Even ardent supporters of the German war literature often betrayed a paternalistic strain of superiority, such as a parent might use in encouraging a gifted child. Regularly throughout the period, we find English reviewers stating that this or that might be acceptable in Germany, but not in England. The implication was that it may be all right for the German barbarian but not for the civilized Englishman.

The critics' traditional position as leaders of public opinion was being undermined by the new trend in war books. Their reviews indicate a fear of a loss of control of the reading public. Reviewers commonly derided the public's low taste in preferring the German books to English ones: "As for the German translations, one can only say that it is a terrible comment upon British taste that *Undertones of War*—very successful as it has been—should have had a sale actually trifling by comparison with that of *All Quiet on the Western Front*. Perhaps it is natural that the crowd should prefer a Doré to a Rembrandt."[59] The appeal of the German books was ascribed to the "young who knew not the war" and to rhapsodizing "women curious about the life of men."[60]

Their opponents, on the other hand, with equal fierceness strove to expose the futility and dangers of an outdated system of beliefs and style of writing. Accordingly, such reviewers searched for a view of the war from sources outside the code and perhaps, by logical extension, a view of the entire postwar world from a new perspective.

The popularity of the German war novels began to recede in 1932. In England, attitudes toward war literature in general were changing. The rise of fascism in Italy and Spain and of Nazism in Germany provoked British awareness that another war might have to be fought again in the near future. By the second half of the 1930s, most of the British intelligentsia were sympathetic to the Republican struggle in Spain. The tables had turned and English intellectuals of the left, many of whom volunteered to fight on the Republican side, were urging their Conservative government, content with a noninterventionist policy, to take military action in Spain. In this atmosphere, antiwar novels lost their charm.

Notes

1. Wohl, *Generation of 1914*, p. 103.

2. MacCarthy, "The End of War?"

3. Bennett, *Evening Standard*, January 23, 1930, p. 6.

4. G. Gould, "The Boom in War Books," *Daily Herald*, March 20, 1930, p. 6.

5. A. Bennett, "People Who Are Tired of War Books," *Evening Standard*, December 6, 1928, p. 9.

6. Bennett, "The Topmost Peaks of War Fiction."

7. Graves and Hodge, *The Long Week-End*, p. 205.

8. For a detailed examination of the "code," see Mark Girouard, *The Return to Camelot: Chivalry and the English Gentleman* (New Haven: Yale University Press, 1981). Also Isabel Quigly, *The Heirs of Tom Brown: The English School Story* (Oxford: Oxford University Press, 1984).

9. O. F. Christie, *A History of Clifton College* (Bristol: Arrowsmith, 1935), cited in P. Howarth, *Play Up and Play the Game* (London: Methuen, 1973), p. 14.

10. T. Hughes, *Tom Brown's Schooldays* (London: Macmillan, 1857), p. 72.

11. Ibid., p. 206.

12. Ibid., p. 219.

13. Tomlinson, "War Books," p. 419.

14. Graves, *Goodbye to All That*, p. 157.

15. *Daily Herald*, November 18, 1929, Front Page.

16. Ibid.

17. V. Williams, "The Unhappy Warriors and their Unhappy Books," *Morning Post*, February 11, 1930, p. 10.

18. Jerrold, *The Lie About the War*, p. 33.

19. Ibid., p. 29.

20. J. C. Squire, "German and English War Books," *London Mercury*, 1929–1930, pp. 2–3.

21. Ibid.

22. *TLS*, "The Garlands Wither," June 12, 1930, pp. 485–486.

23. R. Graves, *But It Still Goes On* (New York: J. Cape and H. Smith, 1931), p. 32.

24. Jerrold, *The Lie About the War*, p. 10.

25. Ibid., p. 21.

26. Ibid., p. 10.

27. C. Wilkinson, "Recent War Books," *London Mercury*, 1929–1930, p. 230.

28. *TLS*, April 28, 1929, p. 314.

29. *London Mercury*, January 1930, p. 3.

30. Falls, *War Books*, p. 294.

31. *TLS*, November 21, 1929, p. 938.

32. Ibid., October 3, 1929, p. 794.

33. Ibid., April 18, 1929, p. xx.

34. Ibid., July 10, 1930, p. 567.

35. Read, *Criterion*, 1928–1929, p. 549.

36. Ibid., p. 547.

37. Tomlinson, "War Books," p. 408.

38. Graves, *Goodbye to All That*, p. 282.

39. *Spectator*, November 13, 1929, p. 780.

40. M. Muggeridge, *The Thirties: 1930–1940 in Great Britain* (London: Hamish Hamilton, 1940), p. 33.

41. *Listener*, October 1, 1930, p. 526.

42. *Spectator*, November 13, 1929, p. 780.

43. *Daily News*, March 7, 1929, p. 4.

44. Bennett, *Evening Standard*, December 6, 1928, p. 9.

45. Major General Sir Ernest Swinton, "Introduction," C. Douie, *The Weary Road* (London: Strong Oak Press, 1988).

46. Orwell, "My Country Right or Left," *Collected Essays*, p. 589.

47. Brittain, *Testament of Youth*, p. 292.

48. Douie, *The Weary Road*, p. 151.

49. R. West, "Journey's End Again," *Ending in Earnest* (Garden City, N.Y.: Doubleday, Doran and Co. 1931), p. 77.

50. Orwell, "My Country Right or Left," p. 592.

51. Bostock, *Some Well-Known German War Novels*, p. 24.

52. *TLS*, June 20, 1929, p. 485.

53. *Spectator*, June 22, 1929, p. 974.

54. Wilkinson, "Recent War Books," p. 237.

55. I. Evans, *English Literature Between the Wars* (London: Methuen, 1948), p. 108.

56. R. Lynd, "An Attack on War Books," *Daily News*, July 26, 1929, p. 4.

57. Douie, *The Weary Road*, p. 8.

58. Tomlinson, "War Books," p. 419.

59. Falls, *War Books*, p. 183.

60. J. C. Squire, "Editorial," *London Mercury*, 1929–1930, pp. 2–4.

DAVID MIDGLEY

Remembering the War

"The war, my dear doctor, has been forgotten." "Worse than that, Herr
Pont, it has been repressed."

Arnold Zweig, "Pont und Anna", 1925[1]

The time is fast approaching when the war will become a myth.

Joseph Ponten, 1927 (*LW* 3, 4, 1)

The narrative accounts of the First World War warrant a chapter to themselves for two reasons. They testify to the ideological contest that took place
in the 1920s over the way the war should be interpreted in retrospect, and in
doing so they illustrate the senses in which the post-war mood in Germany
should not be viewed simply in terms of disillusionment or a retreat from
ideologies.

There is, of course, a sense in which the war literature of other combatant nations can also be interpreted as a reconstruction of the experience
in the terms of particular ways of looking at the world. The publication of
Paul Fussell's book *The Great War and Modern Memory* in 1975 made readers
generally more keenly aware of the senses in which the well-known English
war memoirs by Robert Graves, Edmund Blunden, and Siegfried Sassoon,
for example, were moulded by literary preconceptions as well as by personal
experience. Cruel ironies and stark contrasts may have been among the com-

From *Writing Weimar: Critical Realism in German Literature 1918–1933* by David Midgley, pp. 226–259. © 2000 David Midgley.

monly shared experiences of the effects of protracted and static warfare, but
the narrative structures in which such memories are recalled can also be seen
to relate to one or another kind of fictional prefiguration. In Sassoon's case it
is the highlighting of symbolic contrasts, in the case of Graves it is the structure of comic anecdote. Fussell rather overstated his case when he tried to
relate Erich Maria Remarque's *Im Westen nichts Neues* (*All Quiet on the Western
Front*) to a German baroque tradition in imaginative writing, although he
is certainly right in principle to contrast the contrived eeriness of some of
Remarque's effects with the comic tradition he had recognized in the works
of English writers.[2] But it is not my purpose here to take issue with the interpretation of details in depictions of the war by German authors. Rather
I wish to emphasize the contrasts among those depictions, the implications
of the narrative strategies adopted by particular authors, and the manner in
which, in the context of Weimar Germany, the issue of how the war should
be depicted became heavily politicized.

*   *   *

When reviewing some right-wing writings in 1930, Walter Benjamin commented that the Germans had lost the 1914–18 war in a double sense: first as
a matter of historical fact, and secondly in that they had tried to forget it (*GS*
III, 242). Benjamin's remark contained a polemical thrust, and a character-
istically paradoxical point about the function of literature. He was blaming
the forgetting of the war on the dull-mindedness of the bourgeoisie, while
also implying that the fictionalization of the war in itself constituted a
retreat from the reality of it. But he was also drawing attention to a pattern
in German public responses to the war which might not be readily apparent
from the standard historical accounts of the Weimar period.

There are obvious senses in which the war was never far from public
consciousness. Commemoration of the war dead naturally became part of
ceremonial state practice under the Weimar Republic; the cost of war pen-
sions and the problem of caring for the war wounded remained abiding political issues throughout the period; and the perception of the Versailles Treaty
as an unjustly imposed and punitive peace settlement provided right-wing
politicians with a never-failing opportunity for agitation (cf. Whalen). At
the same time, the awareness of the Great War as a major historical turning
point and a source of opportunities for revolutionary change was nurtured
on the radical left, and was kept before the public mind by Piscator's productions of the mid-1920s, for example. But there was something about the
literary responses to the subject after 1920 which nevertheless made the war
look like a forgotten experience. In the epochal novels of Thomas Mann and
Robert Musil the war represents a kind of vanishing point for the narrative, a

threshold beyond which the text does not venture; and in Döblin's *Berlin Alexanderplatz* it represents a concealed memory which lies behind some aspects of the behaviour of the protagonist Franz Biberkopf, but without being explicitly evoked. There is even evidence that in the mid-1920s German publishers thought the subject had become unsaleable. Joseph Ponten, in the article of January 1927 that is quoted at the head of this chapter, was protesting at the exclusion of the subject of wartime experience from a literary competition announced by the S. Fischer publishing house.[3] Ponten, a nationalist and a deeply conservative writer, envisaged the war as the potential subject-matter for a great German epic in the manner of the *Iliad* or the *Nibelungenlied*, and within a very few years other nationalist authors were to attempt just such a treatment. But his comment about the war becoming the stuff of myth might also alert us to the senses in which the spectacular wave of war novels which did appear at the end of the 1920s represented a struggle for control of the memory of the war.

The phases in the literary treatment of the war to which Benjamin alludes have been reconstructed by Martin Travers in his 1982 book *German Novels on the First World War and their Ideological Implications, 1918–1933*. The immediate post-war years had seen the publication of many a volume of memoirs by high-ranking officers, largely concerned with the justification of their own strategic role, and insistent that, however things had turned out politically, Germany had not been defeated in the field. Particularly influential were the memoirs of the Grand Admiral of the Fleet, Alfred von Tirpitz, and those of the chief architect of Germany's campaign during its final year, Erich Ludendorff (soon to be associated with Hitler's attempted Munich putsch of 1923). Later historical analysis was to show how Ludendorff in particular had used his position in 1918 to ensure that responsibility for political decisions which looked like the actions of a defeated nation were safely entrusted to parliamentarians, as opposed to representatives of the imperial establishment. The effect of his actions at the time, however, was to create the potent political legend that the German army had been 'stabbed in the back'—a legend which the most painstaking investigations of a government commission in the early 1920s were unable effectively to dispel (cf. Travers, 30; Bessel 1988, 22).

Another popular form of publication between 1915 and 1919 was the diary-style account of front-line action. The perspective that dominates here is that of the more junior officer, the platoon or company commander, concerned with limited battlefield objectives and the personal qualities needed to accomplish them. Some of the most vivid accounts of the emotional experience of infantry action ever written are to be found in one of these works, Ernst Jünger's *In Stahlgewittern* (Storm of Steel, 1920). Such diary-style literature continued to be published in small editions well into the mid-1920s, and two examples written from more lofty perspectives were to be commended to English schoolboys for many a year to come as representing the humanity of the German officer and gentleman: Hans Carossa, *Rumänisches Tagebuch* (Rumanian Diary, 1924), and Rudolf Binding, *Aus dem Krieg* (From the War, 1925). Carossa writes as a medical officer, and shows sensitivity towards the human predicaments of war from within a staunchly unpolitical ethos which accepts the war as something inflicted as if by fate. Binding is eloquently critical of the devastation entailed by the High Command's strategy of attrition, and of the distortion of truth in official reports; but he writes as a staff officer for whom the rationale of the war and its sustaining ethos again remain beyond question (cf. Travers, 38–41).

Both the glory and the horror of war had found direct expression in the lyric poetry written between 1914 and 1918. But censorship, and probably also the sheer nearness of the experience, impeded the broader depiction of war as a social phenomenon. Even those Expressionist dramas which placed their treatment of the subject on the plane of existential spirituality and universalized grief could only be performed in private in 1918 (Patterson, 194). Reinhard Goering's *Seeschlacht* (Sea Battle) confines its action to the gun turret of a battleship, and its dramatic argument to the search for meaning in the face of death. Fritz von Unruh stylizes the experience of bereavement in *Ein Geschlecht* (A Noble Family). While the memory of gas warfare clearly influenced Georg Kaiser's choice of the title *Gas* for his dramatic trilogy of 1917–20, what that text provides is a highly intellectualized and notoriously abstract vision of humanity's inexorable progression through industrialization to eventual mutual annihilation. A clear sense of outrage at the relentless destruction of war is to be found in Toller's *Die Wandlung* (Transfiguration) of 1919, and equally clear echoes of it are to be found in some of his later plays. But while *Die Wandlung* makes use of both harrowing battlefield images and political satire, what it is primarily articulating is that volatile mood of social cataclysm and utopian counter-current which was all-pervasive in the literature of the immediate post-war phase.[4]

The one work of that time which stands out as an attempt to encompass the social behaviour of the German and Austrian nations at war—notwithstanding its openly apocalyptic title—is *Die letzten Tage der Menschheit* (The Last Days of Mankind) by the Viennese author Karl Kraus. Written by a process of slow accretion between 1917 and 1922, it suffers from compositional and ideological inconsistencies, but it captures aspects of the political responsibility for the war and the psychological collusion of society in it by presenting in dialogue form statements which had actually appeared in print during the course of the war (cf. Tims, 371–402). Running to over 600 pages, the work poses enormous problems for stage presentation (Kraus himself describes it in his preface, sardonically, as being conceived for a "Martian theatre"). But in its self-conscious use of montage and ironic juxtaposition it may be seen as pioneering a form of documentary technique which was to be used to some effect by later novelists and campaigners who sought to defend humanitarian values against the cynicism and the emotional appeal of the Nationalist right.

Those who attempted to promote views which were critical of Germany's wartime leadership faced repressive measures in the 1920s. The statistician and social democrat E. J. Gumbel published a pamphlet in 1919 entitled *Vier Jahre Lügen* (Four Years of Lies) which indicated, amongst other things, that the Kaiser's government had deliberately frustrated international peace initiatives since 1915. A leading member of the German League for Human Rights, Gumbel went on to chart the record of political violence in the early 1920s and to demonstrate the nationalist bias in the judiciary's response to it. But in common with other leading pacifists of the time, he faced a series of attempts to stifle him with law suits—all eventually dismissed—as well as a campaign to remove him from his university post at Heidelberg for his outspokenness. He was driven into exile by Nazi agitation in 1932 (Holl and Wette, 113–34). The revolutionary pacifist Ernst Friedrich mounted his campaign on an international level and with a multilingual text. In his book *Krieg dem Kriege!* (War against War, 1924) he combined two kinds of documentary evidence. He printed a unique collection of previously unpublished photographs exposing the horrors of the war, and interspersed them with complacent and bombastic utterances by military leaders and imperial politicians. Ernst Friedrich, too, suffered frequent litigation for alleged defamation, and a period of imprisonment in 1930–1 under a charge of high treason for the intended dissemination of anti-militarist literature among members of the army and the police.[5]

Judicial suppression faced others who—perhaps naively—sought to present their wartime experiences as symptomatic of the inhumanity of the old imperial regime. Heinrich Wandt assembled a veritable catalogue of corruption, iniquity, and brutality among German officers in occupied Belgium under the title *Etappe Gent* ("Etappe" implying the extended system of military administration behind the front lines). His book was initially banned in 1920, published in expanded form in 1924, and went on to sell over 200,000 copies in popular editions by 1929. Officers whom Wandt had portrayed in the book were unsuccessful in seeking a legal injunction prohibiting its sale, but Wandt was instead charged with military treason in 1924 and sentenced to six years in prison.[6] Bruno Vogel set about the systematic deflation of wartime clichés in a passionate tract, *Es lebe der Krieg!* (Long Live War!), but it was confiscated and banned on grounds of blasphemy, again in 1924 (Momber, 31–3). And the Communist J. R. Becher researched the effects of chemical warfare and its development during and since the war, working his findings into a novel in which he imagined its potential impact on civilian populations in a future war against the Soviet Union. His novel, which took its title from the formula for the poison gas Levisite, was also confiscated, and Becher was subjected to a protracted and inconclusive prosecution for high treason on the basis of this and other publications, which turned him into a literary cause célèbre between the years 1925 and 1928.[7] Coupled with the election of Field Marshal Hindenburg as President of the Republic in 1925, the judicial suppression of critical writings on the war has been seen as one of the clearest indicators that the economic stabilization in the years after 1923 was accompanied by a restoration of authoritarian power structures in German society (Bornebusch, 72 ff.; Bessel 1988, 33 f.).

Such was the background to the sudden resurgence of German public interest in the war at the end of the 1920s, and it helps to account for the palpable difference between the pattern of publications about the war in Germany on the one hand and that in Britain, France, and America on the other. While there had of course been painful and bitter memories to assimilate in the victorious western countries, too, there had at least been a certain continuity in the way that these had been articulated. Henri Barbusse's famous disillusioning novel Le Feu (Under Fire, 1916) had been published while the war was still in progress, and was promptly awarded the Prix Goncourt. (An English translation appeared in 1917; a German translation was published in neutral Switzerland in 1918, but military censorship prevented the immediate dissemination of it in Germany itself.) Roland Dorgelès was able to publish his novel Les Croix de bois (The Wooden Crosses) in 1919, but a German translation had to wait until 1930. The war novels of John Dos Passos and E. E. Cummings appeared in America in the early 1920s, and in England both R. H. Mottram and Ford Madox Ford were publishing trilogies about the war between 1924 and 1928.[8] Even Hollywood moved rapidly through a documentary phase in the immediate post-war years, and by 1925 King Vidor's The Big Parade was openly exploring the cruel ironies of war; it might not have been a runaway box-office success in America, but in Germany it was banned.[9] In so far as accounts of the war were available to the German reading and cinema-going public in the mid-1920s, by contrast, they constituted a mixture of military self-glorification and romantic nostalgia.[10]

The "return" of the war in German fiction which occurred at the end of the 1920s was thus in part a response to a genuine thirst for information which had been denied to the German public, but it was not without its aspect of cynical calculation. Remarque's Im Westen nichts Neues began to be serialized in the Vossische Zeitung precisely on 10 November 1928, the eve of the tenth anniversary of the armistice. It was not the first of the German war novels to appear. The liberal Frankfurter Zeitung had serialized Arnold Zweig's Der Streit um den Sergeanten Grischa (The Case of Sergeant Grischa) in the summer of 1927, and had followed this in the course of 1928 with Siegfried Kracauer's *Ginster* and Ludwig Renn's *Krieg* (War). Remarque was also acquainted with the novel *Soldat Suhren* (Soldier Suhren, 1927) by Georg von der Vring which he reviewed, together with some earlier works by Ernst Jünger, at the time he was preparing his own novel.[11] But publishers were evidently still cautious about the prospects for war novels, and when Remarque approached them in 1928 he had difficulty persuading them to accept his manuscript. Even when he signed up with Ullstein in August 1928, the contract contained clauses which insured the publisher against the possibility of poor sales (Howind, 58). At the same time, however, this influential publishing house threw its efforts into promoting *Im Westen nichts Neues* as *the* novel which, ten years after the event, was finally going to tell the truth about the war. The book version was deliberately held back until 31 January 1929 in order to keep appetites keen and to avoid competition with the Christmas market; and on the day of the launch, three different Ullstein papers carried full-page articles about Remarque by well-known authors, using the novel's title as a banner headline. Finally, when sales took off, the book's commercial success was itself presented in the promotional literature as proof positive of the truthfulness of what it depicted—the hype was complete.[12]

As Angelika Howind notes, it was the advance publicity for the novel that was also responsible for creating a cynical legend. In an announcement of the serialization, published in the *Vossische Zeitung* of 8 November 1928, Remarque was stylized into a simple soldier with no literary background, who had just sat down one day to write down his wartime experiences: his novel was to be "the first true monument to the Unknown Soldier". Documentary authenticity was evidently considered a prime selling-point; and in the interests of this, the publisher also insisted on deleting a sentence from the prefatory note to the book. In the form in which readers are familiar with it, that note describes the book as neither an indictment nor a confession. As Remarque had originally typed it, it also denied—above all—that the novel represented an *experience*, "for death is not an experience for him who is confronted by it" (Howind, 59, 63). Even the small amount of laconic self-awareness that these words convey was incompatible with the image of the author as naive autobiographer which the marketing strategy required. The publisher's imposition of an inauthentic identity on the author (on the pretext of promoting the 'authenticity' of his book) is one reason, incidentally, why Remarque's subsequent statements about his intentions in writing the novel must be treated with particular caution. Another is his evident difficulty in coping with the political controversy that arose around his novel.

What we find if we strip away the misleading claims of Remarque's publisher is—in the words of Herbert Bornebusch (p. 118)—the artful reconstruction of an ostensibly personal experience from the stuff of collective memory. What prompted the controversy was the way the text persistently deheroicized the war.[13] Each chapter is carefully organized around its own particular constellation of themes which were to become commonplaces in the depiction of the experiences of the common soldier. The soldier's most fundamental concern, as evoked in the opening chapter, is not the fighting, but the fulfilment of bodily needs. The company is tucking into double rations; only as we read on is it gradually disclosed that the reason for this good fortune is that half their force was killed or wounded in the previous day's action. Apart from eating, their concerns are with catching up on sleep and providing as best they can for the rigours that lie ahead. The second half of the chapter takes us on a visit to a comrade whose leg has been amputated in the field hospital. Only here do we begin to get a sense of the background of the characters we have been reading about, in the shape of recollections of schooldays and the teachers who had dinned patriotic sentiment into them until they had joined up. Only gradually, again, does the unpleasant truth emerge that the survivors have an ulterior motive for their visit, namely to scavenge the dying man's boots. The picture of army life that Remarque is building up is one that is reduced to the horizons of basic material need: these young men are alienated from the standards of home and civil institutions, not so much in the sense that they have discovered the nationalist clichés to be a cruel delusion (they prefer not to think too deeply about what has got them into the situation they find themselves in), but by simple habits of mind.

The story that follows is similarly composed of ironic juxtapositions. The pathos of watching the amputee Kemmerich die is set against the impersonal routine of death in the military hospital. The first account of the experience of artillery bombardment and gas attack is followed by the carnivalesque episode in which the group celebrates the incarceration of one of their number for a deliberate act of insubordination by stealing and roasting a goose. The long, central sixth chapter, which evokes the experience of trench warfare—the remorseless logic of attack and counter-attack, the violent rage engendered by an atmosphere of kill-or-be-killed, and the nerve-racking cries of the wounded by night—is framed by examples of the macabre humour of men accustomed to the ever-presence of gruesome death. It is followed again by relaxation: a period at rest, an illicit night of love with some French women, and a spell of home leave which serves only to reinforce the sense of a gulf of misunderstanding between serving men and civilians. The closing stages of the narrative renew the depiction of the intensity of experience at the front, with the narrator telling of his first experience of hand-to-hand combat, and of the slow death, at his hand, of a Frenchman with whom he shares a shellhole. "What war really means", in this account, is the mutilation and debilitation he observes while hospitalized with a leg-wound; and back in the trenches, he finds his comrades eliminated one by one around him until we are informed, in the short final paragraph, that he too was killed, a month or so before the armistice, on a day when activity was so typical of the war routine that all was reported to be quiet on the Western Front. In a very deliberate way, the fiction constructs its account of a young generation cut off from their pre-war roots, isolated from the population at home, and relentlessly destroyed by a carnage that no one had anticipated and no one seems to understand.

The narrator has a name—Paul Bäumer—but his social identity is only vaguely defined. He is characterized as sensitive and artistic, and accustomed to a higher social perspective than "the poor" (although his own parents are described as worn down by labour and privation). But it is not his character that matters to the way the novel works so much as his constant presence as an accompanying voice, guiding us through events in the present tense. It talks us through the army routine, the sensations of exposure to attack, the fear and apprehension, the physical oppression, and the special sense of intimacy with the earth and of group solidarity associated with those experiences. At the same time it retains, in its moments of lyrical reflection, an awareness of the now distant promise of youth, innocence, and cultured civility. In short, it is a voice which guides the reader on an imaginary journey into a realm which is by definition remote from the shared reality of peacetime society. The contrived pathos of Remarque's final paragraph reinforces this impression by intimating that Bäumer's is a voice speaking to us from beyond the grave. In an important psychological study of the soldier's experience at war, Eric Leed has described the transition by which the infantryman in particular becomes separated from his former identity and from the community to which he used to belong, and initiated into a new one (Leed 1979). A crucial factor, surely, in the enduring popularity of Remarque's novel is the contrivance by which it gives an uninitiated readership the illusion of participating in the infantryman's experience of separation, alienation from his home background, and integration into a community defined by the distinctive varieties of suffering it had shared.

*　*　*

In the wake of Remarque's spectacular success, the German book market became swiftly flooded with narrative accounts of the war. The Viennese scholar Ernst Jirgal, who surveyed the literary treatment of the war in 1931, listed over 200 such publications in German between 1928 and 1930. It was characteristic of this wave of war literature that it placed a high priority on the claim to first-hand 'authentic' experience, and it became a commonplace to speak of these writings as the testimony of a 'war generation' that had finally found its voice. Reviewers were for the most part concerned to judge these works from the point of view of whether or not they created a sense of how the war had 'really' been (cf. Prangel, 61–4). The atmosphere of tense controversy in which these critical assessments took place is reflected in the terms of the questionnaire in which the Ullstein Verlag, at the end of 1929, invited readers to evaluate Remarque's novel: did they or did they not find it truthful, pacifistic, offensive, a danger to youth, and a threat to religion and morality (H.-H. Müller, 66)? The question of literary merit was simply not a major concern at the time. But if we want to develop an adequate sense of the terms in which wartime experience was being reconstructed, then we need to consider the distinctive narrative approaches which authors adopted for that purpose, as well as the manifest ideological content of particular works.

To start at the most simple level of depiction, Ludwig Renn's *Krieg* (War), which was written in the early 1920s and published shortly before Remarque's novel in 1928, aspires to do nothing more than give a mundane account of what the physical experience of wartime service had been like for the ordinary infantryman. But in the circumstances of the time, that alone was sufficient for the work to be recognized as a self-conscious break with the tradition of self-justifying officer memoirs. The author was in fact himself an officer and aristocrat by the name of Arnold Friedrich Vieth von Golssenau, who had served in the war in the rank of Captain, and had subsequently joined the Communist Party. It appears that the *Frankfurter Zeitung*, keen to emphasize what was new and different about the work, insisted that it be published under a pseudonym and that the author's true identity be kept secret for six months after the start of serialization (H.-H. Müller, 186 f.). The pseudonym he chose was the name of his protagonist. Nothing in the text itself betrays any sign of political allegiance, and the work was initially reviewed in positive terms in the nationalist press as a faithful depiction of the war.[14] The first-person narrator is a common soldier who works his way up through the ranks between the moment of mobilization in 1914 and the armistice of 1918, and is decorated for bravery along the way. He takes part in various battles on the western front, and describes the distinctive experiences of the front-line fighter: advancing, coming under fire, taking casualties, the euphoria of attack, the recognition of one's own shock responses, and the apathy that results from protracted exposure to danger. His emotional responses and the conclusions he draws from his experiences are reported only in lapidary fashion, and there is liberal use of onomatopoeia in the evocation of events on the battlefield. In so far as there is any sense of conscious literary orientation in the work, it comes with the brief allusion to Grimmelshausen's *Simplicissimus* novel, which Renn's protagonist is given as a birthday present. The implication, in context, is that the wartime experience of the persona Renn has created is that of a simple figure buffeted by the events of world history and the decisions of others, and for whom the ignorance and uncertainty surrounding those decisions is part of the characteristic experience. Renn's professed intention was to break with the insistence of the memoir tradition that there had been a higher purpose behind the carnage, and foremost among the conclusions he draws from the experience of battle is that sacrificing lives is in itself pointless. But the inescapable consequence of the narrative stance he maintains is that the reader is not provided with any explanation of what is happening and why.

Of all the German writers of the period, the one who is most commonly referred to nowadays in discussions of the immediate experience of battle is Ernst Jünger, and the substance of his writings undoubtedly provides justification for this situation. But although he worked doggedly throughout the early 1920s at his diary-style accounts of battlefield experience (and continued to revise them subsequently), his writings received relatively little attention until after Remarque's success. Even then it appears that they were more sympathetically received in England, where Remarque's novel had stimulated interest in the German side of the picture, than in Germany.[15] Jünger's narrative stance is that of the participant—he tells the story of his own wartime service as an infantry officer, in the course of which he was wounded several times and highly decorated—and of the unflinching observer. His texts bear vivid testimony to the heightening of sensory awareness that comes with living in the face of perpetual danger. As a contemporary reader commented, his descriptions are distinguished by a clinical quality, as if he has gone about the battlefield carrying a bag of quick lime, but then forgot at the decisive moment to scatter it.[16] A soldier's first encounter with a dead body, Jünger notes, leaves a precise image seared on the mind, and he specifies: the black crust of blood in the hair, the bluish lips set off against the whiteness of the teeth, the hand driven like a claw into moss and soil.[17] His narrative reconstructions are consistently frank and undeluded about what this war between industrialized nations entails. In the early stages, the adjustments that need to be made are to a life of dirt, physical labour, and vigilance. The fighting, when it comes, is the application of a learned craft, intensified in its effects by the release of pent-up vital energies. By the time we reach the campaigns of 1918, Jünger is describing sustained artillery bombardments as the unleashing of elemental destructive forces (the "storms of steel" evoked in the title of his first volume), but affirming all the more strongly in that connection his faith in military strategy and the ability of his own troops to prevail. Often he adopts the perspective of a superior vantage point from which to describe the activity of stormtroopers overwhelming a defensive position or the devastating impact of artillery fire, and the more practised his writing becomes, the more stylized his descriptions. By the time we reach *Feuer und Blut* (Fire and Blood, 1925), the reconstruction of momentary perceptions is palpably moulded by the technique of literary analogy. From the edge of a crater he observes the after-effects of a direct hit on his company. A pack of shadowy figures is clambering up the sides of the crater, and from the bottom a "magical light" shines forth, which his next sentence identifies as the combustion of machine-gun ammunition. He goes on to recognize a mass of bodies seriously wounded by the exploding shell. But in his evocation of them they are "squirming like amphibians in a boiling sea, like the damned in a Dantesque vision" (*Feuer*, 81).

It became fashionable in the 1980s to view Ernst Jünger as a major representative of literary modernism. The basis for that view was provided by Karl Heinz Bohrer, in his book *Die Ästhetik des Schreckens* (The Aesthetics of Terror, 1978), in which he constructed a cultural lineage for Jünger which ran back to the aesthetic play on the imaginative power of terror in works by Oscar Wilde, Edgar Allan Poe, and E. T. A. Hoffmann. More specifically, Bohrer argued that the sense of reality as dissolved into isolated and terrifying images, which Jünger's writings undoubtedly convey, places him in a tradition which runs from the dandyism of Baudelaire to the literary shock techniques of French Surrealism (Bohrer, 140–3). What was misleading about Bohrer's argument was not so much the account it gave of Jünger's descriptive practice (which no doubt does evoke physical sensations with a directness that excludes the intervention of moral control, as Bohrer says), but the way it appeared to turn amoral sensationalism into *the* defining feature of the modernist heritage. It did so by excluding from that heritage the dimension of rational self-critique and self-irony which can be found in Baudelaire, in Wilde, in Nietzsche, and even in André Breton (to say nothing of Musil and Döblin), and by excluding from its own analysis the ideological perspective of Jünger's depiction of war.

Jünger presents the war of attrition as a process of quasi-Darwinian selection, from which the front-line fighter emerges, tempered and vulcanized, as a new breed. Intellectually he was seeking to uphold the ideal of heroic individualism with which he had entered the war in the face of the collective experience of indiscriminate destruction. The collection of essays in which he attempted to resolve this intellectual problem, *Der Kampf als inneres Erlebnis* (Battle as an Inner Experience, 1922), is highly eclectic. It contains passing allusions to the aesthetic theories of Kant and Schiller, as well as to the Nietzschean conception of intoxication (*Rausch*). The assertion early in the text that war is "the father of all things" is merely a simplistic version of what Nietzsche has to say in *The Gay Science* about cultural achievements as the outcome of ruthless struggle. Jünger also draws selectively on Spengler's *Der Untergang des Abendlandes* (The Decline of the West), insisting repeatedly that fighting is something fundamental to human affairs, an elemental expression of the life-force, and thus an essential means of cultural renewal. The political thrust of his argument is directed against the liberalism of the

Republic, against the Enlightenment principle of tolerance, and against any belief in a rational path of historical progress. To experience war only in a spirit of suffering and negation, he concludes, is to experience it only contingently, "externally", and thus to endure it "as a slave". His construction of the memory of the war is thus fundamentally related to that current of existential 'decisionism' with which the radical nationalism of the 1920s sought to justify political action in terms of an unbridled assertion of the will.[18]

These intellectual attitudes are already manifest in the way he describes the infantry war in his first volume, *In Stahlgewittern*. He speaks of the modern battlefield as a machine that draws ever increasing numbers of men and supplies into a maelstrom of destruction, but he expressly denies that the infantry war has become degraded to a mass slaughter; on the contrary, the actions of the individual remain decisive and the hand-to-hand fighting has found its men of the hour, "princes of the trenches" in whose grim determination "the blood" speaks (pp. 107, 210 f.). Their heroism is a blend of the animal and the divine; the vital will of the nation expresses itself in the unleashed drive to kill (pp. 227, 134 f.). Danger is an occasion for experiencing the virtues Jünger associates with "enhanced manliness", and the hardened fighter is someone who has braved every terror and learned to regard it with contempt (pp. 24 f., 84). A page later he describes the "landscape of horror" created by an artillery bombardment, including the body of a small girl lying in a pool of blood. A toast to fallen companions at the end of a day is simply a part of the fighter's routine (p. 127). A man endures out of a sense of duty, but he does so because his individual will has become invested in the fate of nations that is being decided by the massive deployment of destructive forces in which his personal death has become an irrelevancy (pp. 162, 226 f.). The fighting has acquired its own rationale, independent of strategic or political, to say nothing of humane, considerations.[19] Those who are tempted to read Jünger's writings as if they yielded a more 'authentic' account of the war than the novels of the late 1920s ought to take note of the senses in which he, too, is subjecting the experience to a retrospective stylization. It was in a spirit of almost anarchic individualism and vitalism that Jünger celebrated the war; that is what distinguished his attitude from that of more conservative nationalists. Only gradually did he adjust his intellectual outlook to accommodate the aspect of political organization in the modern state, and even then it was his experience of military organization at the front that provided his model for a totalitarian state of the future.[20]

Jünger did not contribute directly to the wave of war fiction that appeared in 1929–30, but something of his ethos is apparent in the writings of other authors who responded to the challenge of Remarque's novel by constructing alternative myths of the war from a nationalist perspective. Werner Beumelburg, who had previously contributed a number of volumes to the nationalist historiography of the war,[21] published *Die Gruppe Bosemüller* (1930), which tells of the fate of a small group of fighting men in the battle of Verdun. The circumstances in which these men are placed yields an ideal setting for an imagined test of survival instinct, discipline, and comradeship. They know they are involved in a battle which takes an enormous toll of lives, in which they are up against huge odds, in which platoons are buried alive and men are driven mad. Against that background, the officers Beumelburg depicts come across as model leaders: a major who can restore the confidence of others with his tactical planning, a captain who exudes "icy" logic, and a giant of a lieutenant, who has self-consciously made the battlefield his home and moves about it with the unfailing self-assurance of a phantom. Beumelburg's one foil for the valour of his protagonists is a martinet sergeant-major who becomes a figure of fun in much the same way as the equivalent character in Remarque's novel.[22] His common soldiers may experience moments of doubt, confusion, or indolence, but only in order to overcome them. Once committed to the task of storming strongly defended positions, they are characterized exclusively in terms of single-mindedness, the euphoria of assault, and a capacity for exemplary loyalty and self-denial. The figure of Bosemüller himself is presented as a dreamer, a bit of a poet, and a proud father, but also as a fearless fighter who, having visited his wife and new-born son, returns to his platoon with a renewed sense of commitment to its group ethos and common destiny. In Beumelburg's representation of the comradeship of battle, it is precisely that experience of group loyalty that paves the way for a new sense of national identity.

Verdun had been the site of the first attempt of the war, initiated by the German High Command early in 1916, to conduct a campaign of attrition. By concentrating a massed artillery and infantry assault on Verdun, General Falkenhayn hoped to break French morale by drawing increasing numbers of their troops through the "mill" of his bombardment in defence of a stronghold heavily imbued with symbolic significance for either nation. The battle had remained in public memory for the deployment of previously untried technological weapons—poison gas and flame-throwers, as well as large calibre guns—and for the huge numbers of casualties on either side.[23] For the Catholic author Josef Magnus Wehner, as for Beumelburg, Verdun provided a legendary setting, and in *Sieben vor Verdun* (Seven before Verdun, 1930) Wehner set out to write precisely the sort of epic vision of the war that Josef Ponten had anticipated in 1927. He did so by combining a sense of prophetic foreboding—five of his seven warriors are destined to meet a gruesome death—with the heavy inference of an opportunity lost. Wehner prefaces his narrative with an explicit critique of the reticence of Falkenhayn, precisely because his strategy had not made it a supreme objective to capture the citadel of Verdun; and he illustrates the point in the course of his narrative by describing the frustration of stormtroops who are ordered to hold their position rather than press home their advantage, or who advance so quickly that they come under fire from their own artillery. By way of contrast, Wehner stylizes the Crown Prince (who is otherwise remembered for having warily kept his distance from the front and for maintaining a lifestyle of leisured luxury during the war) into an embodiment of the will to achieve that objective by all-out assault, and presents the enormous sacrifice of lives at Verdun as an expression of the subliminal yearning of all Germans for unification into a greater German Reich. Wehner's characterization is still cruder than Beumelburg's. His infantrymen carry stereotyped traits of emotional and artistic sensibility, as well as valour, but they are above all presented as victims of a vicious and barbaric enemy (capable of bayoneting unarmed prisoners) as well as of the incompetence of an old-fashioned military leadership. Ennobled by its allusion to Aeschylus' *Seven against Thebes* and by religious intimations of life after death, Wehner's novel celebrates its dead heroes as lives sacrificed for the redemption of an ancient dream of pan-German unity (cf. Travers, 180–92).

Clearly, such novels as these are not simply commemorating the experiences of the past war. They belong to the retrospective cultivation of the legend of a 'front generation', and of the unified sense of purpose in what that generation had fought for, which came to play an important role in the defining of political allegiances in the early 1930s.[24] Another contributor to this vein of war writing was the National Socialist Hans Zöberlein, whose *Der Glaube an Deutschland* (Faith in Germany, 1931) appeared with a foreword by Hitler evoking the "heritage of the front". Zöberlein writes in the first person, and from the perspective of a simple soldier for whom allegiance to his group is never at issue. He describes the battles on the western front in which he participated between 1916 and 1918, and does so at great length, in order to emphasize the aspect of heroic endurance in that participation. His Nazi belief in German racial superiority is explicit in the text, his evocations of the enemy are frequently tinged with contempt, and he recalls the actions of revolutionaries and striking munitions workers as a direct betrayal of 'the front'. For Zöberlein, as for Beumelburg and Wehner, the front-line fighter is not simply sustained by his faith in the national cause, he is the true embodiment of that cause and the harbinger of a new spirit which will transcend decadent 'civilization'. But the most accomplished, as well as the most ambitious of these attempts to present the war as the source of a new nationalist mythology is Franz Schauwecker's *Aufbruch der Nation* (The Nation on the March, 1929).

Schauwecker, like Jünger, had emerged from the First World War with the conviction that the soldiers it had produced were a new breed characterized by the ultimate refinement of manly virtues.[25] What distinguishes his *Aufbruch der Nation* from the common run of nationalist war fiction of 1929–30 is the sense of historical context he gives to his narrative. In the process he also reveals more of the social pathology behind the nationalist mythology of the war than is immediately apparent from the other authors discussed so far. The persona through which Schauwecker reconstructs the learning experience of war is Albrecht Urach, a professional-class young man who breaks off his university studies in 1914, welcoming the outbreak of war as a liberation from the constraints of a peacetime society dominated by materialism, calculated careerism, and the intellectual discipline of academic specialization. At the front, Urach embraces the surrender of intellect in a double sense: he relishes the spontaneity of his own instinctual responses to danger, and he enjoys becoming blended into the collective, the mass of German fighting men. For Schauwecker, as for Jünger, the confrontation with horror is an important element in the forging of a new heroic identity, and he lingers over the description of the mass of pulped flesh left behind by an exploding shell. (Once more, the scene is Verdun.) But what matters above all for him is the stylization of front-line experience into a more authentic expression of 'life' than anything that can be found in the world of the civilian. The gulf of understanding between the front and home, which is described by many veterans of twentieth-century wars, is presented here as the difference between the fighters who have discovered their 'true nature' and the abstract patriotism of those who have no real appreciation of what the fighters are defending because they cannot share their experience. The nationalism Schauwecker evokes for readers in 1930 is one which is no longer defending the homeland of 1914, but projecting a new sense of collective identity for the future derived from the surrender of individuality and critical rationality on the battlefield. That is the sense that lies behind the paradoxical conclusion his protagonist reaches at the end of the novel, namely that Germany had to lose the war in order to discover itself as a nation. Through his sustained characterization of Urach and the depiction of his concrete experiences, Schauwecker lends substance to the otherwise abstract impressions conveyed by the anti-rational existentialism of radical right-wing thought in the period.[26]

    The radical nationalists did not have the field to themselves, indeed their sales figures before 1933 failed to rival those of the more successful of the anti-war novels.[27] We have already seen the sense in which Ludwig Renn's *Krieg* (1928) was attempting to counter the tendencies of a heroic recollection of war. In other specific ways, too, works published before Remarque's novel can be seen to be challenging the glorification of war. Siegfried Kracauer's *Ginster* (1928) contrives a particularly marked critical distance towards wartime events by adopting from the outset the perspective of a self-conscious outsider. The title-figure has acquired his nickname (the German word for gorse or broom) as a schoolboy. Whether he is witnessing attitudes at home or in the army, Ginster confronts wartime clichés with that sharpness of gaze that is characteristic of so much of the new writing of the later 1920s. He is a persistent sceptic towards patriotic sentiment, is bemused by the way military saluting becomes a conditioned reflex among his contemporaries, and notes with irony that Germany's internal political differences have been laid aside in favour of the ferocious denunciation of foreign nations. A prime example of the satirical edge to Kracauer's narrative is the section midway through the text in which Ginster responds to the news that his home town is planning to dedicate a cemetery to the honour of its fallen sons. As he notes, many of the dead would thus be better accommodated than when they were alive, but the bronze that might have gone into the creation of their monuments has gone into the manufacture of armaments, and in any case, "it was unfortunately not possible to return the soldiers in the desired state of completeness". Ernst Glaeser's *Jahrgang 1902* (Generation of 1902, 1928), which ranked among the best-sellers of 1928–9, presents the adult society of wartime through the eyes of an adolescent protagonist and exposes the operation of personal motives under the cloak of patriotic euphoria, although the focus of the narrative is on the emotional and psychological tensions at work in the youthful narrator himself. In *Soldat Suhren* (Soldier Suhren, 1927), Georg von der Vring also adopts something approaching a childlike perspective in his depiction of the process by which the war relentlessly destroys the personality and sensibility of his self-pitying poet-protagonist.[28] (Arnold Zweig's *Sergeant Grischa* novel, which also appeared a full year before *Im Westen nichts Neues*, will be discussed together with other works by Zweig at the end of this chapter.)

Remarque's example provided an impetus for more directed counter-attacks from the left. Theodor Plievier, who was to go on to write epic accounts of major battles of the Second World War as well as a documentary novel about Germany's political transition in 1918, was prompted to write *Des Kaisers Kulis* (The Kaiser's Coolies, 1929), which was hailed in the press as a "nautical Remarque". Based on a combination of research into the naval mutinies of 1917 and Plievier's own pre-war experience in the merchant navy, the work was too political for the Kiepenheuer Verlag, but not political enough for the Communist *Linkskurve*, whose reviewer would have liked to see the story extended to the insurrection of 1918–19 (cf. Travers, 111 f.). In so far as the work expresses a political orientation, it is that of the anarchist movement to which Plievier had remained close throughout the 1920s. This comes out particularly in his stylization of the stoker Albin Köbis, who was executed for an alleged infraction of military discipline in 1917, into an anarchist martyr committed to a negotiated peace without annexations.[29] *Des Kaisers Kulis* gives a graphic account of shipboard life, emphasizing the stark contrasts between the luxuries enjoyed by the officer class and the regime of repetitive drill and privation suffered by the ratings. Whatever the precise relationship between Plievier's plot and his historical sources, the work was received in the liberal and left-wing press as a welcome critique of militarism, and on the right as a defamation of the German fleet.

The most self-conscious reconstruction of wartime experience from a proletarian viewpoint is Adam Scharrer's *Vaterlandslose Gesellen* (1930), the title of which is a phrase coined by Wilhelm II in order to denounce the pre-war Social Democrats as an unpatriotic crew. Narrated in the first person, this heavily autobiographical novel tells the story of Hans Betzoldt, who is a factory worker in Hamburg at the start of the war, and someone accustomed to taking part in socialist anti-war demonstrations. As the newspapers begin to carry stories of Belgian and Cossack atrocities, Betzoldt is made increasingly aware of his political isolation in the circumstances of the moment, given that his own party has voted to support the war effort. His wartime experiences are divided between spells of work in munitions factories and service on both the western and the eastern front. In the army, as well as at home, he witnesses at first hand the perpetuation of social injustice behind the veneer of wartime solidarity. He particularly denounces the 'comradeship of the front' as a sham which is only maintained in the face of imminent death; the old class distinctions and privileges reassert themselves as soon as his company withdraws from the front line. Elucidating the familiar tag that the war would soon be forgotten if the combatants received equal pay and provisions, which is cited by Remarque and others, Scharrer identifies a hierarchical social structure as responsible for keeping men at their military tasks, particularly behind the lines.[30] But his narrator also testifies to the increasing depredation of skilled labour and the demoralization which sets in after the destructive campaigns of 1916. The narrative ends with his participation in the munitions strikes and revolutionary insurrection of 1918.

Edlef Koeppen's *Heeresbericht* (Higher Command) invited comparison with the technique of Karl Kraus when it appeared in 1930 because of the satirical use it makes of authentic wartime documents. In addition to quoting from military and governmental proclamations (the ruler of each combatant nation claims, for example, that he has God on his side), Koeppen opens up ironic perspectives on the perceptions of the war being cultivated among the general populace by reproducing circus and music-hall programmes which include representations of the sinking of the *Lusitania*, or of "our heroes in France" followed by a spectacular "final apotheosis". As the text progresses he also blurs the boundaries between history and fiction by including ostensibly documentary material relating to the young soldier who provides the personal storyline in the work, Adolf Reisiger. Reisiger shares certain biographical details with Koeppen himself. He enthusiastically volunteers for service in 1914 and advances to the rank of lieutenant, but is ultimately confined to a mental asylum after openly condemning the senselessness of the slaughter. As the narrative is constructed, Reisiger is the reader's naive witness to situations and military procedures, the purpose of which remains a mystery to him, but the effects of which he can observe at first hand. Assigned to an artillery battery, he experiences the men's relief as the tension and uncertainty of the anticipation of an attack give way to mechanical activity when they are ordered to give rapid fire. Seriously wounded, he learns of the gruesome routines of a field hospital, but can find no other rationale in his life than to return to his unit. As an observer in the front trenches, he witnesses the combination of mechanized routine and desperation required to repel a frontal infantry attack under covering artillery fire. Assigned to desk duties behind the lines, he discovers to his horror that, here too, he is directly implicated in the preparation for murderous acts. He becomes gradually initiated into the material realities behind such abstract notions as 'the front', 'the enemy', and 'the chain of command'. But what he never loses—and it is this that lends the work its emotional poignancy—is his sense of the value of individual lives sacrificed, something which is obscured by the statistics published in the daily bulletins.

Koeppen prefaces his text with a statement by the military censors of 1915 proscribing the publication of extensive accounts of the war by persons who are not in a position to assess the significance of specific events in their broader context. By confronting the personal (and necessarily limited) experiences of Reisiger with fragments of documentation which point to the broader historical context of those experiences, he achieves two ends: he demonstrates the need for any assessment of overall significance to take the form of active interpretation of the connections between fragmentary items of information, and he keeps alive the sense of glaring disparity between the official manipulation of information and the devastating effects of wartime experience at a personal level.[31] That is the sense in which Koeppen's novel makes a positive and substantial contribution to the task of constructive disillusionment with regard to the memorialization of the war in the context of its time. But as Herbert Bornebusch (p. 152) has noted, it is a mode of composition which presupposes "a (bourgeois) public of critically reflecting individuals" capable of recognizing the irrationalities that sustained the war and willing to respond to an appeal to their consciences on behalf of its victims. The effects of *Heeresbericht* depend chiefly on the pathos generated by the discrepancy between the suffering of individuals and the relentless momentum of the military machine which exacts that suffering.

Arnold Zweig, too, built on that sense of discrepancy between the suffering individual and the machinery of power, but his novels distinguish themselves from other German war fiction of the time by their extensive exploration of the social and political dimensions of the war. The means by which he conducts that exploration is the technique of omniscient narration cultivated by the major nineteenth-century European novelists. The elevated character of his literary style, particularly in the first of his war novels, *Der Streit um den Sergeanten Grischa* (The Case of Sergeant Grischa, 1927), did not endear him to critics of the time whose expectations were attuned to the public demand for 'sachlich' reportage.[32] But that novel was among those which enjoyed a printrun of over 100,000 within a very few years, and both in that work and in the volumes he added in the early 1930s Zweig conferred social and psychological depth on the depiction of situations which were part of the common experience of participants in the war.

Der Streit um den Sergeanten Grischa tells the story of a Russian prisoner of war who tries to make his way home in the spring of 1917, is captured using a false identity, and is ultimately shot as a spy even though his true identity (and implicit innocence) has been established. Zweig presents that story as a test of the moral probity of the German imperial regime. The exercise of arbitrary authority by the overall commander in occupied Eastern Europe, General Schieffenzahn (who is modelled on Ludendorff, and whose draconian approach to the issue is fuelled by his fear of Bolshevik infiltration), is opposed by an array of figures whose sense of a moral imperative makes them determined to defend Grischa to the limits of their capabilities. The group includes a divisional commander, General von Lychow, whose strong sense of traditional Prussian values makes him insistent that the exercise of power should have a demonstrable moral foundation, but also means that he will ultimately confine his actions in the matter to 'official channels'. The divisional legal officer under Lychow's command is a Jew by the name of Posnanski, whose ethical commitment to the case is expressly related to the strength of his belief in Mosaic law. Posnanski in his turn is assisted by a young intellectual, Werner Bertin, who is moved by a sense of fellow-feeling as well as moral outrage and who, on the eve of Grischa's execution, conceives the idea for a drama based on the affair which will present it as a danger sign overlooked by the authorities of the time.[33] An impulse which these three figures share is to interpret the case of Sergeant Grischa as a manifestation of hubris on the part of the regime, as the "writing on the wall" for imperial Germany. And that interest in the individual case as a sign of the times is extended in the text into interpretations along both Marxist and Talmudic lines by members of the local population: the fact that the narrated events reach their conclusion in November 1917 enables the text to carry discrete allusions to the Balfour Declaration, which promised the establishment of a Jewish homeland in Palestine, as well as to the Bolshevik Revolution in Russia (cf. Midgley 1980, 48–52).

The fact that Zweig's novel (in accordance with his own experiences of military service) focuses on the operation of authority behind the lines brings certain advantages when it comes to an extended depiction of the nation at war. He treats each phase in Grischa's story as an opportunity to highlight the position of particular individuals within the overall structure of authority. The power of command which keeps men at their posts and impels them, under certain circumstances, to carry out inhumane acts is sharply evoked at various stages of the action. The conflicting personal motives of the combatants as the third winter of the war comes to an end are initially intimated, not through the thoughts of Grischa himself, but through those of a German soldier on sentry duty. Fear of execution or transfer to the front weighs heavily in the minds of the ordinary soldiers who find themselves directly or indirectly implicated in Grischa's fate, particularly in the case of the man on guardhouse duty who forestalls a last-minute attempt to abduct the prisoner. The suppressed rage of those who have witnessed the horrendous sacrifice of lives in pursuit of national self-aggrandizement erupts, ironically, at an officers' party held to mark the third anniversary of the outbreak of war (more precisely, of the British declaration of war in response to the German violation of Belgian neutrality). But Zweig also investigates the mentality of those who exercise power and influence in the circumstances of the time. He explores the psychology of Schieffenzahn, a career soldier who, unusually in the German context, comes from a middle-class background, and who has cultivated the extraordinary intellectual skills required for the strategic conduct of the war as a way of compensating for his low social status and winning the favours of his aristocratic fellow-officers. He works into his text references to the socioeconomic dimension of the war, particularly through the figure of Albin Schilles (based on the industrialist Hugo Stinnes), a guest at Schieffenzahn's table who has read the fortune of the German war effort in the falling value of the mark on international exchanges, and is taking care to transfer his personal assets into foreign currency. As a counterpart to the manipulations of the capitalist, Zweig ends the work with an intimation of the growing power of skilled labour under the conditions of war: it is not so much the fact that an engine-driver dares to halt his train in order to pick up a straggler bound for home leave as the nature of the comments his act attracts that leaves the reader with a pronounced sense of the significance of the closing date of the novel, late November 1917.

These are the ways in which *Der Streit um den Sergeanten Grischa* lays bare both the operation of power structures which contribute to the perpetuation of the war and the factors which make those power structures vulnerable in the longer term. But Zweig also has a distinctive way of dealing with the question of how to 'make sense' of the war. The anti-war novels of Remarque and Renn have no answer to that question: for their protagonists it can only represent a dangerous distraction from the immediate task of surviving under the conditions of front-line fighting. Koeppen's protagonist, devastated by the evident senselessness of the slaughter he has witnessed, turns his back on the world for as long as the war lasts. The radical nationalists filled that vacuum of 'meaning' by stylizing the fighting itself into an expression of the struggle for life and collective (racial) dominance. One way in which Zweig addresses the issue is by extricating it from the context of the battlefield and presenting it as a personal and psychological adjustment to the prospect of death. He shows Grischa 'making sense' of his impending execution by relating it to his own complicity in the slaughter, embracing the Talionic principle that whoever has spilt blood shall have his blood spilt in turn. It is a principle that has been articulated for him by the pious Jewish carpenter alongside whom he finds himself working, articulated moreover in a context which emphasizes once more the symbolic significance of Grischa's death for the regime which kills him rather than for himself. But in his acts and his private thoughts, Grischa becomes identified in the closing stages of the novel with the willed acceptance of atonement, the forgiveness of iniquity, and the dream of a more equitable future life which might transcend the terrible divisions of a world at war. The other way in which Zweig addresses the issue is by presenting the war as an educative experience.

The two further volumes which Zweig published respectively in 1931 and 1935 focus on the personal development of Bertin between the outbreak of war and his transfer to the position of legal clerk that he occupies in *Der Streit um den Sergeanten Grischa*. In the first of these novels, *Junge Frau von 1914* (Young Woman of 1914), Bertin participates in that seemingly liberating experience shared by many young intellectuals of the combatant nations in 1914. He is swept along by the patriotic fervour of the moment, and unashamedly seeks to justify the war as a "tragic" confrontation in the terms of the philosophical idealism with which his education has imbued him: he would happily give orders to fire on the Strasbourg Minster if called upon to do so because that is what the situation seems to demand. He welcomes the physicality of military service and the sense of being incorporated into a social collective, although the detached narrating voice also brings out the irony of the mindless conditioning to which Bertin is subjected in the course of his military training. The abandonment of civilized restraint which this process encourages becomes apparent when he dominates and violates the fiancée with whom he has enjoyed a rich and mutually fulfilling relationship in the months preceding the war. Although the novel ends with the endorsement of that relationship in a highly conventional wedding, this is not before the consequences of Bertin's act have been extensively depicted, namely the humiliation and suffering of the fiancée, who is left alone to face the rigours of terminating an unwanted pregnancy and the potential menaces of a censorious society. Bertin's own path to self-recognition and critical self-awareness leads through the active service he experiences, not in the front line, but as part of that supportive machinery sustaining the ferocity of the fighting, once more, at Verdun.

In an essay he published in 1929, Zweig was insistent that the only appropriate way to depict the social behaviour of a nation at war was as an extension and intensification of peace-time conflicts.[34] That principle is especially well observed in *Erziehung vor Verdun* (Education before Verdun), where Bertin is brought face to face with the administrative dimension of the war, and with the opportunities it provides for petty bureaucrats to exercise the power and authority that is denied them in civilian life. He experiences this aspect directly when his humanitarian behaviour towards French prisoners exposes him to ridicule and victimization at the hands of his immediate superiors; and he experiences it indirectly when he becomes a witness to the way the Captain of a supply unit contrives to bring about a man's death under enemy fire in order to conceal the truth about his own corrupt administrative practices. In the figure of the dead man's brother, Lieutenant Kroysing, Zweig creates a character who embodies precisely those 'manly' attributes which the radical nationalists had emphasized and heroized in their novels.[35] Kroysing is an imposing presence and the epitome of a technocratic warrior who survives in the devastated landscape and subterranean fortifications of Verdun by adopting an unashamedly amoral view of life, and who thinks nothing of drawing the entire supply company concerned into the 'mill' of the Verdun battlefield in order to exact vengeance on his brother's killer. It is through the agency of Kroysing above all that Bertin is enabled to recognize that the prosecution of this war depends on the unleashing of primitive instincts on the one hand, and on the systematic exercise of social subjugation on the other. It is in the company of Kroysing's sappers that Bertin visits the front-line trenches. He approaches the occasion as a sensational escapade, and it provides him with a moment of participation in the exhilaration of destruction as he peeps over the breastwork to observe the artillery barrage. But in the dugout where the troops await the call to attack, Bertin makes a discovery which undermines the heroic expectations he has brought with him. What he recognizes, as the earth groans above him and the wan-faced infantrymen smoke their cigarettes, is that these men, too, are just carrying out orders. They are the "proletarians" of war. But the truth that hurts is that what determines the actions of men going into battle is ultimately no different from the oppressive command structure he knows from his own company (*Erziehung*, 245).

The 'education' Bertin experiences in the novel is neither consistent nor conclusive. He learns of the contradictory impulses lurking within himself, and within human nature generally; and he learns of the unbridled ruthlessness at work in the world around him; but at the end of the text he is still digesting his wartime experiences and working at the interpretation of them under the

fraught political circumstances of post-war Germany. In the course of showing what Bertin goes through during his months at Verdun, however, Zweig
explores the appeal of precisely those opposing tendencies we have seen to be
at work in the wave of war novels published in 1929–30. For as he struggles
to make sense of his situation and the iniquities he witnesses, Bertin is wooed
by competing ideological factions. To the right there is Kroysing, who remains
doggedly committed to the national struggle for dominance, and to the pursuit
of a personal position of dominance within that struggle. To the left there is a
pair of class-conscious workers in Bertin's company, Pahl and Lebehde, who
recognize in him a brand of intellectual who could with profit be recruited to
the class struggle. What Zweig depicts in *Erziehung vor Verdun*, in other words,
is more than the outcome of his own personal experiences as a soldier and a
writer. From the vantage point of his all-seeing narrator, he gives a critical ex-
position of the various standpoints from which the contest for the meaning of
the war had been fought during the crisis years of the Weimar Republic. Of all
the anti-war novelists of the Weimar period, it is Arnold Zweig who provides
the most effective conceivable refutation of the nationalist heroization of the
war because he makes the psychological and social dimensions of the behaviour of men at war transparent to the reader, and thus contributes directly and
self-critically to an understanding of the personal and ideological factors which
made the interpretation of the war such a sensitive issue after the event.

NOTES

1. Arnold Zweig, *Der Regenbogen* (Berlin: J. M. Spaeth, 1915), 307.
2. Paul Fussell, "Der Einfluß kultureller Paradigmen auf die literarische
Wiedergabe traumatischer Erfahrung", in Vondung, 175–87. Fussell's allegations of
Gothic fantasy in Remarque have been effectively refuted by Brian Murdoch (1993,
176 f.).
3. Both Georg von der Vring and Ludwig Renn, who wrote their war novels
in the early 1920s, had their works rejected by a succession of publishers before they
finally appeared in 1927 and 1928 respectively: see H.-H. Müller, 95, 186.
4. The same may be said of many prose works which appeared around the end
of the war, including Andreas Latzko, *Menschen im Krieg* (1917), Leonhard Frank,
Der Mensch ist gut (1918), Bernhard Kellermann, *Der 9. November* (1919), and Hermann Hesse, *Demian* (1919).
5. See Douglas Kellner's introduction to Ernst Friedrich, *War against War!*
(London: Journeyman, 1987).
6. Cf. U. Baron and H.-H. Müller, "Weltkriege und Kriegsromane",
Zeitschrift für Literaturwissenschaft und Linguistik, 19 (1989), Heft 75, 14–38 (18).
Wandt published his own account of his imprisonment under the title *Der Gefangene
von Potsdam* (The Prisoner of Potsdam) (Vienna: Agis, 1927).
7. Cf. Kaes, 145–7. A full documentation of the Becher case can be found
in F. Albrecht et al., *Aktionen, Bekenntnisse, Perspektiven* (Berlin: Aufbau, 1966),
65–127.

8. On the steady output of war novels in English during the 1920s, see Bruno Schultze, "Fiction and Truth: Politics and the War Novel", in Stanzel and Löschnigg, 297–311.

9. See Kevin Brownlow, *The War, the West, and the Wilderness* (London: Secker & Warburg, 1979), 176–90; Hans Sochaczewer, "Der verbotene Film 'The Big Parade'", *LW* 3, 18, 7.

10. See Rüter, 13–24; Bornebusch, 37–60; H.-H. Müller, 29–35. When the literary scholar Ernst Jirgal published a broad survey of war literature in 1931 under the suggestive title *Die Wiederkehr des Weltkrieges in der Literatur* (The Return of the World War in Literature), he listed well over 200 war books by German and Austrian authors which had appeared in the course of 1929 and 1930, whereas the titles which dated from before 1928 were predominantly by foreign authors.

11. Erich Maria Remarque, *"Soldat Suhren—Ringen an der Somme—Das Wäldchen 125—In Stahlgewittern—Das Frontbuch"*, *Sport im Bild* (Berlin) 1928, no. 12, 895–6. In addition to the evidence of textual borrowing from nationalist authors discovered by Rüter (pp. 47 ff.), it is conceivable that the section in Remarque's chapter 8 about Russian prisoners of war and the "Befehl" that makes them enemies of the German soldier was influenced by Zweig's *Grischa* novel, and that his description of injuries owes something to the publications of Ernst Friedrich or J. R. Becher.

12. Further details of the publication history of *Im Westen nichts Neues* are given by Eksteins (pp. 276 f.), but his account is marred by a curious animus against Remarque for aspects of the publicity for which he was clearly not responsible. The fullest study of the publication and subsequent reception of Remarque's novel is Johannes Brautzsch, "Untersuchungen über die Publikumswirksamkeit der Romane *Im Westen nichts Neues* und *Der Weg zurück* von Erich Maria Remarque vor 1933", Diss. Potsdam, 1969.

13. For a summary of the critical reception of Remarque's novel, see Gollbach, 293–305; H.-H. Müller, 66–93.

14. It is only at the very end of Renn's sequel, *Nachkrieg* (1930), that he makes his political allegiance explicit, but in the course of 1929 he had explained his sense of ideological purpose in the Communist journal *Die Linkskurve* (1, 1, 11–14 *et seq.*). Cf. Bornebusch, 91–7.

15. See Hans-Harald Müller, "'Herr Jünger thinks war a lovely business': On the Reception of Ernst Jünger's *In Stahlgewittern* in Germany and Britain before 1933", in Stanzel and Löschnigg, 327–39.

16. Erik Reger, *Kleine Schriften*, vol. i, 80.

17. *Der Kampf als inneres Erlebnis*, 12.

18. For a critical analysis of political decisionism, and of Jünger's contribution to it, see Christian Graf von Krockow, *Die Entscheidung: Eine Untersuchung über Ernst Jünger, Carl Schmitt, Martin Heidegger* (Stuttgart: Ferdinand Enke, 1958).

19. This sense that the fighting has become its own rationale is indeed made explicit in Jünger's original foreword to *In Stahlgewittern*: "Das war der deutsche Infanterist im Kriege. Gleichviel wofür er kämpfte, sein Kampf war übermenschlich."

20. Cf. Prümm 1974; H.-H. Müller, 283–95; Harro Segeberg, "Technikverwachsen: Zur Konstruktion des 'Arbeiter' bei Ernst Jünger", *Der Deutschunterricht*, 46 (1994), 3, 40–50. Jünger's political tract *Der Arbeiter* is discussed in Chapter 8, below.

21. Beumelburg's chronicle of the war, *Sperrfeuer um Deutschland*, which appeared in October 1929, rapidly became a best-seller: see Vogt-Praclik, 60 f.

22. The fact that this character goes by the name of Benzin, and that his bowel control regularly fails him when danger approaches, suggests that he is also conceived as a scurrilous parody of Renn, who is similarly frank about his spontaneous physiological responses to danger.

23. For a recent account in English of the thinking behind the battle of Verdun, and of its consequences, see Holger H. Herwig, *The First World War: Germany and Austria-Hungary 1914–1918* (London: Arnold, 1997), 179 ff.

24. For a discussion of the role this notion played in the politics of the Weimar Republic, see the final chapter of Bessel 1993.

25. In his memoir *Im Todesrachen* (1919), Schauwecker writes of the war veteran as "eine neue Art von Mensch, ein Mann in höchster Steigerung aller männlichen Eigenschaften": quoted in U. Baron and H.-H. Müller, "Weltkriege und Kriegsromane", *Zeitschrift für Literaturwissenschaft und Linguistik*, 19 (1989), 75, 14–38 (17).

26. The terms in which Schauwecker characterizes the pre-war civilian world strongly suggest that he is participating in that current of post-war anti-modernism which consciously repudiated Max Weber's characterization of modern society as inescapably "disenchanted" (cf. Bolz).

27. Kornelia Vogt-Praclik (p. 48) notes that the nationalist war novels generally lagged far behind the anti-war novels in terms of sales, and only achieved best-seller status in the course of the 1930s, with the aid of official promotion by the National Socialists. For indications of sales figures in particular instances, see Gollbach; H.-H. Müller.

28. Hans-Harald Müller (pp. 94–104) also discusses Alexander Moritz Frey's medical orderly novel *Die Pflasterkästen* and Karl Federn's *Hauptmann Latour*, as well as the works of Glaeser and von der Vring, as critical accounts of wartime service which were written before *Im Westen nichts Neues*, although they were not published until 1929.

29. Cf. Hans-Harald Müller's introduction to Theodor Plievier, *Der Kaiser ging, die Generäle blieben* (Hamburg: Konkret Literatur Verlag, 1979), 16. The background circumstances to the execution of Köbis are explained in F. L. Carsten, *War against War: British and German Radical Movements in the First World War* (London: Batsford, 1982.), 118 f.

30. "Es ist längst ausgemacht—auch für den stupidesten Sohn des Vaterlandes—, daß gleicher Lohn und gleiches Essen die Disziplin derer, die den Krieg als eine Badekur ansehen, so völlig zersetzen würde, daß der Krieg auch nicht einen Tag länger dauern würde. So ist denn überall dafür gesorgt, den hohen und weniger hohen Herren das Durchhalten zu ermöglichen." (*Gesellen*, 182.) For a full account of the political background to Scharrer's novel, see Hans-Harald Müller, "Kriegsroman und Republik: Historische Skizze mit einer Interpretation von Adam Scharrers proletarischem Antikriegsroman *Vaterlandslose Gesellen*", in M. Brauneck (ed.), *Der deutsche Roman im 20. Jahrhundert* (Bamberg: Buchner, 1976), 222–52.

31. For detailed discussion of the effects created in Koeppen's novel, see Brian Murdoch, "Documentation and Narrative: Edlef Koeppen's Heeresbericht and the Anti-War Novels of the Weimar Republic", *New German Studies*, 15 (1988–9), 1, 23–47; Jutta Vinzent, *Edlef Koeppen—Schriftsteller zwischen den Fronten* (Munich: iudicium, 1997), 114–43.

32. Ernst Jirgal (p. 222) described *Der Streit um den Sergeanten Grischa* as "arg literarisiert" by comparison with the other war novels he was reviewing; Kurt

Tucholsky (*GW* 5, 410) also objected to the contrived nobility of Zweig's style. On the relationship between Zweig's self-conception as a writer and the background culture of 'Neue Sachlichkeit', see David Midgley, "Schreiben um der Vergeistigung des Lebens willen: Das Verhältnis Arnold Zweigs zur Neuen Sachlichkeit", in D. Midgley et al., *Arnold Zweig-Poetik, Judentum und Politik* (Berne: Peter Lang, 1989), 97–110.

33. Zweig himself originally used the case as the basis for a drama in the immediate post-war years, and something of the Expressionist spirit of protest on behalf of a universalized conception of suffering humanity remains apparent in the novel.

34. Arnold Zweig, "Kriegsromane", *Die Weltbühne*, 16 Apr. 1929, 597–99.

35. For a detailed analysis of the characterization of Kroysing, see Hans-Harald Müller, "Militanter Pazifismus: Eine Interpretationsskizze zu Arnold Zweigs Roman *Erziehung vor Verdun*", *Weimarer Beiträge*, 36 (1990), 12, 1894–1914.

HILTON TIMS

All Quiet on the Western Front

Germany's bookshops were awash with novels and memoirs of the war and by the end of the decade there was a perception in the publishing business that the book-buying public was satiated. In those ten years following the armistice more than 200 war-related titles with respectable sales had appeared, twenty-four of them in the twelve months of 1927/28 alone.

Remarque made no attempt to submit his manuscript. His reluctance remains a mystery he never publicly clarified. Involved as he was in publishing, he may have discerned the prevailing trend, or merely regarded his book as a personal rite of exorcism, for private consumption only. More likely, his chronic lack of confidence prevented him from gauging the true measure of its merits and potential. Billy Wilder allegedly warned him while he was writing it that nobody would want to read 'a grim piece of anti-war realism' and urged him not to jeopardize his job.[1]

At least Jutta had faith in it. Remarque welcomed her comments as he wrote and passed the pages to her for correction and editing. There is evidence that he ultimately made her a gift of the original manuscript. When it mysteriously surfaced for auction at Sotheby's in London in 1995, the anonymous vendor was rumoured to have acquired it from Jutta's estate following her death twenty years earlier.

From *Erich Maria Remarque: The Last Romantic* by Hilton Tims, pp. 51–61, 217. © 2003 Hilton Tims.

The manuscript lay undisturbed in Remarque's desk drawer for six months until, pressed by Jutta and others, he decided to seek a publisher. Tactfully—though with negative consequences later—he discounted his own employers. The Hugenberg organization with its increasingly Fascist stance had no sympathy for anti-war sentiment. Only that year its owner Alfred Hugenberg had been elected leader of the German Nationalist People's Party and would throw in his lot with Hitler five years later.

Instead Remarque sent the manuscript to the Berlin house of S. Fischer Verlag, publisher of Thomas Mann's *Buddenbrooks*. Their reaction to it foreshadowed the impact it was to make. One of the firm's directors Bermann Fischer read the novel at a single sitting, passed it on to his brother and company chairman Samuel Fischer the following morning and urged him to read it at once and draw up a contract with the author without delay 'before any other publisher got sight of it'.[2]

The response of the all-powerful Samuel Fischer was more cautious. He hedged his bets by suggesting they would take the book if no other publisher was prepared to accept it, on the grounds that sales were questionable because nobody wanted to read about the war any more. Privately he felt the novel's style and content did not accord with the Fischer house-image of publishing 'literature' by established authors, a view he maintained even after its spectacular success.

If Remarque was disappointed, Bermann Fischer's enthusiasm compensated and spurred his determination. He promptly sent it to Propyläen Verlag, the book arm of the vast Ullstein publishing company. There have been many versions of the chain of circumstances that turned an unsolicited manuscript into one of the publishing sensations of the twentieth century—and just as many claimants to the honour of 'discovering' it. In a 1963 Berlin television interview—the only one he ever gave—Remarque recollected that a friend, Dr Fritz Meyer, who had contacts with Ullstein, asked his permission to show it to Fritz Ross, one of the firm's editors. 'That did it. I received a letter from Ullstein. Would I like to go along to them?' he said.

But other accounts suggest it was not quite so straightforward as that. Fritz Ross was certainly among the first to read it and recommend buying it. Where the legends diverge is in what happened next. According to some eye-witnesses, Ross's superiors did not share his enthusiasm and it lay, unheeded, on various readers' desks until the production manager Cyrill Soschka, leaving the office one evening, randomly took it home as something to read that night.

The next morning he thrust it to the editorial team, saying: 'I know war, and this is the real war, the truth about war, naked and honest.' And he vowed that if no publisher was prepared to take it, he would found his own company to publish it.

Not without some of Samuel Fischer's trepidation, Ullstein offered Remarque a contract, paying him 24,000 marks in monthly installments of 1,000 over two years, with a proviso that if the book failed to cover the publishing costs the author would be required to cover the deficit by submitting further writings without payment. Unofficially, however, they signalled a vote of confidence in the book's quality by not demanding any alterations or corrections.

Until the 1995 Sotheby's auction, it was generally believed that *All Quiet on the Western Front* had been originally published exactly as Remarque had written it. In fact the rediscovered autograph manuscript revealed a previously unsuspected opening chapter in which the protagonist Paul Bäumer described his home life and family.

Susan Wharton, Sotheby's specialist in continental manuscripts, said: 'This manuscript shows how it was originally envisaged ... his second thoughts were really much better than his first.'[3]

* * *

While the book was being typeset Cyrill Soschka had galley proofs pulled and sent to the editors of twelve newspapers and periodicals in the Ullstein group, inviting them to bid for serialization rights. Only one responded, Monty Jacobs, the editor of the leading liberal daily *Vossische Zeitung*, the favoured reading of Berlin intellectuals and affectionately known as *Tante Voss* (Auntie Voss). Pre-publication serialization was scheduled to start in November. Ullstein, sensing the expectation that was building up in a book they had been so hesitant about taking, began to plan a promotional campaign unprecedented in German publishing. From press advertising and street hoardings the public quickly became aware that a literary event was in the offing. Booksellers received publicity window displays.

As always, Remarque's reaction was ambivalent: elated by the growing excitement and the justification of his abilities as a writer, enjoying the putative aura of celebrity, yet dismayed by the reality of the media interest it was focusing on him personally. He would later claim to have had no preconception of the book's success.

He had already started work on a so-called sequel *The Road Back* (*Der Weg zurück*) dealing with the immediate post-war problems—loosely his own—that confronted the young veterans of the trenches returning to civilian life in a defeated homeland. But in the run-up to publication of *All Quiet on the Western Front* he found it impossible to write in Berlin and decided to return to Osnabrück. Not, however, to the family home. His advertisement for lodgings in an Osnabrück newspaper brought a reply from a Frau Maria

Hoberg, a well-to-do war widow, who would briefly assume the near-status of a surrogate mother to him.

The rooms she offered him in her house on Süsterstrasse were perfect for his writing requirements and state of mind: spacious, quiet, with a terrace fronting a peaceful garden which he could look out on from his desk in the window. Ironically, a neighbour on the opposite side of the street was one of the Vogt brothers who had employed him five years before. Leaving Jutta in Berlin, he moved in on a four-week rental—the period during which his book was appearing in *Vossische Zeitung*. Karla Hoberg, his landlady's daughter, later recalled that he seemed to be in a state of deep depression.

* * *

The circulation of *Vossische Zeitung* shot up threefold during the serialization. The installments carried the title *Nichts Neues im Westen*, a sardonically bitter annexation of the phrase used in official war bulletins meaning 'nothing new on the Western Front'. In the weeks preceding the book's publication Ullstein reversed the words to the sharper, more mellifluous *Im Westen nichts Neues*. The initial print-run was to be 30,000, unusually large for a 'first' novel by an unknown author, but as serialization continued, booksellers' orders increased to avalanche proportions. Another 20,000 copies were added to the run.[4]

Five days after the first instalment appeared Remarque was summarily fired from his job with *Sport im Bild*. Not only had he flouted Hugenberg house rules by failing to give them first refusal on the novel and serialization rights, but the tone of the book was anathema to the company's political ethos. It was a minor indignity in the context of what the future held for him.

By publication day, 31 January 1929, Germany was engulfed in *All Quiet* fever. No book until then in the history of literature had created such excitement. The first print run sold out on the first day. The mighty Ullstein, unable to cope with the printing demand, was forced to sub-contract six outside printers and ten book-binding firms. In the first few weeks sales were estimated at 20,000 a day. By the end of 1929 nearly 1 million copies had been sold in Germany alone.

The pattern, though less frenzied, was repeated abroad. *All Quiet on the Western Front* became an international publishing phenomenon, selling in its first year 300,000 in both Britain and France, 215,000 in the United States and proportionate numbers in smaller markets such as Spain, Italy and the Scandinavian countries.

In Germany, however, the book, unlike elsewhere, quickly became a literary and political *cause célèbre*, polarizing opinion and drawing aggressive critical fire from 'old school' nationalists and military traditionalists for what they perceived as its defeatist, inglorious depiction of German soldiery. Remarque had portrayed life in the trenches as he had observed it, in harsh realism and cryptic neo-documentary sentences. The style of writing, raw, stark and uncompromising, frequently shocking, was unprecedented in fiction. In many respects it prefigured the idiosyncratic style Ernest Hemingway was developing with his First World War novel *A Farewell to Arms* published nine months later in the United States. Even after seventy years Remarque's descriptions of battle and the physical and psychological wounds of its victims still convey a disturbing, piteous immediacy. It speaks for all common soldiers in all warfare and it was this universality that commended it to readers of all ranks and classes.

It was this aspect, too, which determined its impact among politically motivated critics as subversive. They came not only from the right wing. Leftists, too, found cause to attack the book and its author for failing to take an overtly political stance or challenge the social and economic agenda of the ruling classes.

Overwhelmed by the scale of his success, Remarque was totally unprepared for the ensuing controversy, the vehemence of the attrition directed at him personally, not least from fellow authors, impelled no doubt by professional jealousy. Count Harry Kessler noted in his diary the reaction of the left-wing pacifist Arnold Zweig, himself the author eighteen months earlier of a bestselling novel about the war, *Der Streit um den Sergeanten Grischa* (*The Case of Sergeant Grischa*). Zweig 'was venomous about Remarque', Kessler wrote, dismissing the upstart as 'slapdash' and 'a good amateur' who had failed to see the angle from which he should have tackled his subject.

In Remarque's depressive state of mind the onslaughts outweighed the approbations. 'When this success suddenly came upon me last spring, it led to an almost annihilating crisis,' he said later that year, 'I felt that I was finished, vanquished for good. I thought, whatever I write from now on, I would always remain the author of *All Quiet on the Western Front*. And I knew only too well, this book could just as well have been written by anyone else. It was no achievement of mine to have written it.'[5]

More than thirty years later, asked what his reaction had been, he would still remember: 'The feeling of unreality. It never left me ... I found it to be totally out of proportion. And that it was! Fortunately I always realized this and it prevented me from developing delusions of grandeur. On the contrary, I became insecure.'[6]

The Press clamoured to interview this new literary lion. Veterans organizations and literary groups inundated him with speaking invitations. Remarque went to ground. He had tried to co-operate all he could in Ullstein's pre-publication publicity but the resulting furore cowed him. There was to be no let-up in the months ahead, nor, indeed, were his perceived transgressions to be forgotten in the years to come. The author of the world's most famous anti-war novel was to be hounded by it, sometimes perilously and once shockingly, into middle age. His book became the catharsis of the contradictions in his character: the celebrity and material rewards he revelled in duelling with his lurking sense of inadequacy and instinct for anonymity. He recoiled from the invasion of privacy his sudden fame now triggered.

'I wrote *All Quiet on the Western Front* to escape from something that was depressing me, and when I had finished it I felt free of a dreadful weight of those experiences,' he told an English journalist. 'But now this new terror is hanging over me. I cannot escape from this interest in my own person. People ... manuscripts ... the postman ... everybody I meet, everywhere I go.'[7]

The National Socialists were on the rise and one of the most scurrilous attacks on him was mounted by Hitler's mouthpiece newspaper, the *Völkischer Beobachter*, averring that his real name was Kramer—Remark spelt backwards—and that he was Jewish. It was a myth he tried half-heartedly to correct but which would persist even into some of his obituaries nearly half a century later. Another, with marginally more basis in fact, was that he had never served on the front line and his depiction of conditions and attitudes of the troops there were a falsification.

This touched a nerve. 'The details of my book are real experiences in spite of all the rumours spread to the contrary, which I will not take the trouble to contradict. I was at the front long enough to have experienced personally just nearly all I have described,' he insisted.[8]

He was somewhat placated by the reviews from London when Putnam published A.W. Wheen's superlative English translation in March. Unconcerned with internecine German political polemic, the British Press judged the novel according to Remarque's own ethos, as a commentary on the ordinary soldier in combat, and hailed it as a masterpiece. 'It has marks of genius which transcend nationality. There are moments when the narrative rises to heights which place it in the company of the great,' observed *The Times*. 'So dreadful that it ought to be read by every man and woman who is doubtful about the need for preventing the Next War,' was the prescient advice of the Manchester *Evening News*.

The distinguished critic Herbert Read wrote: 'It is terrible, almost unendurable, in its realism and pathos. But it has swept like a gospel over Germany and must sweep over the whole world because it is the first completely satisfying expression in literature of the greatest event of our time. It is a superb piece of construction.' Demand for the book in Britain necessitated no fewer than eight reprints in the first month and more than twenty by the end of the year.

In the United States some passages in the Wheen translation, mainly referring to bodily functions, were deleted by the publishers Little, Brown to satisfy demands of a lucrative Book-of-the-Month Club contract which they would otherwise have lost. Although the novel has never been out of print in America, the cuts were not restored until 1978 for a new paperback edition.

The world's Press announced in July that the film rights had been sold to Hollywood for $40,000, a record sum for that time. 'A talking film based on the book is to be produced, partly in Germany and partly in Hollywood, in two versions, German and English,' reported *The Times*. In the event it was filmed entirely in California.

Carl Laemmle, the German-born head of Universal Studios, travelled to Berlin to clinch the deal with Ullstein and persuade Remarque to work on the screenplay. Legend has it that he also wanted the author to star in the film as Paul Bäumer. Remarque reluctantly agreed to prepare a treatment but after a half-hearted attempt abandoned the project.

* * *

A sequence of coincidences at this point produced a curious alignment of interests and frustrated cross-purposes between the authors of the two great classic works from opposing sides of the First World War.

On 21 January 1929, ten days before *All Quiet on the Western Front* was published in Germany, *Journey's End*, a play depicting a group of British army officers in the Flanders trenches, opened in London at the Savoy Theatre. Its author R.C. Sherriff, like Remarque, was unknown before overnight success thrust him into the public eye. So was its leading actor, Laurence Olivier. Robert Cedric Sherriff was two years older than his German counterpart but they shared a June birthday.

On its opening night, the play was acclaimed for its realism and anti-war credo, and mirrored the excitement in Germany over Remarque's novel. It was translated into every European language and through countless re-vivals since has established itself as one of the definitive English-language dramas of war.

Productions of *Journey's End* quickly followed throughout Europe and the United States. Remarque, in the first flush of celebrity, was approached to adapt it for the German stage under the title *Die andere Seit* (*The Other Side*) even though he did not speak or read English. He declined. 'I read it and felt it agreed completely with my own attitude,' he explained, 'But I don't want to be identified with the war and books and plays the war has brought about. I can't escape from my own book.'[9]

Meanwhile Sherriff, in New York for the July premiere of his play, was being approached to write the screenplay for *All Quiet on the Western Front*. Following Remarque's aborted effort, he was the first writer to be considered.

'It was a tempting offer ... what lured me was the magic spell of Hollywood, a spell I'd been under since my schooldays,' he wrote in his autobiography,

> But there was something pulling harder in a different direction. I was longing to get home. Before I'd sailed we had decided to give the house a face-lift. It was a big old place and we'd never had much to spend on it, but now I'd given my mother a free hand, and all the money she needed ... I had promised to be home in three weeks and my mother had promised to have everything done and ready for my return. It would be a bitter disappointment for her if I cabled to say I was going to Hollywood instead. So I sent my regrets to Carl Laemmle and booked a passage on the *Mauretania*, sailing the following night.[10]

Two years later he would finally be lured to Hollywood to work on the screenplay of Remarque's *The Road Back*, launching his distinguished career there as a screenwriter.

The two writers were never to meet or communicate with each other, although Sherriff was in Berlin for the German premiere of *Die andere Seit* in the summer of 1929. Years later Remarque hinted that he had regretted turning down the offer to adapt *Journey's End*. 'Had I done it at that time, I would probably have written further theatre pieces, for the theatre fascinates me,' he admitted. So why didn't he? 'Because I thought to rebel. From all sides I was being abused for doing this and that to the poor German soldier. I didn't want to make a business of the war and write about it a second time. Quite stupid!'[11]

Over the years he would attempt and abandon a number of plays before finally making it to the Berlin stage with *Die letzte Station* in 1956.

* * *

As income from *All Quiet on the Western Front* soared to unimagined levels, a grateful Ullstein presented Remarque with a bonus—a grey six-cylinder Lancia Cabriolet convertible. Nothing could have pleased him more. It was a dream car. He called it Puma, a pet-name he would recycle in the future.

At Ullstein's insistence he reluctantly submitted himself to a number of Press interviews during the summer months, but avoiding public scrutiny took on a near-paranoid urgency for him. 'I think I should like to disappear, grow a beard and begin a new kind of existence altogether,' he told a journalist that summer.[12] Cars, especially fast cars like the Lancia, became even more central to his life, subconsciously representing, perhaps, a speedy means of escape. 'I spend my free time trying out cars. That's something I do understand. Cars and dogs and fish . . .'[13] He had privileged access to the Avus race-track where he could test-drive various models and where in early 1930 he survived the first of many serious motoring accidents.

In the weeks following publication he and Jutta fled to Davos in Switzerland where she frequently underwent treatment for her tubercular condition. Later he picked up his old friend Georg Middendorf in Osnabrück for an away-from-it-all driving tour through France from Brittany to the Pyrenees, covering 3,750 miles.

But there was no escape from the shockwaves that his book continued to create. It was banned in Italy, already a Fascist dictatorship under Mussolini. In August the Austrian Minister of Defence ordered its removal from all army libraries and 'prohibit[ed] its dissemination anywhere within the precincts of a cantonment'.

Another flurry of controversy followed reports in September that Remarque was to be nominated for the Nobel Prize, with some confusion as to whether it would be in the categories of Literature or Peace. The German Officers' Union promptly announced that it had 'addressed to the Nobel Prize committee an indignant protest against what can only be regarded as an insult to the Army', adding that the book was 'a feeble attempt to misrepresent and discourage the heroic struggle of the united German stock during four years of war.'[14]

Remarque found this rebuke particularly wounding. '[It] makes it difficult for me to imagine how any German officer can really have read into my book an accusation against the heroic spirit Germany showed,' he said. 'The war certainly gave us enough heroes and the only officer I mention is a splendid one who sacrificed his life for his men.'[15]

Like most Germans, he was unaware that the armed forces (*Wehrmacht*), and especially the new younger element of the officer class, was being subtly infiltrated by National Socialist ideology. Such was official concern that General Wilhelm Groener, the Minister of Defence, found it necessary in January 1930 to issue an order of the day. The Nazis, it said, were greedy for power. 'They therefore woo the *Wehrmacht*. In order to use it for the political aims of their party, they attempt to dazzle us [into believing] that the National Socialists alone represent the truly national power.' Soldiers were enjoined to refrain from politics and remain 'aloof from all party strife'.[16]

Far from enjoying his success, Remarque was becoming increasingly soured by it. 'I know nothing of politics and I can only say that the atmosphere of political recrimination which is that of Germany today is hateful to me.'[17]

Notes

1. Zolotow, *op. cit.*

2. P. de Mendelssohn, *S. Fischer und sein Verlag*, cited in Barker and Last.

3. *Daily Telegraph*, London, 30 October 1995.

4. Owen, *op. cit.*

5. EMR interview with *Kölnische Zeitung*, 6 November 1929, cited in Owen, *op. cit.*

6 EMR interview in *Die Welt*, 31 March 1966, cited in Barker and Last, *op. cit.*

7. EMR interview in the *Observer*, *op. cit.*

8. *Ibid.*

9. *Ibid.*

10. R.C. Sherriff, *No Leading Lady.*

11. Television interview, *Das Profil*, Berlin, 1963, transcribed in *Ein militanter Pazifist.*

12. EMR interview in the *Observer*, *op. cit.*

13. *Ibid.*

14. *The Times*, London, 16 September 1929.

15. *The Observer*, *op. cit.*

16. William L. Shirer, *The Rise and Fall of the Third Reich.*

17. *The Observer*, *op. cit.*

HELMUTH KIESEL

Introduction

This volume 68 of The German Library in 100 Volumes presents two novels: Erich Maria Remarque's *Im Westen Nichts Neues* (*All Quiet on the Western Front*, 1929) and a generous selection from Joseph Roth's *Hiob* (*Job*, 1930).

Written during the last years of the Weimar Republic, they reflect widely discussed issues and urgent problems of that age. In particular, the significance of the First World War to the front line troops, who were to play an important part in the Weimar Republic; and further, the problem of Jewish identity in a newly mobilized society with dreams of a modern nationalism. Both novels were extremely successful and were widely distributed in Germany and elsewhere. Both novels are examples of a more traditional narrative style than that of the avant-garde approach used so effectively by Alfred Döblin in *Berlin Alexanderplatz* (1929), and take a prominent and important place in modern German literature.

Erich Maria Remarque—whose name was in fact Erich Paul Remark—was born June 22, 1898, the son of a bookbinder. On completing basic schooling, he attended the Catholic Teacher Training Institution in Osnabrück. Two years after the beginning of World War I, in November 1916, he was called up and began his military service with hard training in a camp in the Luneburg Heath. In the beginning of June 1917, his Unit was

From Erich Maria Remarque, *All Quiet on the Western Front* and Joseph Roth, *Job: The Story of a Simple Man*, Helmuth Kiesel, ed., pp. vii–xvi. © 2004 by Helmuth Kiesel and the Continuum International Publishing Group.

commanded to undertake trench duties on the Western Front, at Flanders. Although frequently under fire, the Unit was not involved in dangerous battles. The trench warfare and assaults described in *All Quiet on the Western Front* were not, therefore, part of the author's immediate experience. Remarque's unit was mobilized against the attacking English forces toward the end of July 1917, but Remarque was seriously wounded early in the advance. He spent a long period in the Field Hospital, and was finally released to clerical duties in the Hospital offices. After the War, Remarque worked for two years as an advertising copywriter for a rubber factory in Hannover. He then worked as a Sports Editor in Berlin.

Remarque had begun to gather material for a book during the war, but it was not until the period 1927–1928 that he could begin to work on it. It may be that Remarque needed this ten-year gestation to develop the necessary writing skills. It may also be that the approaching ten-year anniversary of the War was stirring public memories. In 1928 and 1929, a number of books appeared that dealt with the Great War, as it was then known, and which considered the War in the light of the political developments that had followed it.

This distance is equally fundamental to Remarque's novel. On the one hand, *All Quiet on the Western Front* is a report of experiences, speaking of immediacies, and recounted throughout in the present tense. However, this novel is also unmistakably the speech of a man who had become aware of how much he, and those of his generation who had survived, had been affected by the trauma of the Great War. In suffering from and practicing brutal violence, they had been separated from the normal processes of individual development, and had become estranged from civilian life. *All Quiet on the Western Front* is, not least, a novel of those age groups which, during the '20s, became what the American writer Gertrude Stein referred to as the "Lost Generation."

The hero and storyteller of this novel does not have to continue the tale, having fallen in the last weeks of the War—as is made clear in the use of the preterit tense in the last paragraph. For him, though, the awareness of having been spoiled by war for "normal" life had already crystallized during the War itself.

All Quiet on the Western Front describes the War from the viewpoint of the so-called simple soldier, the *Muschkoten*, as the Infantry was then known. It is described by its hero, Paul Bäumer, a man of good education with literary aspirations. He is absorbed by the colorful mix of comrades in his Unit, and brings their collective experiences to life. Not for nothing does the novel begin with the pronoun "we." This "we" is a group of eight Infantrymen who develop a particularly close relationship born of the time shared on the Front, of which this story reports. The group consists of four high school students, a fitter and turner, a turf-cutter, a farmer, and a forty-year-old soldier of wide experience and considerable insight. Of course, we are best informed about Paul Bäumer, the storyteller. We also hear from him, though, of the experiences and sufferings of his comrades, of the dangers, difficulties, losses, hardships, and the astonishing events they underwent, and of their reactions, based on character and on social and occupational backgrounds. It was apparently Remarque's wish to display as broad as possible a spectrum of typical situations and behavior patterns.

According to a *New York Times* Book Review from January 27, 1946, he described his novel, with a certain understatement, as being "simply a collection of the best stories I told, and that my friends told, as we sat over drinks and relived the War." Remarque, then, derived the novel from a series of stories and episodes. These he recounts with masterly control of facet, to produce a scintillating, precise account of the War.

We become acquainted with the group when, after weeks at the Front, they have withdrawn to the rear and are attempting to recuperate. We are observers as they dig trenches, come under artillery fire, are wreathed in gas vapors, and are plagued by lice and rats. We live through offensive and counter-offensive with them. Hear, as they become death-seeking animals. We endure with the storyteller, who can only survive by stabbing a French soldier seeking shelter in the same bomb-crater to death. We see those who, frenzied by war, begin to rebel, perhaps even run away, probably to later be shot as deserters. We read also of how easy life in the rear can be—especially when one can come by piglets, or a goose. Particularly, too, when a couple of hungry Frenchwomen, for the sake of a little bread and sausage from the debilitated soldiers' rations, give them a good time. We even join the protagonist on home leave—but, of course, merely to see how mothers fear and grieve. We are with him at the end, in the military hospital, to see in detail what weapons and military medicine do to people.

The first half of the novel (up to the beginning of the home leave) is marked by the fatalistic, sarcastic heroism the soldiers adopt as a shield against the horrors to which they are exposed. The second half is filled with descriptions of suffering and grievance. More and more, the War loses the initial adventurous overtones. But such moments still occur in the military hospital—above all, happiness is found in comradeship. So from beginning to end in this description of the war, its horrors of destruction and complexities of suffering are set against such moments of trial and proven friendship, of good luck and survival. This juxtaposition is in part responsible for the extraordinary force of Remarque's novel. The effect is not only forbidding; it also shows war as something which can be endured, and which offers a unique experience in life. This accords with the hero's acceptance, without regret, of a return to the Front, from home leave or from the military hospital. He is prepared to share his comrades' fate, and is an admirer to the end of those

"Magnificent Officers of the Front Line" who "in every difficult situation are in the vanguard" and who sweep the troops along with them.

In brief, the novel allows for an identification with the heroism that ignores pain and death—as does the novel's hero, who naturally expects to survive. That he dies in the end—apparently painlessly, undramatically—carries the sense of the pacifist message Remarque wished to express. It seems forced, however, and not readily believable.

On completing the manuscript, which is said to have taken only six weeks, Remarque offered it to Germany's then most reputable publisher, Samuel Fischer. For unknown reasons, the script was rejected, it was then accepted by Ullstein, initially for publication in the widely read "Vossische Zeitung." The series began on November 10, 1928, ten years to the day of the Kaiser's abdication, which had made possible the end of the Great War, to which the book now called attention.

Propyläen Publishers, a branch of Ullstein, released the book at the end of January 1929. An extraordinary number were sold in a short time: 600,000 copies in the first three months, and over a million within half a year. This became an enduring success: *All Quiet on the Western Front* was reprinted constantly, and in an increasing number of languages, until the rise to power of National Socialism. Today the novel appears in some fifty languages, and between fifteen and twenty million copies have been sold. It qualifies as the most successful German-language book of the twentieth century.

This success is no doubt also due in part to Lewis Milestone's melodramatic film version. Produced in Hollywood in 1930, it drew crowds all around the world, provoked debate, and was banned in some places. Fierce argument accompanied the film, particularly in Germany. The German premiere, in a renowned cinema in Berlin, was bombed by a group of Nazis, led by Goebbels, later the Minister of Propaganda. This occurred during other attempts to show the film, until December 12, when, by order of the Reichstag, the film was banned.

Early in 1933, the National Socialists ordered a large-scale "cleansing" of Germany's libraries. *All Quiet on the Western Front* belonged to the list of banned books, which, on the tenth of May, were ritually burned in all German Universities. As reasons were given that the book exercised "literary betrayal of the soldiers of the World War" and the danger the book posed to "the education of the people in the spirit of military valor." By this time, Remarque was already out of the country—he had left Germany a few days before Hitler took power. Until 1939, he lived mainly close to Ascona, in Italy, and in Paris. In 1939 he moved to the United States. He died on September 25, 1970, in Locarno, Switzerland.

* * *

Like Erich Maria Remarque, so can Joseph Roth be characterized as a member of the so-called Lost Generation. Often, and with justice, Roth said that World War I had cost him his homeland and turned him into a nomad. He tried to turn this loss to advantage, in that he lead a European existence and adopted cosmopolitan manners; but the constant pain of his loss is clearly reflected in his most famous and important novels, in *Hiob* and *Radetzkymarsch*.

(Moses) Joseph Roth was born on September 2, 1894, in Brody. Then a middle-sized merchant township marked by a strong Jewish influence, it lies about a hundred kilometers east of Lemberg, and today belongs to the Ukraine. At the time of Roth's birth, Brody was part of the Kingdom of Galizia and Lodomeria. This was the most easterly province of the multi-cultural State of Austria, which was a result of the first division of Poland in 1772.

Roth's father Nachum was a Jewish grain handler, who, before his son was born, fell mentally ill during a business trip and spent the rest of his life in care. Thus, Roth grew up without a father. After initial study at an enlightened Jewish school, he was able, thanks to his mother's wealthy family, to attend the public Gymnasium in Brody. He subsequently studied Germanistics, in the Winter Semester of 1913–14 in Lemberg, and beginning in the Summer Semester of 1914 in Vienna. In September 1916, Roth was called up. After basic training, he was commanded to serve in Lemberg—not in a fighting Unit, however, but as part of the Press Service.

After the war he returned to Vienna and began to work as a freelance journalist. In 1920 he moved to Berlin, where he worked on a succession of respected newspapers. These included the liberal *Berliner Tageblatt*, and the equally liberal *Prager Tagblatt*. Also, the social democratic newspapers *Vorwärts* (Berlin) and *Arbeiterzeitung* (Vienna) in 1923, and then the most respected of German newspapers, *Frankfurter Zeitung*. Roth wrote not only feature articles, but also modern novels. The topical contents and short chapters made these ideal for serialization in daily newspapers, and as such paid good fees.

In his early years as a journalist he presented a Socialist viewpoint, and made his stand clear by calling himself "Joseph the Red." It is to be noted that Roth's socialism was purely a matter of emotion, derived from the observation of daily life and not bound by theory or Party dogma. Subsequent to the mid-'20s, this socialist tendency was overlaid by a development of socially critical and conservative ideas, which were fed by memories of the Austrian Monarchy, and by an inclination to Catholicism as the tie between the conservative and the cosmopolitan. In Chapter 13 of *Radetzkymarsch*, the famous description of a Viennese Corpus Christi procession gives this new attitude a concentrated aesthetic expression.

Roth never forgot his Jewish origins; nor did he overlook the problems of Jewish existence in a nationalistic Europe. Indeed, he dedicated a series of essays reflecting the situation of Jews in the European capitals of Vienna, Berlin, and Paris, in America, and in the Soviet Union. These were published in book form as *The Wandering Jew*. The title was not merely descriptive, but also a statement of policy. Roth saw Jewish existence as being a matter of constant migration.

Whilst understanding the Zionist longing for a Jewish Homeland in Palestina, nonetheless to him it seemed to be mistaken, given historic persecution and current Pogroms, as being founded on the same concept of a nation-state as had already brought much suffering to Europe and indeed to the world. As he put it in *The Wandering Jew*, "The Epoch of Jewish Nationalism has passed for the Jews. Do they really seek this again? Do they really envy the European States?"

From 1925 on, Roth traveled extensively throughout France (1925), the Soviet Union (1926), Albania (1927), Poland, and Italy (1928), and sent detailed reports to the *Frankfurter Zeitung*. Roth had married in 1922. In 1928, his wife was diagnosed as schizophrenic, and had to be consigned to a clinic for nervous diseases. In the following years, Roth was particularly productive as a novelist, and with *Hiob* (1930) and *Radetzkymarsch* (1932) he reached the apex of his abilities. At the same time, his life became much more complicated. Roth lived with a sequence of different women, and had to take care of their financial needs. His work did not always provide him with the means to do so.

In 1933, immediately after Hitler took power, he left Germany, and lived by choice in a small Parisian hotel. He had been an enthusiastic drinker in the '20s, and now developed into a serious alcoholic, apparently wishing to drink himself to death.

He was in the Parisian café Tournon on May 23, 1929, when he learned of the suicide of the German-Jewish revolutionary and poet, Ernst Toller. In despair over the political situation, Toller had hanged himself in New York the day before. At this, Roth broke down, and was taken to the Hospital Neckar, where he died four days later, on May 27, 1939. On May 30, Joseph Roth was buried in the "Thiais" Cemetery. It is said that an altercation occurred at the graveside between Austrian Monarchists and communist writers, as well as between Jews and Catholics, as each of these groups claimed Roth to have been exclusively one of their own.

Roth's novel, *Hiob* is the story of the sufferings of an average but good Jewish citizen at the time of World War I. There are probably two motivating factors which led to the novel. In the first instance, after 1928, the negative affect on Roth's life of his wife's sickness. In the second, the knowledge, reflected in *The Wandering Jew*, of the lack of any really secure place, in the modern world of that time, for a traditional Jewish lifestyle.

The "simple man" of whom the story tells is a pious and God-fearing Jew living with his family in a Wolhynish village, on the border of Czarist Russia and Galizia-Austria. Mendel Singer—for such is his name—is a teacher, and has a family: his wife Deborah, two strong sons, called Joseph and Schemarjah, and a very pretty daughter called Mirjam. The youngest child, another son called Menuchim, has been marked from birth by a disease that prevents both physical and mental development.

Mendel rejects treatment in a Russian hospital suggested by the district doctor, as he does not want his son associating with Russian children, and eating non-kosher food. So it is that Menuchim remains an apathetic gnome, with a huge head, a skinny body, and bent limbs, unable to control himself, or to talk. It is impossible for Mendel to protect his other children from the influence of their Russian environment. It is not necessary at this point to give a detailed account of how this influence is manifested; suffice it to say that one of the sons has cause to escape across the border and emigrate to America. Mendel fears that his family's Jewish identity will be completely lost under the influence of Russian society. Several years later, leaving the sickly Menuchim behind, he and the rest of the family follow his son.

Of course, America isn't the Promised Land either. Hardly has Mendel settled in New York that he realizes he has not found Canaan, but simply exchanged one form of Egypt for another, and is living still in a Diaspora that threatens his identity. This situation is made more acute by the First World War, which causes the deaths, one after the other, of Mendel's immigrant family, and brings him, parallel to the biblical Job, into dispute with his God. Indeed, Mendel goes one step further than Job. He turns away from God, and begins, in demonstration of his stance, to eat pork. Mendel's life now takes a turn for the better. Unexpectedly, Menuchim, left behind in Russia, appears in New York, giving his father the feeling that God does still work miracles and that Jewish life will endure.

This wondrous end to Roth's *Hiob* was the cause of several extremes in critical reviews. Some saw the happy ending as being completely unrealistic, and therefore kitsch and illegitimate. As an allegory of traditional Jewry in a modern mobile society, it was held to gloss over the inherent pressure for the surrender of Jewish lifestyle, and to ignore the exercise of persecution.

Others understood the conclusion to be Utopian, the sense and justice of it lying precisely in the way in which the difference between the wish for an undisturbed Jewish existence and the reality of the Diaspora is shown. This version is held to be verified by the use Roth makes of the legendary Utopian and the ironically distanced tones with which he tells the story of his Hiob.

Still others saw in *Hiob* a song of praise for the dangerous obstinacy of those Jews who let nothing, neither the threats of Nationalism nor the temptations of modern life, distract them from the observance of the rites of their fathers and who did so in the one place where only the Jews, grown wise politically, could, according to Roth, inhabit: the Diaspora. The novel makes it clear that to achieve this can be self-destructive. Whether this achievement is possible and purposeful is not clearly stated. Then, looked at closely, Mendel Singer has failed at almost all points. He loses not only his homeland, but also his profession as a teacher, his family, and his faith, to which last he returns only at the very end.

Furthermore, this happy end should not distract from the point that his son Menuchim is an exponent of a different way of Jewish life. He is not only the product of traditional Jewry, but also of just that modern medical treatment from which his father, in Czarist Russia, had tried to protect him. In addition, he had received an education in music in the Czarist Army. The international musician, as he arrives in New York and meets his father, leads a very different life from that of the small Wolhynish village schoolmaster, Mendel Singer.

An American edition of *Hiob* appeared in 1931, an English edition in 1933, and other translations followed. A stage version was produced in Paris in 1939, and, also in the thirties, a film was produced in Hollywood. In this version, the story was set in Catholic South Tyrol and of the Jewish teacher was made a Catholic sacristan. . . .

* * *

. . . Remarque and Roth . . . are the subjects of a number of studies, which have been used for this preface but to which only inadequate justice could be done here. For additional detail of the authors and their works, reference should be made to three extensive biographies:

Wilhelm von Sternburg: *"Als wäre alles das letzte Mal": Erich Maria Remarque: eine Biographie*. Köln: Kiepenheuer & Witsch, 1998 (und 2000 als KiWi-Pocket-book).

David Bronsen: *Joseph Roth: eine Biographie*. Köln: Kiepenheuer & Witsch, 1974 (und 1993 als KiWi-Pocket-book mit gekürztem Text).

Helmuth Nürnberger: *Joseph Roth in Selbstzeugnissen und Bilddokumenten*. Reinbek bei Hamburg: Rowohlt, 1981 (9. Auflage 1999).

Finally, there is a new edition of *All Quiet on the Western Front* planned for 2004, with different text versions and a detailed history of its conception and its controversial early reception: Thomas F. Schneider: *Erich Maria Remarques Roman "Im Westen nichts Neues": Text, Edition, Entstehung, Distribution und Rezeption (1928–1930)*. Tübingen: Niemeyer, 2004.

BRIAN MURDOCH

From the Frog's Perspective:
Im Westen nichts Neues
and Der Weg zurück

T he title of this chapter, which considers Remarque's two novels of the
First World War, is a literal translation of the German phrase *aus der
Froschperspektive*, which is usually translated as "worm's eye view," although
frogs, unlike worms, have harsh voices as well as eyes. Remarque treated
the First World War in both novels from this perspective, and although the
second of them is set for the most part after the cessation of hostilities, the
war informs it so completely that *Der Weg zurück* (*The Road Back*), is not
simply a sequel to *Im Westen nichts Neues* (*All Quiet on the Western Front*), but
almost a second part of its famous predecessor.[1]

Im Westen nichts Neues made its first appearance in serial form in Germany in 1928, and then, with a great deal of sometimes not entirely truthful
publicity (its composition and the revision process had taken longer than was
claimed), in a slightly changed and expanded book version in January 1929.
It sold a million copies by 1930,[2] was translated into an enormous number
of languages,[3] and provoked personal attacks, parodies, and imitations. It
remains a bestseller and has been filmed twice, both times in English, and
the first version remains one of the classics of early sound cinema. When it
was first shown in Berlin in 1930 it was famously disrupted, on the orders of
Goebbels, by Nazi activists releasing mice.[4] Remarque was later condemned

From *The Novels of Erich Maria Remarque: Sparks of Life* by Brian Murdoch, pp. 31–65.
© 2006 Brian Murdoch.

by the Nazis for "betraying the front-line soldier" and his novel was publicly burned in May 1933.[5]

The popularity of the novel seems sometimes to have baffled the critics. In 1985, for example, Jost Hermand wrote a piece with the revealing title "Versuch, den Erfolg von Erich Maria Remarques *Im Westen nichts Neues* zu verstehen" (An attempt to understand the success of Erich Maria Remarque's *Im Westen nichts Neues*), while a few years earlier, Alan Bance, having noted that "perhaps because of its phenomenal commercial success, it has received relatively little serious discussion," went on to state that "no one would want to claim for the novel a place in the ranks of first-class literature." But there precisely *is* a case for placing the work in the category of first-class literature. There is no critical law defining a great work as one that can be read or understood only by an intellectual elite, and the focus on the work as a commercial phenomenon has often distracted from proper considerations of style, structure, and content.[6]

Some basic misunderstandings were associated with *Im Westen nichts Neues* from the start. Some of the first critics assumed somewhat unreasonably (given the death of the narrator) that Remarque was completely identifiable with Paul Bäumer.[7] Of the literary responses—many of which appeared with covers imitating Remarque's novel—Klietmann's *Im Westen wohl was Neues* (Not Quiet on the Western Front) is the most extreme example of a parodistic attack (carrying the heading *Contra Remarque*), with Nickl's *"Im Westen nichts Neues" and sein wahrer Sinn* (The True Meaning of "All Quiet on the Western Front") the most nationalistic and anti-Semitic in its attack on the publisher, Ullstein. Otto's *Im Osten nichts Neues* (All Quiet on the Eastern Front) is a simple imitation, and *Vor Troja nichts Neues* (All Quiet on the Trojan Front) by "Emil Marius Requark" a not uninventive parody that manages one or two telling blows against the marketing strategy adopted for the work.[8] The influence of Remarque's novel was enormous, not only in German, as is clear even from the novel title *Not so Quiet . . .* by Evadne Price, for example, writing as Helen Zenna Smith in 1930.[9]

In 1931 Remarque published *Der Weg zurück*. The first war novel is set in 1917 and 1918, and its sequel begins with a prologue set immediately after, and referring to, the death of the narrator of *Im Westen nichts Neues* in October 1918. The main part takes place in 1919, immediately following the last month of the war, although an epilogue takes us briefly into 1920. The work is set, then, in the period of the establishment of the Weimar Republic.[10] The new first-person narrator is so similar to that of the first novel in name, background, and attitude that he could be Bäumer brought back to life, but this reinforces the point that the young soldiers of the First World War were both representative *and* individual. *Der Weg zurück* did not meet with the same enthusiasm as the first war novel, although it too was widely translated and also filmed.

Both novels are part of an international body of literature concerned with the war and produced in the late 1920s and early 1930s. The universality of the experience of the trenches was emphasized by the appearance in Germany during the Weimar period not only of many native novels, but of German translations of numbers of war novels from abroad. Most of the contemporary German war novels, even the more obscure ones, were also translated into English, French, and other languages. In Germany the novels included both pacifist anti-war works and novels that took the opposite stance and presented the war as a heroic, and as a testing and strengthening of German virtues in the storm of steel.[11] The emergence of the pacifist *Im Westen nichts Neues* as the leading war novel in an international context is all the more impressive.

Im Westen nichts Neues

That a historical event of the magnitude of the First World War, which cost around ten million lives from most nations of the world, could be encapsulated to any extent in a novel the paperback edition of which has little more than two hundred pages is an achievement in itself.[12] The fact that the body of the novel is a convincingly presented first-person narrative means that it *does* still need to be spelled out that Bäumer is not Remarque, who drew without doubt upon his own experiences in the war and at home in Osnabrück. But *Im Westen nichts Neues* is a work of fiction, and most importantly it has only one character. With two small but significant exceptions, the young soldier Paul Bäumer delivers the work directly to the reader, and therefore everything we see or hear is through him. It testifies to Remarque's skill that Bäumer remains consistent throughout the work, and it is Bäumer's character and background that dictates the style.[13] The choice of a narrator is significant; because Bäumer, drafted in 1916, was still a schoolboy in 1914, he bears no personal responsibility for the war itself, nor indeed does he understand much about it. Equally, Remarque does not permit him any prescience (although of course he speculates) about what happens *after* the war. This has an effect on the way in which other figures are presented to us, and criticism has been leveled at the book for the apparent one-sidedness of some of the characters encountered, or for the limited view of the fighting troops. But since they are all presented through Bäumer, his close friends would clearly be in far sharper focus than an anonymous and unpleasant major, or even an attractive French girl met on one occasion only. Bäumer would in reality have been unlikely to know the names of either of them. Nor would he have had much of a view of the war beyond company level, and his immediate experience with senior or even junior officers would be limited. The most senior officer glimpsed in the work is in fact Kaiser Wilhelm, when he comes to review the troops, but apart from one major and his own second lieutenant, Bäumer mentions no one else above the noncommissioned ranks. *Im Westen nichts Neues*, and to an extent the sequel, seem by this approach to claim the advantages of a diary—that is, its immediacy—with none of the drawbacks of a precise chronology, and Bäumer (and Birkholz in *Der Weg zurück*) present their thoughts, experiences, and reflections directly to the reader.[14]

The individual private soldier Paul Bäumer nevertheless sees himself for most of the novel as part of a group, so that it is the first person plural that predominates much of the work, and the move away from it at the end to Bäumer as an individual gains in significance thereby. Nor, of course, must we forget Remarque as the (concealed) structuring author behind the character, controlling the work as a whole in the variation in chapter lengths, or in the balance of action and periods of inaction, of reported discussion and private reflection. Remarque allows Bäumer to send signals to the reader to consider how single events need to be multiplied by thousands, for example, or indications that a particular train of thought will be able to be taken to a logical conclusion only after the war.

It is also sometimes overlooked that *Im Westen nichts Neues* is not a contemporary account of the First World War. Although both novels contain episodes based upon historical reality,[15] *Im Westen nichts Neues* was not written in 1918, but in 1928, recreating within the Weimar Republic events that had happened ten or more years before, even if those events were part of the experience of many of those living in the new postwar German state. *Im Westen nichts Neues* is historical fiction, and so is *Der Weg zurück*, although by the time of the latter, the sense that history was moving on was more apparent.[16] That Remarque chose to set the two novels during and just after the war itself means that they cannot be historically reflective in themselves, but both raise questions to which the narrator was never in a position to give answers. The burden of finding answers is thus placed upon the reader, whether in 1930 or in the present, and wherever he or she may be responding to the work.[17] In the first instance the target audience was the Weimar Republic itself, because both novels reflect the shared history of those reaching maturity in a postwar Germany that was already beginning to look insecure. But they were addressed, also, to the contemporary world, sending out a specifically pacifist message to Germany's former enemies. Beside these two time levels—that of the action and that of the contemporary reception—stands a third, the time of the present reader. They are addressed also to an international posterity and remain important in their general implications.

There are two places in *Im Westen nichts Neues* in which Bäumer is not in control of the narrative. There is a prefatory statement by the author that was omitted in some translations and appears in others with a significant variation from the text of the first German edition. It may be cited in German from a prepublication version, with the translation by A. W. Wheen, who included it in full in his 1929 translation; the sentence in italics was left out of the first German book edition:[18]

> Dieses Buch soll weder eine Anklage noch ein Bekenntnis, *vor allem aber kein Erlebnis* sein, *denn der Tod ist kein Erlebnis fur den, der ihm gegenübersteht.* Es soll nur den Versuch machen, über eine Generation zu berichten, die vom Kriege zerstört wurde;—auch wenn sie seinen Granaten entkam.

> [This book is to be neither an accusation nor a confession, and least of all an adventure, for death is not an adventure to those who stand face to face with it. It will try simply to tell of a generation of men who, even though they may have escaped its shells, were destroyed by the war.]

The statement in its original form was necessary because there were many examples of literature that did present the war in that light. More importantly though, it categorizes the work as a *Bericht*, a report, reminding us that although the fictive narrator would have been dead for ten years when the book appeared, other soldiers had survived. As a parallel with this opening statement, the final half-dozen lines of the novel are spoken by a new third-person narrator within the historical fictionality of the book, commenting on the death of Bäumer.

It was argued early in the criticism of the novel that the presentation of the war by a single individual could not portray a valid picture of the war.[19] There are various responses to this: one is that the first person in the novel is, as indicated, frequently the plural *wir*, so that Bäumer speaks for other soldiers and their experiences. Furthermore, even the notion of "other soldiers" can mean a variety of things, ranging from just Bäumer and Katczinsky (Kat), his mentor, to his immediate groups of school or platoon comrades, to his company, to the German army, or even the Germans as a whole. Refining it again, it might refer to the ordinary German soldier, or indeed to the ordinary soldier as such. Remarque permits Bäumer and his comrades to stress their representative status by pointing out that most of the soldiers of all countries are also ordinary people, and also by introducing overtly what might be seen as a multiplication factor at key points. Thus Bäumer says of the teacher, Kantorek, who had bullied them into signing up: "Es gab ja Tausende von Kantoreks" (18, there were thousands of Kantoreks), and more significantly towards the end of the novel, of the military hospital, which shows the true measure of war: "es gibt Hunderttausende in Deutschland, Hunderttausende in Frankreich, Hunderttausende in Russland . . ." (177, there are hundreds of thousands of them in Germany, hundreds of thousands of them in France, hundreds of thousands of them in Russia).

The *Froschperspektive* need not, then, be as restricted as it might appear.[20] But the narrator is also an individual; wars may be expressed in terms of the often unimaginably large numbers of those who fought or were killed, but such statistics are always made up of individuals. Remarque reduces the *wir* element gradually throughout the work in parallel to what was a war of attrition that ultimately reached the single individual, when at the end Paul Bäumer is not just left alone, but is thrown onto his own inner resources without support from any side. The ultimate expression of Bäumer's existentialist realization of the nature of life in the face of the extreme situation of war links this work with Remarque's oeuvre as a whole.

The fictional time of the novel begins in 1917, well after the outbreak of the war, and the reader is aware of time—more specifically of the seasons—passing until October 1918. Bäumer's own thoughts and conversations with others take the reader back to earlier periods, but in the fictional present the deadly monotony and constant attrition is completely established. The first chapter begins with *wir*, which refers on this occasion to a company of 150 men, just back from what was supposed to be a quiet sector after heavy losses, and with only eighty survivors. The battle has not been an important one, and the reason for the losses is casually put:

> Nun aber gab es gerade am letzten Tage bei uns überraschend viel Langrohr und dicke Brocken, englische Artillerie, die ständig auf unsere Stellung trommelte, so daß wir starke Verluste hatten und nur mit achtzig Männer zurückkamen. (11)

> [But then, on the very last day we were taken by surprise by long-range shelling from the heavy artillery. The English guns kept on pounding our position, so we lost a lot of men, and only eighty of us came back.]

The slang (*Langrohr und dicke Brocken* cannot really be imitated in translation) and the offhand manner of describing the death of nearly half the company is striking, and even more so is the stress on the pure mischance that there just happened to be unexpected heavy shellfire. The impression is one of passivity. The role of Bäumer and the other ordinary soldiers as victims rather than warriors is immediately established.

The first person plural now shifts to two smaller groups: Bäumer and three former classmates, Kropp, Müller, and Leer, who have joined the army straight from high school, then four more friends who were workers—Tjaden, a locksmith; Westhus, a peat-digger; Detering, a farmer; and finally

Katczinsky, the father figure of the group, who is already forty and who is presented as someone with enormous capabilities for spotting and avoiding trouble and for finding things that are needed. We have, therefore, a cross section of those fighting at the lowest and largest level, although, for different reasons, none of them understands precisely why they are fighting.

Paul Bäumer is nineteen when the action of *Im Westen nichts Neues* begins, and we learn that he joined up directly from a *Gymnasium* (classical high school). He is educated along traditional lines, is thoughtful, but does not have enough experience to draw full conclusions, especially since he has been thrust into the extreme situation of war. The consistency of the character is made clear in numerous small ways: when wounded and on a hospital train, he is still too embarrassed to ask a nurse when he needs to relieve himself, although he has been under heavy shellfire. On another occasion he describes how Tjaden, his ex-locksmith friend, insults their drill corporal, Himmelstoss, who has been sent to the front: "Tjaden erwidert gelassen und abschliessend, ohne es zu wissen, mit dem bekanntesten Klassikerzitat. Gleichzeitig lüftet er seine Kehrseite" (64, Tjaden gives an unworried and conclusive reply, quoting, though he doesn't know he's doing so, one of Goethe's best-known lines, the one about kissing a specific part of his anatomy. At the same time he sticks his backside up in the air). The quotation is from Goethe's *Götz von Berlichingen*, and it is often truncated in print anyway, though the sense ("you can kiss my ass") is clear and is here even made graphic. The passage is difficult to translate, because the quotation is not known in English, but the real point of Bäumer's report of this small incident is that Tjaden has used the literal expression, but does not know about any literary allusions. Bäumer, on the other hand, uses the literary reference to avoid actually saying what Tjaden has said, and even in describing Tjaden's gesture he uses a euphemism. Bäumer notes several times that everything they learned at school has now become worthless, and this is true; but he cannot escape from his background.[21]

Im Westen nichts Neues presents the war as such being shown with the vivid and deliberately shocking realism associated with the term *neue Sachlichkeit* (new objectivity). The approach here and in many comparable war novels is a quasi-documentary one, but the style is not only one of objective authenticity.[22] The structure is episodic, something that would become a hallmark of Remarque's novels, holding the interest by moving rapidly from one scene to another and alternating the kinds of scenes presented, while picking up themes from one episode to another in twelve chapters that vary in content, emphasis, and length. This enables the work to present a wide range of experiences of the war: we see the soldiers recovering behind the lines, visiting and being treated in a military hospital, on wiring duty, on reconnaissance patrol, under fire in a dugout, going over the top and attacking another trench, going on leave. Further experiences, including a soldiers' brothel, are filled in by *Der*

Weg zurück. Movement from the immediate present to the remembered past also enables Bäumer to give us scenes of basic training as well.

The first three chapters are set behind the lines, the work opening with an apparently trivial incident in which Bäumer and his associates receive a double ration of food; we soon discover, however, that it is because they have just sustained the loss of half of the company, and the attrition continues when the reinforcements sent to bring them back to strength are raw recruits, who fall in large numbers. Discussions between the soldiers take us back to the training period under the martinet Himmelstoss as drill corporal, and then in the third chapter the soldiers recollect the satisfactory revenge that they had taken, beating him up when he is drunk, and thus utilizing the pragmatism of violence that he has instilled in them, and in fact is vital for their survival. Revenge on the noncommissioned officer (NCO) is probably part of the fantasy of any soldier, and it certainly has literary antecedents in German.[23] The character of Himmelstoss, however, is developed in the work. Initially frightened when forced to go into battle, he is shamed into gathering his courage, and eventually becomes friendly towards the former recruits. The first two chapters each end, however, with a visit to one of Bäumer's school-friends, Fritz Kemmerich, who is badly wounded in a field hospital in the first, and dead by the end of the second.

Various key themes are voiced in these early chapters. Attention has been paid to a comment by Bäumer describing the feeling of solidarity engendered first by their training, which "im Felde dann zum Besten steigerte, was der Krieg hervorbrachte: zur Kameradschaft" (27–28, grew, on the battlefield, into the best thing that the war produced—comradeship in arms). It is possible to make too much of this comment, and most certainly the development of a close comradeship is not to be taken as a justification for the war; it is just that the war, as an extreme situation, permits it to develop more strongly. The comradeship in *Im Westen nichts Neues* is born of mutual help in battle, and in *Der Weg zurück* Remarque would make clear that while it is a necessity in war, it does not necessarily always survive in peacetime. Equally important is a motif first voiced at the end of the third chapter, in response to someone's reference to them as *eiserne Jugend* (22, iron youth), Bäumer comments that none of them is young, even if they are only nineteen or twenty. Their youth has been taken away from them, and they feel that they are—this is a common literary motif with other writers, too—a betrayed, a lost generation.[24]

The novel now shows the young soldiers in action, first on duty laying barbed wire, and then, after a further period behind the lines, in the field, although we rarely see the soldiers engaged in actual fighting. The episode when they are laying wire shows them being fired upon, rather than firing. Various striking incidents remain in the mind from this section of the work: the young recruit who loses control of his bowels under fire; the slow and grotesque death of a horse (in a scene that once again has literary parallels before and after Remarque), a gas attack, and the fact that the men come under fire in a cemetery and have to take cover against death among the graves and coffins of the fairly recently dead (a sleeve is apparently still intact on one of the bodies). The symbolism of the cemetery scene is clear enough, but it is not gratuitous, nor grotesque sensationalism, as has been suggested.[25] In this incident, too, the young recruit from the earlier scene who soiled himself under fire, is fatally wounded. Kat wants to shoot the horribly wounded soldier, but cannot do so because other soldiers are around. The irony in his being prevented from mercy killing, when they are forced to kill otherwise, is underlined again in the reaction of Detering, the farmer, who wants to shoot the wounded horse, but cannot, because this would draw fire upon them.

The fifth chapter, which contains the arrival of Himmelstoss at the front and Tjaden's insult, is set behind the lines, again a respite from the horrors of the previous chapter. A discussion between the young soldiers focuses upon the realization of the high school recruits that their knowledge has become worthless and they are now unable to think beyond the war. The atmosphere of a more or less flippant conversation gradually gives way to something close to despair in Bäumer's thoughts. He reports one of his friends as saying: "Der Krieg hat uns für alles verdorben" (67, the war has ruined us for everything), and sums up for the reader—in the Weimar Republic and afterwards—their collective state of mind, developing the idea of the loss of youth: "Wir sind keine Jugend mehr. Wir wollen die Welt nicht mehr stürmen. Wir sind Flüchtende. . . . wir glauben an den Krieg" (67, We're no longer young men. We've lost any desire to conquer the world. We are refugees . . . we believe in the war). The chapter concludes, however, with a scene in which the ever-resourceful Kat, aided by Bäumer, requisitions—steals—a couple of geese and roasts them. The incident may have adventurous, or even comic elements, but the long process of cooking the geese permits Bäumer to think further, and to comment for the benefit of the reader upon what he has become. He and his older mentor are close, and although Kat, too, will fall before the end of the work, for the moment Bäumer is aware of them both simply as "zwei Menschen, zwei winzige Funken Leben, draußen ist die Nacht und der Kreis des Todes" (72, two human beings, two tiny sparks of life; outside there is just the night, and all around us, death). That spark of life—possibly the most important recurrent theme in Remarque's novels—will survive in Bäumer to the end.

The central sixth chapter is one of the longest in the work, two dozen pages in the standard paperback, as against the final chapter, which is barely two pages long, and although it does show the soldiers fighting, the concept of the soldier as victim as well as aggressor is maintained. The precise nature of the enemy is important, too. The realistically presented fighting makes a deliberate assault on all of the senses, in particular that of hearing. The massive and permanent noise of war is probably the feature that those who experienced it recollected most.

> Plötzlich heult und blitzt es ungeheuer, der Unterstand kracht in allen Fugen unter einem Treffer, glücklicherweise einem leichten, dem die Betonklötze standgehalten haben. Es klirrt metallisch und fürchterlich, die Wände wackeln, Gewehre, Helme, Erde, Dreck und Staub fliegen. Schwefeliger Qualm dringt ein. (81)

> [Suddenly there is a terrible noise and flash of light, and every joint in the dugout creaks under the impact of a direct hit—luckily not a heavy one, and one that the concrete blocks could withstand. There is a fearsome metallic rattling, the walls shake, rifles, steel helmets, earth, mud, and dust fly around. Sulphurous fumes penetrate the walls.]

Cinema audiences in the early 1930s were horrified when films with a realistic soundtrack were first shown. The sound of war in particular, but also sight, feeling, and smell are all invoked in a chapter that makes clear the physical aspects of front-line warfare. The soldiers fight like automata when they go over the top, and they suffer from *Unterstandsangst* otherwise, driven crazy in the confinements of a dugout under heavy shelling. A severely wounded man calls out constantly for some days, but cannot be reached, large numbers of untrained recruits, referred to as *Kinder* (children), are killed, as are some of Bäumer's friends. Tjaden, however, has to be stopped from trying to knock the fuse off a dud shell; a natural survivor, he appears in *Der Weg zurück*, the only member of the group to do so. The novel began with the return of eighty out of 150 men, and this chapter, at the halfway point, ends with the return of only thirty-two. In terms of actual plot, the ironic major achievement in this part of the offensive is the welcome capture of five cans of corned beef.

The physical realism is balanced by Bäumer's thoughts. In an earlier chapter, the front was for Bäumer a whirlpool, sucking him in as a helpless victim, and now it is a cage, again an image of external entrapment, while later on it will be an inescapable fever. Dominating everything is *Zufall* (chance), another key theme throughout the work. An indifferent universe can inflict upon any human being what it will, and in the war a bullet may strike at any time, which leaves the soldier believing in chance and chance alone. The soldiers themselves become not men but dangerous animals, who fight to stay alive, something that also—significantly—distances their actions from those of hatred for any specific human enemy.

Aus uns sind gefährliche Tiere geworden. Wir kämpfen nicht, wir verteidigen uns vor der Vernichtung. Wir schleudern die Granaten nicht gegen Menschen, was wissen wir im Augenblick davon, dort hetzt mit Händen und Helmen der Tod hinter uns her . . . (83)

[We have turned into dangerous animals. We are not fighting, we are defending ourselves from annihilation. We are not hurling our grenades against human beings—what do we know about all that in the heat of the moment?—the hands and the helmets that are after us belong to Death itself . . .]

The breathless style of the passage is noteworthy, and the length of the chapter also underlines the comments by Bäumer that the horror seems to go and on with no sign of relief. Episodic variation permits us to see periods of waiting, which can be as bad as the fighting, killing rats, and preventing the dugout-crazy recruits from running out into the open. There are calmer moments—at one point two butterflies are seen near their trenches—but the return is always to the fighting, until the few remaining exhausted soldiers return behind the lines.

The next chapter matches this in length; after a brief incident when some of them visit some French girls, Bäumer returns home on leave, and is confronted with his now unimaginably distant earlier life. Here he has to cope with the uncomprehending worries of his dying mother, and with the differently uncomprehending attitudes first of the military—an unpleasant major is critical of Bäumer's *Frontsitten* (front-line manners)—and of civilians, as a group of well-meaning middle-aged men at an inn instruct him on what the army ought to do. Neither the major nor the civilians have any idea of the realities of life at the front, which have just been shown so graphically to the reader. Bäumer also has to report to Franz Kemmerich's mother how he died, swearing (ironically) on his own life that Kemmerich died instantly. Bäumer and the others may feel that they are no longer young, but Kemmerich's mother reminds us sharply of the real situation when she asks why "you children" are out there. The conclusion Bäumer draws is that he should never have gone on leave.

A brief interlude in which Bäumer is detailed to guard some Russian prisoners of war reminds us that this was a war on more than one front, and is followed by a return to his unit and the ceremonial visit by the Kaiser, which provides occasion for the soldiers to discuss the nature of the war once again. It is followed, however, by a reconnaissance patrol in which Bäumer kills in terror a French soldier—the only enemy soldier seen closely, and certainly the only one named, Gérard Duval—against whom he is quite literally thrown in a shell hole and whom he stabs. His experience, trapped in no man's land

while Duval dies slowly, brings Bäumer close to madness as he realizes that
this is a real person, with a name and a family. While trapped with the dying
French soldier, Bäumer makes promises to him, declaring that "Es darf nie
wieder geschehen" (154, It must never happen again). That last statement is
directed at the outside world, of course, from a Weimar Republic concerned
to remove the image of Germany as the aggressor. However, when he finds
his way back to his own trench, Bäumer is made to watch a sniper at work,
and to find a kind of comfort in the circular notion that *Krieg ist Krieg*, war is
war. That might during the war itself be enough, but whether it would work
afterwards is left open.

The original version of the prefatory statement warned against seeing
war as an adventure, and that criticism has been leveled at the incident when
Bäumer and his comrades are placed in charge of a food supply dump. They
take advantage of this and organize a feast, but Bäumer points out the need
for the soldiers to seize any opportunity of light relief, contextualizing this
passage as a respite, rather than as an adventure. It is the same reflex action
that makes the soldiers use jokey slang evasions for the idea of being killed.
The meal, which gives the participants diarrhea, is conducted under heavy
shellfire, and immediately afterwards Bäumer and others are wounded and
hospitalized, giving him the opportunity to see and to comment upon for
the reader another aspect of the war. He enumerates soberly and in detail the
various types of wounds—a long list of all the places in which a man can be
hit by a bullet—and notes that this is the real indicator of the reality of war:
"Erst das Lazarett zeigt, was Krieg ist" (177, only a military hospital can really
show you what war is).

Bäumer's mood seems to reach complete despair in the two final short
chapters. The penultimate chapter is still characterized by the *wir* opening: "Wir zählen die Wochen nicht mehr" (183, we've stopped counting
the weeks), but not many of Bäumer's friends are left, and the war seems
neverending. Again some incidents stand out: the farmer Detering's apparent desertion, although he is actually heading homewards towards his farm,
rather than trying to escape to the Netherlands; the attempt, also caused
by front-line madness, by another soldier to rescue a wounded dog. The
horrors of war have been shown in telegrammatic enumeration at earlier
points, and here again the style sounds almost like an expressionist poem
by, say, August Stramm:[26]

Granaten, Gasschwaden und Tankflottillen—Zerstampfen,
Zerfressen, Tod.
    Ruhr, Gruppe, Typhus—Würgen, Verbrennen, Tod. Graben,
    Lazarett, Massengrab—mehr Möglichkeiten gibt es nicht. (190)
[Shells, gas clouds and flotillas of tanks—crushing, devouring, death.

> Dysentery, influenza, typhus—choking, scalding, death. Trench, hospital, mass grave—there are no other possibilities.]

A further stylistic variation stressing the apparent endlessness of the war is seen in a sequence of four paragraphs beginning: *Sommer 1918* (Summer 1918), full of the desire not to be killed at this late stage, coupled with the desperate feeling that surely it has to end soon?

Bäumer is still able to voice comments on the nature of the war, castigating the profiteers, for example: "Die Fabrikbesitzer in Deutschland sind reiche Leute geworden—uns zerschrinnt die Ruhr die Därme" (188, the factory owners in Germany have grown rich, while dysentery racks our guts). He also comments on why the war is ending for the German army. It is simply because they are tired and hungry, yet are faced with a well-provisioned and stronger opposition force—America had finally joined the war in 1917, and the allied blockade had affected supplies to Germany itself. But the German army, says Bäumer—and the *wir* voice is highly significant here—has not been defeated in a purely military sense:

> Wir sind nicht geschlagen, denn wir sind als Soldaten besser und erfahrener; wir sind einfach von der vielfachen Übermacht zerdrückt und zurückgeschoben. (192)

> [We haven't been defeated, because as soldiers we are better and more experienced; we have simply been crushed and pushed back by forces many times superior to ours.]

Historically Germany had in any real terms been defeated; but Bäumer's wartime interpretation, while certainly not in line with the famous notion that she had been "stabbed in the back" by left-wing political forces (the *Dolchstosslegende*),[27] may still have struck a chord with the former soldiers in the Weimar Republic who were the first audience for the book. The Nazis, who accused the work of insulting the front-line soldier, presumably overlooked this passage. Remarque himself, however, was specific enough on Germany's actual defeat later, and in a piece written in 1944 he criticized the plethora of books published in the years after the First World War with titles like *Im Felde unbesiegt* (Undefeated in Battle). In *Der Weg zurück* the idea is neatly countered when the new narrator thinks of an essay he wrote at school on the subject of why Germany is bound to win, and considers that the low grade it received was probably about right in the circumstances.[28]

Juxtaposed with the comments and thoughts of Bäumer in the penultimate chapter is a quickening of the final attrition, as the last of his friends are killed. Müller leaves to Bäumer the boots he had inherited from Kemmerich, and which became probably the most commented-upon motif in the work—Tjaden will get them next, and he of course survives.[29] Then Kat is killed by a random piece of shrapnel while Bäumer is carrying him to a dressing station to have another minor wound treated. The loss of the man with whom he had shared the moment of isolation in the battlefield as the spark of life leaves him with an immense feeling of isolation, and means that Bäumer is alone in a final two-page chapter.

Had they returned in 1916, Bäumer thinks that they could have unleashed a revolution—the idea will be developed in other novels—but now he feels that there is weariness without hope. However, this state of mind gives way fairly suddenly to a new attitude: this might, he thinks, just be a transitory melancholy, the trees are green, there is much talk of peace, and he himself becomes very calm: "Ich bin sehr ruhig" (197). Whatever happens, there will be inside him an independent spark of life that will carry him onwards, whether his own individuality wants it or not. Bäumer has used the *wir* voice a great deal, but now he is forced into the first person singular as the last survivor of his group. Beyond this, his thoughts move still further away from the individual that he has become to focus on the independent life force, from the *ich* to the *es*. "Aber so lange es [das Leben] da ist, wird es sich seinen Weg suchen, mag dieses was in mir 'ich' sagt, wollen oder nicht" (197, but as long as life is there it will make its own way, whether my conscious self likes it or not).

But things go further. Bäumer is killed, and now he is completely objectivized as *er*, seen by a third party. His death is as random as Kat's in reality, although in literary terms we recall his promise to Kemmerich's mother that he may not return if he is not telling the truth, and there is also perhaps a sense of expiation for the death of the French soldier. He dies in October 1918, on a day when there is—hence the title—"nichts Neues zu melden" (197, nothing new to report). It is difficult to stress enough the importance of this final section of the novel, in which an objective observer not only reports the death, but speculates on Bäumer's mind at the end: he looked, he tells us, "als wäre er beinahe zufrieden damit, daß es so gekommen war" (197, as if he were almost happy that it had turned out that way). The subjunctive "as if he were" and the qualifier "almost" are both warnings that this is only speculation. The reader has been privy to Bäumer's actual thoughts and experiences, and may well think differently. Of course there will always be an ambiguity: no one can know whether another individual was content to have died at any point. Nor, of course, do we know what happens next: there is no indication of whether Bäumer even believed in an afterlife, let alone whether he now enters one, and the work, like most of Remarque's, is agnostic in that sense.

Im Westen nichts Neues provokes thought about the nature of war in various different ways. The most obvious is the direct presentation of the horrors: parts of bodies hanging in trees, the wounded soldier calling out from no man's land, the slow gurgling death of the French soldier. Sometimes the telegrammatic lists of forms of attack, or weapons, or types of wounds make their point. The reader is, however, also prompted to consider the nature of war by being privy to the inconclusive and often humorous discussions by the young or uneducated soldiers. Thus when the visit of the Kaiser leads to a discussion between the *Gymnasium* pupils and the working-class soldiers of how wars come about, one of the former declares that wars happen when one country insults another. The answer comes that it is impossible for a mountain to insult another mountain; when this is countered by the fact that a nation can be insulted, Tjaden—not one of the high school group—points out that he does not feel insulted and should therefore not be there. The only people to profit from war, the soldiers feel at this point, are those like the Kaiser, who need a famous victory. Of course there is no conclusion. Müller comments that it is better that the war should be fought in France than in Germany, and Tjaden responds that the best of all would be no war at all. Eventually a consensus is reached that the discussion is pointless because it will change nothing. This may be true in the immediate historical context; the message to the Weimar reader, though, is that perhaps things might be changed.

Sometimes Bäumer's comments are addressed directly to the reader. In the second chapter the soldiers visit Franz Kemmerich, who is dying in a field hospital, and Bäumer thinks:

> Da liegt er nun, weshalb nur? Man sollte die ganze Welt an diesem Bette vorbeiführen und sagen: Das ist Franz Kemmerich, neunzehneinhalb Jahre alt, er will nicht sterben. Lasst ihn nicht sterben! (29)

> [Now he is lying there—and for what reason? Everybody in the whole world ought to be made to walk past his bed and be told: "This is Franz Kemmerich, he's nineteen and a half, and he doesn't want to die! Don't let him die!"]

The novel has done precisely what Bäumer has asked: the world has been led past that bed. Later, when he is in a *Lazarett* (military hospital) himself, Bäumer makes a personal statement that gradually develops into a philosophical attitude to the war as a whole:

> Ich bin jung, ich bin zwanzig Jahre alt; aber ich kenne vom Leben nichts anderes als die Verzweiflung, den Tod, die Angst und die

Verkettung sinnlosester Oberflächlichkeit mit einem Abgrund des
Leidens. Ich sehe, dass Völker gegeneinander getrieben werden
und sich schweigend, unwissend, töricht, gehorsam, unschuldig
töten. (177)

[I am young, I am twenty years of age; but I know nothing of
life except despair, death, fear, and the combination of completely
mindless superficiality with an abyss of suffering. I see people
being driven against one another, and silently, uncomprehendingly,
foolishly, and obediently and innocently killing one another.]

Most striking is the idea of the victim as killer, the paradoxical *unschuldig
töten* (innocently killing). These almost exculpatory words are again clearly
directed at the ex-soldiers who survived the war. Bäumer also wonders how
the older generation would react if they called them to account. This, too,
is what the novel is doing.

Often Bäumer himself is unable to think things through because, since
he is actually in the war, those conclusions would lead to madness.[30] For the
time being he is forced to cling to the circular statement that "war is war";
sometimes, however, Bäumer decides consciously to store up ideas for later,
and thus Remarque permits him to present ideas directly to the later readership. When on guard-duty over the Russian prisoners, for example, he has
time to speculate.

Ein Befehl hat diese stille Gestalten zu unseren Feinden gemacht;
ein Befehl könnte sie in unsere Freude verwandeln. An irgendeinem
Tisch wird ein Schriftstück von einigen Leuten unterzeichnet, die
keiner von uns kennt; und jahrelang ist unser höchstes Ziel das,
worauf sonst die Verachtung der Welt und ihre höchste Strafe
ruht. (134)

[An order has turned these silent figures into our enemies; an order
could turn them into friends again. On some table, a document is
signed by some people that none of us knows, and for years our main
aim in life is the one thing that usually draws the condemnation of
the whole world and incurs its severest punishment in law.]

Bäumer stops: "Hier darf ich nicht weiterdenken" (I mustn't think along
those lines any more), but the importance of this passage for the novel and
for Weimar is clear. The distancing from responsibility is as marked as the
inclusivity implied by the first person plural, and the questions of guilt and
murder will be raised in *Der Weg zurück* and elsewhere. The question of

responsibility for war on an individual basis, however, is not addressed until we reach the Second World War and *Zeit zu leben, und Zeit zu sterben*,[31] by which time conditions for Germany were very different.

A war implies an enemy. For Bäumer, however, the principal enemy faced by all soldiers is death itself, and after that the bullying noncommissioned officers of their own army. The declared enemy—the British or French soldiers—are usually invisible, although we are aware of their guns. Bäumer himself meets only the *poilu* Duval and the Russian prisoners of war whom he guards. The absence of a specific enemy was a programmatic policy message for the Weimar Republic. The consistent portrayal of Bäumer as a victim, who was too young to be involved even with the hysteria associated with the outbreak in 1914, and who understands little and can influence even less, is also appropriate to the novel's Weimar context and to the generation that survived the war. The Weimar Republic welcomed the realistic and graphic presentation of the horrors of the war in a way that showed the participants free of responsibility, if not of guilt. Other unresponsible and even guilt-free narrators and protagonists in Weimar anti-war novels of the period include stretcher bearers, women, children, or schoolboys too young to join up, and most extreme of all, but most clearly a participant who is an innocent victim of bestial humanity, Liesl the mare, used as the narrator in Ernst Johannsen's unjustly forgotten *Fronterinnerungen eines Pferdes* (Front Line Memoirs of a Horse).[32] What unites all these involved narrators is the complete lack of awareness of the reasons for war as such, or for this war.

Im Westen nichts Neues needs more than any of Remarque's later works to be located in various contexts, first of all in the genre of the war novel. This itself, however, requires some subdivision: *Im Westen nichts Neues* is a novel about the First World War, but not one written either during that war, like Henri Barbusse's *Le Feu* (*Under Fire*), or just afterwards, such as Ernst Jünger's *In Stahlgewittern* (*Storm of Steel*), nor, on the other hand, at a historical distance so far removed as to be completely divorced from the actual experience (as with recent novels by, for example, Pat Barker). It is a historical novel addressing as its first audience Germans who shared the experiences presented in the work and survived, and it can be contextualized therefore as Weimar literature and hence is a German novel for reasons other than the simply linguistic. As one of the many novels produced at around the same time that took a similarly pacifist and anti-war stance, however, it is both national and international. *Im Westen nichts Neues* is a German novel in that it shows us German soldiers worn down to what amounts to a defeat in 1918. The war in the novel has no beginning, nor do we see the end, because Bäumer dies before the armistice, so that questions of responsibility and indeed of whether or not Germany was ultimately defeated are not raised. It is also worth noting—though the Nazi critics again missed the point—that there is no lack of patriotism in general terms on the part of Remarque's soldiers. All these elements would have elicited a response from those in the Weimar Republic trying to come to terms with the war. At the same time, the intentional internationalism of the novel is clear in the presentation precisely from the viewpoint of the ordinary soldier and member of the lost generation. Equally clear is the expressly pacifist message. In fact, some English-language reviews criticized the novel for offering too mild a presentation of the German soldier. Nevertheless, the work is a clear indictment of all wars. Wars are still fought, even if not in the trenches, and they still give rise to political chaos. They are still fought largely by the young and uncomprehending, who are themselves forced by killing to incur a guilt that they do not necessarily deserve, while the major questions, such as why wars happen at all, often still go unanswered. One criticism of the work was that Remarque did not take a political stand, which means that he did not allow Bäumer to do so. This is partly justified by the consistent character of the narrator, but in fact the work does have a political dimension in various respects. Its pacifist stance and the emphasis on the soldiers as victims of the war are both contributions to the political agenda of Weimar Germany, and in general terms, the attacks on a prewar social system embodied in teachers like Kantorek, and the references to the capitalist profiteering are clear. As an antiwar novel, too, its message could hardly be clearer.

Within Remarque's novels as a whole, the fate of Bäumer may also be taken beyond the confines of the war itself. Remarque shows us a historical event, but also makes clear the way in which it faces an individual with an extreme situation. Bäumer is eventually stripped of all support and left alone, which forces him to the existential realization that the life force will carry him onwards regardless, because it is all that there is. That life force is represented by the spark of life that is with Kat on the battlefield at night in the surrounding sea of destruction. The force is there, too, in nature, which saves Bäumer physically—when he presses himself to the earth, praising it in what is almost an echo of an Homeric hymn[33]—and also spiritually at the end, when his near despair gives way after the promptings of the natural world. He is not content to die, his death is a final reminder of the force of chance, seemingly malignant but actually completely impartial, which is heightened in a war, but is always present in Remarque's novels. The same awareness will come to many of Remarque's later figures. The novel is not just a pacifist work. The human theme of the inextinguishable nature of the spark of life is just as significant.[34]

It is overly tempting to view all of Remarque's other novels in the light of *Im Westen nichts Neue*, but themes first found here do recur and are developed. *Zeit zu leben und Zeit zu sterben* has a number of actual echoes, such as the scenes in the hospital, but picks up and develops the idea of the responsibility of the soldier in a later war where this was far more a German issue. The concentration camp novel *Der Funke Leben* (*The Spark of Life*)—the title harks back to *Im Westen nichts Neues*—uses the narrative technique of shocking realism again, and rather than a soldier in a war, we have an even more extreme situation in which the spark of humanity must struggle even harder to survive. There were, however, aspects of the work that Remarque realized could be misunderstood, and there is indeed some danger in his chosen methodology of placing the burden of discourse upon a later reader. Remarque does indeed allow Bäumer to praise *Kameradschaft* in war, but it is offset by the need to cope with the attrition that takes away all of Bäumer's friends one by one. The closest friendship—with Kat—is fortuitous, and it is brought to an end by and in the war. The ties that bound the men together in war, too, are shown to break down in *Der Weg zurück*, and some of the other important ideas—such as what constitutes murder, or whether war is a justification in itself of the deeds done within it—are also brought back and re-examined in the new novel. Remarque called the second work a necessary one.[35]

NOTES

1. Texts cited are the 1998 KiWi editions of *Im Westen nichts Neues* and *Der Weg zurück*, both with afterwords by Tilman Westphalen (Cologne: Kiepenheuer and Witsch, 1998). The earlier KiWi edition of the former (1987) has a slightly different afterword (referring to the first Gulf War) and a useful selection of materials on the work from 1929 to 1980. The first edition of *Im Westen nichts Neues* was published in Berlin under Ullstein's Propyläen imprint in January 1929 after a *Vorabdruck* in Ullstein's *Vossische Zeitung* starting just before Armistice Day in 1928, ten years after the end of the war. *Der Weg zurück* appeared under the same imprint in 1931, also after a preprint in the *Vossische Zeitung* at the end of 1930. For a full bibliography of editions, including picture books, and translations into all languages of *Im Westen nichts Neues*, see Thomas F. Schneider, *Erich Maria Remarque: Im Westen nichts neues: Bibliographie der Drucke* (Bramsche: Rasch, 1992).

2. See Thomas F. Schneider, *Erich Maria Remarque: Im Westen nichts Neues: Text, Edition, Entstehung, Distribution und Rezeption, 1928–1930* (Habilitationsschrift: University of Osnabrück, 2000; now published in Tübingen: Niemeyer, 2004 as a book plus CD), and his booklet *Erich Maria Remarque: Im Westen nichts Neues: Das Manuskript* (Bramsche: Rasch, 1996). Schneider notes on page 12 that Remarque's contract with Ullstein demanded that if the book were not to be a success, Remarque would have to work off the advance paid by working for them as a journalist. Remarque claimed in a 1966 piece for the newspaper *Die Welt* that he worked on the novel for only five weeks: "Grössere und kleinere Ironien meines Lebens," *Ein militanter Pazifist*, 141; *Das unbekannte Werk*, vol. 4, 439; *Herbstfahrt*, 257.

3. The translation by A. W. Wheen as *All Quiet on the Western Front* (London: G. P. Putnam's Sons 1929; Boston: Little, Brown, and Company, 1929) was made, as were other translations, from a typescript and is slightly different from the German book version. It was bowdlerized when first published in the United States,

and the full version was only readily available in a Fawcett paperback after 1979. The quality of Wheen's translation was attacked on publication, although Remarque seems to have liked it, calling it "eine englische Originalarbeit" (an original English work): see the letter by Herbert Read in *Time and Tide* on 26 April 1929. The reviewer for *Time and Tide*, Cicely Hamilton, pointed out gently that Remarque was perhaps not an authority on English. Richard Church praised the translation in the *Spectator* for 20 April 1929. For more detail, see Claude R. Owen, *"All Quiet on the Western Front*: Sixty Years Later," *Krieg und Literatur/War and Literature* 1 (1989): 41–48, and my papers "Translating the Western Front: A. W. Wheen and E. M. Remarque," *Antiquarian Book Monthly Review* 18 (1991): 452–60 and 102, and "We Germans . . .? Remarques englischer Roman *All Quiet on the Western Front*," *Jahrbuch* 6 (1996): 11–34. On Wheen, see Ian Campbell, "Remarking Remarque: The Arthur Wheen Papers," *National Library of Australia News* 8, no. 7 (April, 1998): 3–7, with illustrations of the drafts, showing the shift from "No News in the West" to "All Quiet in the West," with the familiar title only emerging at galley stage. My own translation (London: Cape, 1993) retains Wheen's by now established title. In spite of its flaws (mostly of register), Wheen's translation played an important part in the establishing of the novel as a masterwork of world literature: see the comments by General Sir Ian Hamilton in 1929 in: "The End of War?" *Life and Letters* 3 (1929): 399–411, see 403.

4. Lewis Milestone directed *All Quiet on the Western Front* for Universal in 1930. The script, by George Abbott, Maxwell Anderson, and Dell Andrews, is available in German translation by Jürgen Schebera together with full documentation of its first performance, in *"Der Fall Remarque, Im Westen nichts Neues"—eine Dokumentation*, ed. Bärbel Schräder (Leipzig: Reclam, 1992), 104–73 and 289–409; see 409 on the change from the intended final scene to its famous replacement in which Bäumer is killed reaching out for a butterfly. Much secondary literature has been devoted to the film, including most of issue 3 of the 1993 *Jahrbuch*. See Wagener, *Understanding*, 122, on the United States reissue in 1939 and its showing in Germany in 1952. Examples of secondary studies are: Kevin Brownlow, *The War, the West, and the Wilderness* (London: Secker and Warburg, 1979), 214–19; George J. Mitchell, "Making All Quiet on the Western Front," *American Cinematographer* 66 (1985): 34–43; Andrew Kelly, *"All Quiet on the Western Front*: 'Brutal Cutting, Stupid Censors, and Bigoted Politicos'," *Historical Journal of Film, Radio, and Television* 9 (1989): 135–50—see also his book *Filming "All Quiet on the Western Front"* (London and New York: I. B. Tauris, 1998); John Whiteclay Chambers, *"All Quiet on the Western Front* (1930): the Anti-war Film and the Image of the First World War," *Historical Journal of Film, Radio, and Television* 14 (1994): 377–411. Milestone's film compares well with the exactly contemporary German Nerofilm *Westfront 1918*, based on a novel by Ernst Johannsen and directed by Georg W. Pabst; see Kathleen Norrie and Malcolm Read, "Pacifism, Politics, and Art: Milestone's *All Quiet on the Western Front* and Pabst's *Westfront 1918*" in *Remarque Against War*, ed. Brian Murdoch, Mark Ward, and Maggie Sargeant (Glasgow: Scottish Papers in Germanic Studies, 1998), 62–84. *All Quiet on the Western Front* was remade for television for Norman Rosemont productions, directed by Delbert Mann.

5. There is an anecdotal but interesting historical report on the reading in 1944 of this proscribed book by Klaus Gruhn, "'Wehrkraftzersetzend': Schüler des Gymnasium Laurentianum Warendorflernen 1944 *Im Westen nichts Neues* kennen," *Jahrbuch* 15 (2005): 93–100, and see for the response to exile books in schools after

1945 Hermann Glaser, "Das Exil fand nicht statt," in *10 Mai 1933*, ed. Walberer, 260–84. In a brief resumé of his life and works in 1956, Remarque noted that the book was banned in Italy from 1929–45, in Germany from 1933–45, but that it had subsequently been banned in the Soviet Union in 1947 and at that stage still was: *Das unbekannte Werk*, vol. 5, 167.

6. Jost Hermand, "Versuch, den Erfolg von Erich Maria Remarques *Im Westen nichts Neues* zu verstehen," in *Weimar am Pazifik: Festschrift für Werner Vordtriede*, ed. Dieter Borchmeyer and Till Heimeran (Tübingen: Niemeyer, 1985), 71–78; A. F. Bance, "*Im Westen nichts Neues*: a Bestseller in Context," *Modern Language Review* 72 (1977): 359–73, cited 359, and see the comments by Firda, *All Quiet*, 12, whose book attempts a full-scale "Literary Analysis and Cultural Context." On the work as a bestseller, see Hubert Rüter, *Erich Maria Remarque: Im Westen nichts Neues": Ein Bestseller der Kriegsliteratur im Kontext* (Paderborn: Schöningh, 1980). On the style see Brian Rowley, "Journalism into Fiction: *Im Westen Nichts Neue*," in *The First World War in Fiction*, ed. Holger Klein (London: Macmillan, 1976), 101–11; Brian Murdoch, "Narrative Strategies in Remarque's *Im Westen nichts Neues*," *New German Studies* 17 (1992–93): 175–202; Howard M. De Leeuw, "Remarque's Use of Simile in *Im Westen nichts Neues*," and Harald Kloiber, "Struktur, Stil, und Motivik in Remarques *Im Westen nichts Neues*," *Jahrbuch* 4 (1994): 45–64 and 5–78 respectively; and Thomas Schneider, "Es ist ein Buch ohne Tendenz" *Im Westen nichts Neues*: Auto- und Textsystem im Rahmen eines Konstitutions- und Wirkungsmodells für Literatur," *Krieg und Literatur/War and Literature* 1 (1989): 23–40.

7. Most famously by Peter Kropp, *Endlich Klarheit über Remarque und sein Buch Im Westen nichts Neues* (Hamm: Kropp, 1930), which sold well, as did Wilhelm Müller-Scheld, *Im Westen nichts Neues eine Täuschung* (Idstein/Taunus: Grandpierre, 1929). See the survey by Barker and Last, *Remarque*, 38–44 as well as Owen, *Bio-Bibliography*, and Schräder, *Der Fall Remarque*. See also Thomas F. Schneider on the critical response, "'Die Meute hinter Remarque': Zur Diskussion um *Im Westen nichts Neues* 1928–1930," *Jahrbuch zur Literatur der Weimarer Republik* 1 (1995): 143–70, and Robert Neumann's original "Die Meute hinter Remarque," *Die Literatur* 32 (1929–30): 199–200. I have examined the imitative works in detail in my edition: Erich Maria Remarque, *Im Westen nichts Neues* (London: Methuen, 1984; rev. ed. Routledge, 1988), 4–6 and in my monograph *Remarque: Im Westen nichts Neues*, 2d rev. ed. (Glasgow: Glasgow University French and German Publications, 1995), 1–13. See on the work *Hat Erich Maria Remarque wirklich gelebt* by Mynona [Salomo Friedlaender] (Berlin: Steegemann, 1929): Manfred Kuxdorf, "Mynona versus Remarque, Tucholsky, Mann, and Others: Not So Quiet on the Literary Front," in *The First World War in German Narrative Prose: Essays in Honour of George Wallis Field*, ed. Charles N. Genno and Heinz Wetzel (Toronto, Buffalo, and London: U of Toronto P, 1980), 71–91. The dust jacket of Friedlaender's book calls it "eine Denkmalsenthüllung" (uncovering/unmasking a monument).

8. Franz Arthur Klietmann, *Im Westen wohl was Neues* (Berlin: Nonnemann, 1931); Carl A. G. Otto, *Im Osten nichts Neues* (Zirndorf-Nürnberg: Sanitas, 1929); Emil Marius Requark (M. J. Wolff), *Vor Troja nichts Neues* (Berlin: Brunnen/Winckler, 1930); Gottfried Nickl, *"Im Westen nichts Neues" und sein wahrer Sinn*, published by the journal *Heimgarten* as a *Sonderheft* (Graz and Leipzig: Stocker, 1929), referring to the novel as a *Schandmal* (monument of shame), and subtitled *Antwort auf Remarque* (answer to Remarque). E. Erbelding, *Im Westen doch Neues* (Something New on the Western Front) (Munich: Ebering, 1930), is a pro-war piece that merely

uses Remarque's title. Most of these works do not bear reading, but their existence makes its own point. I have examined Wolff's parody in detail in "All Quiet on the Trojan Front: Remarque's Soldiers and Homer's Heroes in a Parody of *Im Westen nichts Neue*," *German Life and Letters* 43 (1989): 49–62. These imitations must be distinguished from literary texts that did, nevertheless, take a positive approach to the military aspects, such as those by Ernst Jünger; see Thomas Nevin, *Ernst Jünger and Germany. Into the Abyss, 1914–1945* (London: Constable, 1997), 143, also on diaries. There is an important comparison by Heinz Ludwig Arnold, "Erich Maria Remarque und Ernst Jünger," in *Jahrbuch* 10 (1999): 5–17. As an aside on modern reception, Günther Grass allows Jünger and Remarque to discuss the First World War in his *Mein Jahrhundert* (Göttingen: Steidl, 1999), and trans. M. H. Heim, *My Century* (New York: Harcourt, 1999).

    9. Brian Murdoch, "'Hinter die Kulissen des Krieges sehen': Evadne Price, Adrienne Thomas—and E. M. Remarque," *Forum for Modern Language Studies* 28 (1992): 56–74.

    10. For a historical overview see such works as Werner Conze, *Die Zeit Wilhelms II und die Weimarer Republik* (Stuttgart: Metzler, 1964); *Die Weimarer Republik*, ed. Friedrich Krummacher and Albert Wucher (Munich: Desch, 1965, illustrated); Hans Herzfeld, *Die Weimarer Republik* (Frankfurt am Main: Ullstein, 1966). In English, see John McKenzie, *Weimar Germany 1918–1933* (London: Blandford, 1971) and J. W. Hiden, *The Weimar Republic* (London: Longman, 1974).

    11. The best survey remains that by Hans-Harald Müller, *Der Krieg und die Schriftsteller: Der Kriegsroman der Weimarer Republik* (Stuttgart: Metzler, 1986). See also, however, the following selective chronological list: J. K. Bostock, *Some Well-known German War Novels 1914–30* (Oxford: Blackwell, 1931); William K. Pfeiler, *War and the German Mind* (1941; reprint, New York: AMS, 1966); Wilhelm J. Schwarz, *War and the Mind of Germany I* (Bern and Frankfurt am Main: Peter Lang, 1975); Michael Gollbach, *Die Wiederkehr des Weltkrieges in der Literatur: Zu den Frontromanen der späten zwanziger Jahre* (Kronberg im Taunus: Athenaeum, 1978); M. P. A. Travers, *German Novels of the First World War* (Stuttgart: Heinz, 1982); Margrit Stickelberger-Eder, *Aufbruch 1914: Kriegsromane der späten Weimarer Republik* (Zurich and Munich: Artemis, 1983); Herbert Bornebusch, *Gegen-Erinnerung: Eine formsemantische Analyse des demokratischen Kriegsromans der Weimarer Republik* (Frankfurt am Main: Peter Lang, 1985); Ulrich Baron and Hans-Harald Müller, "Weltkriege und Kriegsromane," *LiLi. Zeitschrift für Literaturwissenschaft und Linguistik* 19 (1989): 14–38; Ann P. Linder, *Princes of the Trenches: Narrating the German Experience of the First World War* (Columbia, SC: Camden House, 1996); *Von Richthofen bis Remarque: Deutschsprachige Prosa zum 1. Weltkrieg*, ed. Thomas F. Schneider and Hans Wagener (Amsterdam and New York: Rodopi, 2003).

    12. There is a large body of secondary literature on the novel (some cited elsewhere in this chapter), and it is usually discussed in studies of war novels as such: George Parfitt's *Fiction of the First World War* (London: Faber, 1988) is a study of English-language novels with reference otherwise only to Remarque, Ernst Jünger, Jules Romains, and Henri Barbusse, and this is true too (minus Romains) of Bernard Bergonzi, *Heroes' Twilight: A Study of the Literature of the Great War* 2d ed. (London: Macmillan, 1980). There are monograph-length studies of *Im Westen nichts Neues* by the present writer, *Remarque: Im Westen nichts Neues*, as well as by Firda, *All Quiet*, and Rüter, *Bestseller*. There are various papers in the *Jahrbuch* 10 (2000), and many studies compare the work with other novels of the war: Helmut

Liedloff; "Two War Novels," *Revue de Littérature Comparée* 42 (1968): 390–406 (with Hemingway); Holger M. Klein, "Dazwischen Niemandsland: *Im Westen nichts Neues* and *Her Privates We*, in *Grossbritannien und Deutschland: Festschrift für John W. P. Bourke*, ed. Ortwin Kuhn (Munich: Goldmann, 1974), 488–512 (with Manning); Holger M. Klein, "Grundhaltung und Feindbilder bei Remarque, Céline und Hemingway," *Krieg und Literatur/War and Literature* 1 (1989): 7–22. Some studies are less useful than others: David J. Ulbrich, "A Male-Conscious Critique of Erich Maria Remarque's *All Quiet on the Western Front*," *Journal of Men's Studies* 3 (1995): 229–40 is not enlightening. Given the clarity of the novel it is intriguing to note the continued production of "study guides" in English, which do little more than provide a detailed plot summary (Cliffs Notes, 1965; Monarch Notes, 1966; Coles Notes, 1984; Sparknotes, 2002). See in German however the rather different introductions by Peter Bekes, *Erich Maria Remarque, Im Westen nichts Neues* (Munich: Oldenbourg, 1998), and Reiner Poppe, *Erich Maria Remarque: Im Westen nichts Neues* (Hollfeld: Beyer, 1998). An adapted and abridged version of the English text was published for foreign students of the English language (such has it become part of the English canon): *Remarque: All Quiet on the Western Front*, adapted by Colin Swatridge (London: Macmillan, 1987).

13. As noted by Rowley, "Journalism into Fiction," 108. Rowley also indicates the importance of the chapter division and their varying lengths on 109. Rowley's reference, however, to a "curiously unrealistic cross-section of the fighting-troops" (109) is surely explained by the fact that this, too, is dictated by Bäumer's "frog's eye view," a term Rowley cites, 108.

14. An early subtitle was "Aus den Tagebüchern des Freiwilligen Georg Bäumers" (From the Diaries of the Volunteer Soldier Georg Bäumer—the name was changed later, too). See Schneider, *Text, Edition, Entstehung*, 463. See my paper "Paul Bäumer's Diary" in Murdoch, Ward, and Sargeant, *Remarque Against War*, 1–23.

15. The debate about the actual reality of the presentation of the war in the novel has continued in various forms since the first objections by those critics who wanted it to be autobiographical. See Günter Hartung, "Zum Wahrheitsgehalt des Romans *Im Westen nichts Neue*," *Jahrbuch* 1 (1991): 5–17. See also my "Paul Bäumer's Diary." Paul Fussell, *The Great War and Modern Memory* (London: Oxford UP, 1977), 183, counters the notion that the work is as "real and intimate" as letters from the front.

16. Hans-Harold Müller makes the point clearly in "Politics and the War Novel," in *German Writers and Politics 1918–39*, ed. Richard Dove and Stephen Lamb (London: Macmillan, 1992), 103–20, esp. 112.

17. On Remarque's discourse technique, already apparent in these early novels, see Heinrich Placke on the works of the 1950s: *Die Chiffren des Utopischen: Zum literarischen Gehalt der politischen 50er Jahre-Romane Remarques* (Göttingen: Vandenhoek and Ruprecht, 2004).

18. The much-reprinted French translation and at least one of the recently reprinted Yiddish versions (by Isaac Bashevis Singer) omit the statement, known as "the Motto," entirely. In other translations it is tucked away on the verso of the title page. The English is from Erich Maria Remarque, *All Quiet on the Western Front*, trans. A. W. Wheen (London: G. P. Putnam's Sons, 1929; also in the American edition, Boston: Little, Brown, and Company, 1929). In these and the German first edition it is prominently displayed on a separate preliminary page. Wheen translated from a typescript; my own translation follows the printed German text (thus

omits the italicized parts). For variant versions of the Motto, see Schneider, *Text, Edition, Entstehung*, 465–67 (and I am indebted to Thomas Schneider for guiding me through the complexity of this situation). The translation of *Erlebnis* as "adventure" is not exact, but there were many books that did see the war as an adventure. Gunther Plüschow's *Die Abenteuer des Fliegers von Tsingtau*, another bestseller from Ullstein, originally 1916, but printed in 610,000 copies by 1927, and translated as *My Escape from Donington Hall* (London: Bodley Head, 1929), is adventurous, although a single airman who escapes from a POW camp (hence the English title) is not representative; the publishers added a preface in 1927 claiming that it was being presented *nicht als Kriegsbuch* (not as a war book).

19. As by Rudolf Huch, for example, in a review discussed by Roger Woods in "The Conservative Revolution and the First World War: Literature as Evidence in Historical Explanation," *Modern Language Review* 85 (1990): 77–91, see 86–87. The conservative literature of the war, which justified and to an extent glorified it, objected that the individual could form no overview of the inner sense of the conflict.

20. See Woods, "The Conservative Revolution," 87–88, discussing Rudolf Huch's criticism of Remarque and the *Froschperspektive*. See also Travers, *German Novels*, 134.

21. Various German novels blame teachers: see Caroline Martin, "The Conflict of Education: Soldiers, Civilians, a Child, and a Teacher," in Murdoch, Ward, Sargeant, *Remarque Against War*, 39–61. There is an interesting contrast with the situation in English, where the opposite was (or seemed often to be) the case, soldiers drawing strength from what they had learned at British public (that is, private) schools: see on this Peter Parker, *The Old Lie: The Great War and the Public School Ethos* (London: Constable, 1987), 283–84, with reference to Remarque.

22. See on the style (with comments on "pseudo-authenticity") especially David Midgley, *Writing Weimar: Critical Realism in Weimar Literature 1918–1933* (Oxford: Oxford UP, 2000), especially 14–56. I have discussed the question with regard to Remarque in "Paul Bäumer's Diary," and see Thomas Schneider, "'Krieg ist Krieg schließlich': Erich Maria Remarque: *Im Westen nichts Neues* (1928)," in Schneider and Wagener, *Von Richthofen bis Remarque*, 217–32. On *Neue Sachlichkeit*, see Helmut Gruber, "'Neue Sachlichkeit' and the World War," *German Life and Letters* 20 (1966–67): 138–49.

23. See my "Narrative Strategies," 180, referring to [Fritz Oswald] Bilse's *Aus einer kleinen Garnison: Ein militärisches Zeitbild* (Braunschweig: Sattler, 1903) (*Life in a Garrison Town*, London: Bodley Head, 1904), which contains also a discussion of comradeship and a scene where a soldier fails to salute a superior.

24. See Robert Wohl, *The Generation of 1914* (London: Weidenfeld and Nicolson, 1980) for an international overview of the lost generation. Richard Littlejohns, "'Der Krieg hat uns für alles verdorben': the Real Theme of *Im Westen nichts Neues*," *Modern Languages* 70 (1989): 89–94 takes this as the principal theme of the novel, rather than the war as such.

25. Fussell, *The Great War*, 196 misrepresents the scene, both misunderstanding the text—it is not a civilian cemetery—and by mischievously using phrases, unlike Remarque, such as "graves torn asunder," "stinking cerements" or "the narrator and his chums." There is no doubt of the potential reality of what is clearly also a symbolic scene and it is certainly not a "Gothic fantasia"; the dead were often not left in peace.

26. Stramm (1874–1915) was himself killed in the war: see his brief poems in *Lyrik des Expressionistischen Jahrzehnts* (Munich: dtv, 1962), 133–34. There are translations of two in *The Penguin Book of First World War Poetry*, ed. Jon Silkin (Harmondsworth: Penguin, 1979), 227.

27. Hindenburg, in his memoirs, commented that "unsere ermattete Front" (our exhausted front line) fell like Siegfried, with Hagen's spear in the back: Generalfeldmarschall [Paul] von Hindenburg, *Aus meinem Leben* (Leipzig: Hirzel, 1920), 403. Hitler himself claimed that "Germany was not defeated by the sanctions but exclusively by the internal process of revolutionizing"—thus the English translation of a letter from Hitler to the press baron Lord Rothermere, dated 20 December 1935, in *Fleet Street, Press Barons, and Politics: The Journals of Collin Brooks*, edited by N. J. Crowson (London: Royal Historical Society, 1998), 286. Both recognize a defeat of some sort.

28. As late as 1940 a pamphlet appeared in a World Affairs series by Cyril Falls called *Was Germany Defeated in 1918?* (Oxford: Clarendon, 1940). See also the larger historical studies of 1918 by John Terraine, *To Win a War* (London: Sidgwick and Jackson, 1978); John Toland, *No Man's Land* (London: Eyre Methuen, 1980); Gordon Brook-Shepherd, *November 1918* (London: Collins, 1981). Terraine's book carries a quotation on the title page from David Lloyd-George's war memoirs: "the conclusion is inescapable that Germany and her allies were in fact defeated in the field." H. Essame, *The Battle for Europe 1918* (London: Batsford, 1972) has a final chapter titled "The Politicians Take Over," and Niall Ferguson's *The Pity of War* (Harmondsworth: Penguin, 1998) ends with two chapters titled "The Captor's Dilemma" and "How (Not) to Pay for the War." See on the (sometimes avoided) question of the opening of the war the papers in: *Forging the Collective Memory*, ed. Keith Wilson (Providence, RI and Oxford: Berghahn, 1996). On the literary response to the concept of defeat in the Weimar republic, see Linder, *Princes of the Trenches*, 151–78. Remarque's 1944 comments were in an unpublished piece surviving in English, titled "Practical Education Work in Germany after the War," now in German translation by Thomas Schneider in *Ein militanter Pazifist*, 66–83 (see 72) as "Praktische Erziehungsarbeit in Deutschland nach dem Krieg" (also in *Das unbekannte Werk*, vol. 5, 387–403 and *Herbstfahrt*, 226–42).

29. Even Remarque commented ironically on the boots ("Kemmerichs Stiefel in *All Quiet*") in a diary entry on 1 August 1950: *Das unbekannte Werk*, vol. 5, 427. Of course they are a symbol of death, but the real point, alluded to by Remarque in his diary, is their utilitarian value; only because they are of no use to Kemmerich does Müller take them.

30. This happens in Edlef Koeppen's *Heeresbericht* (Berlin: Horen 1930 and Reinbek bei Hamburg: Rowohlt, 1986). For example, see my "Documentation and Narrative: Edlef Koeppen's *Heeresbericht* and the Anti-War Novels of the Weimar Republic," *New German Studies* 15 (1988–89): 23–47.

31. See Hans Wagener, "Erich Maria Remarque, *Im Westen nichts neues—Zeit zu leben und Zeit zu sterben*: Ein Autor, zwei Weltkriege," *Jahrbuch* 10 (2000): 31–52, see 39.

32. See Brian Murdoch, "Tierische Menschen und menschliche Tiere: Ernst Johannsen: *Vier von der Infanterie* und *Fronterinnerungen eines Pferdes* (1929)" in Schneider and Wagener, *Von Richthofen bis Remarque*, 249–60. The same collection contains articles on many comparable works and also a useful indication of sales figures, 12–11. The other texts referred to here are Ernst Glaeser, *Jahrgang 1902*

(1928; reprint, Frankfurt am Main and Berlin: Ullstein, 1986), translated as *Class of 1902* by Willa and Edwin Muir (London: Secker, 1929); Alexander Moritz Frey, *Die Pflasterkästen* (1929; reprinted in the *Verboten und verbrannt/Exil* series, Frankfurt am Main: Fischer, 1986), translated as *The Crossbearers*, no translator given (London: G. P. Putnam's Sons, 1931); Adrienne Thomas's *Die Katrin wird Soldat* (1930) is in the same series (Frankfurt am Main: Fischer: 1987), trans. Margaret Goldsmith, *Katrin Becomes a Soldier* (Boston: Little, Brown, and Company, 1931).

33. Bäumer draws life and strength from the earth in the fourth chapter. The motif is a classical one, which Bäumer, as a product of a classical *Gymnasium* (see his dismissive references to Plato and to classical history) might have absorbed: the Homeric hymn to the earth as a mother is in Karl Preisendanz, *Griechische Lyrik* (Leipzig: Insel [1936]), 5, for example, a collection the first edition of which had appeared in 1914.

34. Remarque made the point in his "Grössere und kleinere Ironien," *Ein Militanter Pazifist*, 141; *Das unbekannte Werk*, vol. 4, 438; *Herbstfahrt*, 256. See Richard Schumaker, "Remarque's Abyss of Time: *Im Westen nichts Neues*," *Focus on Robert Graves and his Contemporaries* vol. 1, No. 11 (Winter 1990): 124–35.

35. Friedrich Luft, "Das Profil: Gespräch mit Erich Maria Remarque" in *Ein militanter Pazifist*, 118–33, cited 120. The point is made in the perceptive analysis (principally of *Im Westen nichts Neues*) by Modris Eksteins, *Rites of Spring: The Great War and the Birth of the Modern Age* (London: Transworld, 1990), 368–97. See more on the two works in Kathleen Devine, "The Way Back: Alun Lewis and Remarque," *Anglia* 103 (1985): 320–35. The new work was not well received: see Antkowiak, *Remarque*, 53; Jost Hermand, "Oedipus Lost," in *Die sogenannten zwanziger Jahre*, ed. Reinhold Grimm and Jost Hermand (Bad Homburg: 1970), 218, and Wagener, *Understanding*, 41. American criticism thought more highly of the work: see Barker and Last, *Remarque*, 69.

Chronology

1898	Born on June 22 in Osnabruck, Germany, to bookbinder Peter Franz Remark and Anna Maria Stallknecht.
1904	Attends a Catholic primary school, the *Domschule*.
1908–12	Attends the *Johannisschule* and the *Katholische Preparande*, the latter to prepare for admission to the Catholic Teachers' Seminar.
1915–16	Studies at the teachers' seminar; influenced by classical music and German Romantic literature.
1916	Drafted, with many classmates, into the army; undergoes harsh military training in Osnabrück.
1917	Assigned to the Western Front in June; participated in the German offensive at Flanders; wounded at Geite-Sankt-Josef and sent to St. Vincenz Hospital in Duisburg, Germany; mother dies.
1918	Leaves St. Vincenz Hospital; is transferred to a reserve unit in Osnabrück until able to return to active duty in November; Armistice ending World War I signed on November 11; Germany enters period of political and social upheaval.
1919	Passes elementary teacher's examination in June and begins employment as a substitute teacher; writes about art and music for Osnabrück newspaper.

1920	*Die Traumbude* (*Dream Room*), published; not simultaneously published in English and later disowned by Remarque; teaches briefly in Klein-Berssen and Nahne.
1920	Works at odd jobs: as salesman for a stonecutting and gravestone company, and as Sunday organist at mental hospital chapel.
1922	Becomes editor of *Echo Continental*, the trade journal for the Continental Rubber Company, his place of employment at the time.
1925	Moves to Berlin to take a job as a picture editor at *Sport im Bild*, a publication for race car drivers; marries Jutta Ilse Zambona in Berlin.
1927–28	Writes a racing car novel, which is published serially; begins work on *All Quiet on the Western Front*.
1928	*All Quiet on the Western Front* serialized.
1929	*All Quiet on the Western Front*, translated by A.W. Wheen; Remarque begins to emerge as a controversial figure: the Right is suspicious of his apparent lack of overt patriotism and the Left is disappointed; the reading public, however, is enthusiastic; begins spelling his last name "Remarque."
1930	Divorces Jutta; writes *The Road Back* as a sequel to *All Quiet*, writing about his return from the front; film version of *All Quiet* premieres and provokes protests.
1931	*The Road Back*, translated by A.W. Wheen, is published; Remarque officially censored and regarded by the Nazi Party as a betrayer.
1933	Nazis take power of Germany's government; Remarque goes into exile in Switzerland; *All Quiet* and *Road* are among the 20,000 volumes destroyed in the first of the infamous Nazi book burnings (May 10).
1937	*Three Comrades*, translated by A.W. Wheen, is published.
1938	Remarries Jutta; is expatriated by Nazi Party.
1939	Arrives in New York, still in literary and political exile; wife denied entry, goes to Mexico; Remarque goes to Los Angeles.
1941	*Flotsam*, translated by Denver Lindley, is published; Remarque becomes legal resident of the United States.

1942	Moves from Los Angeles to New York.
1943	Paintings exhibited in New York galleries; sister is executed by Nazis.
1945	*Arch of Triumph*, translated by Walter Sorell and Denver Lindley, is published.
1947	Becomes naturalized American citizen.
1948	Begins to reside in Switzerland and the United States.
1952	*Spark of Life*, translated by James Stern, is published, receives criticism.
1953	*Love Thy Neighbour* is published.
1954	*A Time to Love and a Time to Die*, translated by Denver Lindley, is published; father dies.
1957	*The Black Obelisk*, translated by Denver Lindley, is published; Remarque lives in Hollywood and advises at Universal Studios about the adaptation of *A Time* to film; divorces Jutta.
1958	Marries American film actress Paulette Goddard.
1961	*Heaven Has No Favorites*, translated by Richard and Clara Winston, is published.
1963	Has first stroke while in Naples just after the filming of his wife's final movie.
1964	Is despondent and anxious about mortality during his difficult recuperation; *The Night in Lisbon*, translated by Ralph Manheim, is published; Remarque awarded a medal in his hometown for distinguished service.
1965	Has second stroke while staying in Milan.
1967	Awarded the Distinguished Service Cross of the Order of Merit by the West German government; suffers two more strokes.
1968	Elected to membership of the German Academy for Language and Literature.
1970	Has sixth and final stroke in August; dies September 25 in Saint Agnes Hospital in Locarno, Switzerland;
1972	*Shadows in Paradise*, translated by Ralph Manheim, is published posthumously.
1979	A remake of *All Quiet* is shown on American television.

Contributors

HAROLD BLOOM is Sterling Professor of the Humanities at Yale University. He is the author of 30 books, including *Shelley's Mythmaking*, *The Visionary Company*, *Blake's Apocalypse*, *Yeats*, *A Map of Misreading*, *Kabbalah and Criticism*, *Agon: Toward a Theory of Revisionism*, *The American Religion*, *The Western Canon*, and *Omens of Millennium: The Gnosis of Angels, Dreams, and Resurrection*. *The Anxiety of Influence* sets forth Professor Bloom's provocative theory of the literary relationships between the great writers and their predecessors. His most recent books include *Shakespeare: The Invention of the Human*, a 1998 National Book Award finalist, *How to Read and Why*, *Genius: A Mosaic of One Hundred Exemplary Creative Minds*, *Hamlet: Poem Unlimited*, *Where Shall Wisdom Be Found?*, and *Jesus and Yahweh: The Names Divine*. In 1999, Professor Bloom received the prestigious American Academy of Arts and Letters Gold Medal for Criticism. He has also received the International Prize of Catalonia, the Alfonso Reyes Prize of Mexico, and the Hans Christian Andersen Bicentennial Prize of Denmark.

CHRISTINE R. BARKER has contributed essays to the *Journal of European Studies* and is the author of *The Poetic Vision of Fritz Usinger*.

R.W. LAST is the editor of *Affinities: Essays in German and English* (1971).

GEORGE J. MITCHELL was an associate member of the American Society of Cinematographers founded in 1919.

MODRIS EKSTEINS was born in Latvia and came to Canada as a refugee. Now a Canadian citizen, he is known for his interest and expertise in German history and culture. He also published *Walking Since Daybreak: A Story of Eastern Europe, World War II, and the Heart of Our Century* (1999).

HANS WAGENER, a German by birth, is currently teaching German literature at the University of California at Los Angeles. In 1993, he published *Understanding Franz Werfel*.

ARIELA HALKIN was born in Israel and received her B.A. in French and English literature from Hebrew University in Jerusalem and her M.A. and Ph.D. in Western European history from Tel Aviv University.

DAVID MIDGLEY has written extensively on German authors from the years 1890–1945. He is University Reader in German Literature and Culture at Cambridge University. In 2000 he published *Writing Weimar: Critical Realism in German Literature, 1918–1933*.

HILTON TIMS was the first to write a British-authored biography of Erich Maria Remarque; his book, *Erich Maria Remarque: The Last Romantic* (2003), contains many details about Remarque's life in the United States, and, in particular, his involvement in the glamorous Hollywood scene.

HELMUTH KIESEL edited, contributed to, and provided new translations for *Kafka's "The Metamorphosis" and Other Writings* (2002).

BRIAN MURDOCH teaches German at the University of Stirling in Scotland. He is a widely known writer on medieval German and comparative literature as well as the literature of the world wars, specifically Remarque and other pacifist writers.

Bibliography

Ambrose, Stephen E. *Citizen Soldiers*. New York: Simon & Schuster, 1997.

Barker, Christine, and Rex Last. *Erich Maria Remarque*. London: Wolff, 1979.

Baumer, Franz. *Erich Maria Remarque*. Berlin: Morgenbuch Verlag, 1994.

Bostock, J. K. *Some Well-known German War Novels, 1914–30*. Oxford: Blackwell, 1931.

Cockburn, C. *Bestseller: The Books that Everyone Read 1900–1939*. London, 1972.

Dove, Richard, and Stephen Lamb, eds. *German Writers and Politics: 1918–1939*. London: Macmillan, 1992.

Dunaway, David King. *Huxley in Hollywood*. New York: Harper & Row, 1989.

Eksteins, Modris. *Rites of Spring: The Great War and the Birth of the Modern Age*. London: Transworld, 1990.

Fairbanks Jr., Douglas. *The Salad Days*. London: William Collins, 1988.

Firda, Richard A. *"All Quiet on the Western Front": Literary Analysis and Cultural Context*. New York: Twayne Publishers, 1993.

———. *Erich Maria Remarque: A Thematic Analysis of His Novels*. New York: Peter Lang, 1988.

Fischer, Klaus P. *Nazi-Germany: A New History*. London: Constable & Co., 1995.

Friedrich, Otto. *City of Nets: A Portrait of Hollywood in the 1940s*. London: Headline, 1988.

Fussell, Paul. *The Great War and Modern Memory*. London: Oxford University Press, 1977.

Gilbert, Julie Goldsmith. *Opposite Attraction: The Lives of Erich Maria Remarque and Paulette Goddard*. New York: Pantheon, 1995; German trans. Düsseldorf: List, 1997.

207

Gordon, Haim. *Heroism and Friendship in the Novels of Erich Maria Remarque*. New York: Peter Lang, 2003.

Halkin, Ariela. *The Enemy Reviewed: German Popular Literature through British Eyes between the Two World Wars*. Westport, CT: Praeger Publishers, 1995.

Irving, David. *Goebbels: Mastermind of the Third Reich*. London: Focal Point, 1996.

Kiesel, Helmuth, ed. Erich Maria Remarque: *All Quiet on the Western Front* and Joseph Roth: *Job: The Story of a Simple Man* (abridged). New York: The Continuum International Publishing Group, Inc., 2004.

LaCapra, Dominick, and Steven L. Kaplan. *Modern European Intellectual History: Reappraisals and New Perspectives*. Ithaca, NY: Cornell University Press, 1982.

Leydecker, Karl, ed. *German Novelists of the Weimar Republic: Intersections of Literature and Politics*. Rochester, NY: Camden House, 2006.

Linder, Anne P. *Princes of the Trenches: Narrating the German Experience of the First World War*. Columbia, SC: Camden House, 1996.

Midgley, David. *Writing Weimar: Critical Realism in German Literature 1918–1933*. Oxford: Oxford University Press, 2000.

Murdoch, Brian. *The Novels of Erich Maria Remarque: Sparks of Life*. Rochester, NY: Camden House, 2006.

Murdoch, Brian, Mark Ward, and Maggie Sargeant, eds. *Remarque Against War*. Glasgow: Scottish Papers in Germanic Studies, 1998.

Owen, Claude R. *Erich Maria Remarque: A Critical Bio-Bibliography*. Amsterdam: Rodopi, 1984.

Parfitt, George. *Fiction of the First World War*. London: Faber, 1988.

Pfeiler, William K. *War and the German Mind*. 1941; reprint, New York: AMS, 1966.

Schwarz, Wilhelm J. *War and the Mind of Germany I*. Bern and Frankfurt am Main: Peter Lang, 1975.

Taylor, Harley U. *Erich Maria Remarque: A Literary and Film Biography*. New York: Peter Lang, 1988.

Thornton, Thomas. *A Time to Live: The Life and Writings of Erich Maria Remarque*. New York: Fales Library, 1998.

Tims, Hilton. *Erich Maria Remarque: The Last Romantic*. London: Constable, 2003.

Travers, M. P. A. *German Novels of the First World War*. Stuttgart: Heinz, 1982.

Wagener, Hans. *Understanding Erich Maria Remarque*. Columbia, SC: University of South Carolina Press, 1991.

Willett, J. *The Weimar Years: A Culture Cut Short*. Thames and Hudson, 1984.

Wohl, Robert. *The Generation of 1914*. Cambridge: Harvard University Press, 1979.

Acknowledgments

Christine R. Barker and R.W. Last, "All Quiet on the Western Front." From *Erich Maria Remarque.* © 1979 Oswald Wolff Ltd. Reprinted with permission.

George J. Mitchell, "Making *All Quiet on the Western Front:* Rare Interview with Arthur Edeson, ASC." From *American Cinematographer,* September 1985, vol. 66, no. 9. © 1985 ASC Holding Corporation. Used with permission of the American Society of Cinematographers.

Modris Eksteins, "Memory." From *Rites of Spring: The Great War and the Birth of the Modern Age.* © 1989 by Modris Eksteins. Reprinted with permission.

Hans Wagener, "All Quiet on the Western Front." From *Understanding Erich Maria Remarque,* pp. 9–36. Columbia, SC: University of South Carolina Press, 1991. © 1991 University of South Carolina.

Ariela Halkin, "The Flood." From *The Enemy Reviewed: German Popular Literature Through British Eyes Between the Two World Wars.* © 1995 by Ariela Halkin. Reproduced with permission of Greenwood Publishing Group, Inc., Westport, CT.

David Midgley, "Remembering the War." From *Weimar Writing: Critical Realism in German Literature, 1918–1933.* © 2000 David Midgley. Reprinted with permission.

Hilton Tims, "All Quiet on the Western Front." From *Erich Maria Remarque: The Last Romance.* © 2003 Hilton Tims.

Helmuth Kiesel, "Introduction." From Erich Maria Remarque, *All Quiet on the Western Front* and Joseph Roth, *Job: The Story of a Simple Man.* © 2004 by Helmuth Kiesel and the Continuum International Publishing Group.

Brian Murdoch, "From the Frog's Perspective: *Im Westen nichts Neues* and *Der Weg zurück,*" chapter 2, pp. 31–56, 57–65. From *The Novels of Erich Maria Remarque: Sparks of Life.* Rochester, NY: Camden House, 2006. © 2006 Brian Murdoch.

Index